ROLL TIDE ROLL

Alabama's National Championship Season

Ray Melick

SAGAMORE PUBLISHING
Champaign, IL

Production Manager: Susan M. McKinney
Dustjacket and photo insert design: Michelle R. Dressen
Editors: David Hamburg, Russ Lake
Proofreader: Phyllis L. Bannon

Publisher's Cataloging in Publication
(Prepared by Quality Books Inc.)

Melick, Ray H.
    Roll tide roll: Alabama's national championship season/ Ray
Melick.
    p. cm.
    Preassigned LCCN: 93-84956
    ISBN: 0-915611-79-1

1.   Alabama Crimson Tide (Football team) 2. University of Alabama—Football. I. Title.

GV958.A4M45 1993   796.33′263′0976184
                                  QBI93-1127

Printed in the United States

To Mary Grace, who, when I least expect it, shows me that love has no limits to its endurance, no end to its trust, no fading of its hope, and can outlast anything.

CONTENTS

ACKNOWLEDGMENTS

I would like to acknowledge all the people who are important to me, but space limits me to the following: the 1965 Green Bay Packers; the 1969 Atlanta Braves; the 1972 Los Angeles Lakers; the 1980 Georgia Bulldogs; the 1985 Birmingham Stallions—I won't try to mention you all by name. You know who you are.

And of course others who deserve mention are: my dad the senior golfer, Dick Melick; my brother-in-law, former roommate, and loan co-signer, Tim McGowan; my computer expert brother-in-law who can create programs over the phone, Terry McGowan; my friend and pastor, Doug Walker, who wanted this book dedicated to him (sorry); Shihan Oyama, whose book we never finished; the late Rollie Dotsch and the rejuvinated Gene Stallings, two football coaches very diferent in personality but who both believed in opening practices to beat writers because they knew games weren't won or lost in the newspaper; my favorite interview of all time, Randall "Tex" Cobb; and MST 3K.

Finally, I would like to acknowledge everyone at Sagamore Publishing for their hard work, especially Susan McKinney.

PROLOGUE

Lamar Thomas never saw it coming.

All Thomas knew was that he had executed a perfect hip fake at the sideline that left Alabama sophomore cornerback Willie Gaston reaching for air, and now was looking at a wide receiver's dream — the ball leaving Heisman Trophy winner Gino Torretta's hand on a perfect spiral aimed at a spot somewhere ahead of him, and beyond that, nothing but green until he crossed the goal line, some 89 yards away.

He caught the ball in full stride, and turned his sprinter's speed — Thomas runs the 40-yard dash in 4.5 seconds and is a member of the University of Miami 400-meter relay team — straight down the Miami sideline, past jubilant coaches and teammates who were waving him onward, past lovely cheerleaders who had had so little to cheer about up until this moment, past everyone and everything, already counting on his 11th touchdown of the season, his first of the night, the big play that just might shake the 'Canes from the doldrums and spark them to their 12th victory of the season, 29th in a row, and a repeat as national college football champions.

It was going to be redemption for Thomas, who had done more running with his mouth in the week leading up to the game than he had with the ball in his hands when it counted.

It was Thomas who had walked into a pregame press conference, held up his two national championship rings (1989, 1991) and said the third one, "will be icing on the cake."

It was Thomas who had run down Alabama's league, the Southeastern Conference ("Not what it was," he said), then questioned the ability of Alabama's defensive backs ("Real men play man coverage," he said), and announced that the Miami receiver corps, dubbed the Ruthless Posse by Thomas, was "the best receiving corps ever assembled. Anytime we get a team in man-to-man coverage, it's not fair."

Now Thomas was getting the chance to put up or shut up, and it looked so easy.

What Thomas did not see, what he had no reason to even suspect, was Alabama cornerback George Teague—head down, arms pumping, legs churning—closing the gap between himself and Thomas.

And what happened next will be remembered forever by the 76,789 people packed into the New Orleans Superdome and the millions more watching the game live on ABC-TV.

Teague got to within an arm's reach of Thomas at the Alabama 15-yard line. But instead of tackling Thomas, Teague looped his right arm over Thomas's right arm, the arm in which Thomas was cradling the football, and pulled Thomas's arm behind his back until there was nothing to cradle the ball against.

Then Teague just took the ball away from Thomas, just snatched it away without breaking stride, like the best of Bourbon Street pickpockets.

And even though a penalty flag against Alabama for being off side erased the play from the official record, it was the one play that summed up not just the 1993 Sugar Bowl game, but the entire 1992 season for the Crimson Tide.

No one saw it coming.

But in this, the 100th season of one of the most celebrated football programs in college football, the Alabama Crimson Tide did what everyone else said couldn't be done and captured the 1992 National Championship with a 34-13 victory over Miami.

In some ways this team was a team of destiny. After all, going into the 1992 season, Alabama had claimed 11 national championships in football, with an NCAA-record 44 bowl appearances, an NCAA-record 24 bowl victories, and 19 Southeastern Conference championships. It also had going for it the legend of the winningest Division I coach in NCAA history in Paul "Bear" Bryant and more All-America college football players than there is room to name.

What better way to cap off the Centennial Celebration, a season dubbed "A Century of Champions" long before the first coin toss, than with a 12th national championship?

And yet, who would have believed it?

There was so much working against this team from the beginning: deaths in the families of several players during the season; the off-field problems of its best offensive player, David Palmer, that led to a three-game suspension; and charges of NCAA violations, first by Georgia defensive back Ralph Thomson (who later recanted his story), then later by former Alabama player Gene Jelks.

Throw in an offense that couldn't seem to do anything but run the ball and a quarterback who couldn't seem to do anything but win, and no wonder Alabama head coach Gene Stallings, looking back from the vantage point of January 2, said, "It was a great season, a season nobody really and truly expected us to have."

The total dismantling embarrassment of defending national champion Miami in the Sugar Bowl was as unexpected as the fact that Alabama was even in the Sugar Bowl, in a position to win a national championship.

This was, after all, the first year of the expanded SEC, a conference that had added Arkansas and South Carolina to become a 12-team league that would then divide into two divisions and play the first NCAA Division I-A conference championship game at the end of the season.

The head coaches hated the idea. They were convinced divisional play killed any chance an SEC team had of ever winning another national championship. They said there was no way a team could go undefeated in the SEC anyway, much less go undefeated plus win the conference championship and still win a national title.

And then in the very first year, Alabama did it.

Sure, there were things that fell Alabama's way. It didn't hurt that the Tide would not have to play either defending SEC champion Florida or Georgia during the regular season, since both teams were in the SEC Eastern Division and Alabama was in the SEC Western Division.

It didn't hurt that Alabama would not have to play its biggest challenger in the West, Mississippi State, until late in the season, a time when the Bulldogs were usually starting to weaken because of the lack of depth that had plagued Mississippi State football teams over the last decade.

It certainly didn't hurt that Alabama's intrastate arch rival, Auburn, was a program in disarray due to an ongoing NCAA investigation, or that the SEC championship game would be played in Birmingham, Alabama, at Legion Field, just 60 miles up the interstate from Tuscaloosa — the Crimson Tide's second home — where they played three home games a year.

But any coach will tell you winning a championship of any kind is as much part luck as it is skill, and despite plenty of adversity, Alabama had its share of luck, too.

This, then, is the story of that season, a season that ended in much the same way the first 100 years of Alabama football had been spent — with the Crimson Tide as national champions.

No one could have seen it coming.

But like Teague's play on Thomas in the Sugar Bowl, it won't be forgotten for a long time.

CHAPTER

1

Great Expectations

There were tears in the eyes of Alabama athletic director Cecil "Hootie" Ingram that January day in 1990 when he introduced Eugene "Bebes" Stallings as the Crimson Tide's 23rd head football coach.

When Bill Curry announced he was leaving Alabama after winning the SEC Championship in 1989 — and, incidentally, losing to Miami in the Sugar Bowl — to become head coach at Kentucky, many Tide fans and alumni expected the school to go after such big-name coaches as Florida State's Bobby Bowden or Louisville head coach Howard Schnellenberger, a former Bryant player and assistant who rebuilt the Miami program, winning that school's first national championship in 1983.

But there is no question now that Stallings was Ingram's first choice — albeit a surprising one.

"I'd known Gene since 1958, when he was on Coach Bryant's staff and I was a high school coach," Ingram said. "No matter where I was, Gene would've been prominent in my considerations. But being at Alabama, he was even more so."

Stallings had not coached at the college level since 1971, his final season as head coach at his alma mater, Texas A&M, where he had been fired after only one winning season in seven years.

From A&M, Stallings had gone to the National Football League, where he worked as secondary coach under Tom Landry with the Dallas Cowboys from 1972 until 1985, when he became head coach of the then-St. Louis Cardinals of the NFL.

After four seasons of losing records with the Cardinals, Stallings was fired again. His career head coaching record was a sub-par 50-79-2. No one was more surprised to be offered the head coaching job at Alabama than the 54-year-old Stallings.

Before Ingram came calling, Stallings was sitting on his ranch in Paris, Texas, considering his future. He interviewed for the head coaching job at the U. S. Naval Academy, and he was considering the possibility of doing some television work. Stallings didn't think there would be much demand for a twice-fired head coach with a losing record.

But the University of Alabama was a program in turmoil. Despite the success of Curry's 1989 season, Curry was seen as an outsider by many Alabama fans and alumni, and he had failed to defeat Auburn as a head coach, either at Alabama or at Georgia Tech, his previous head coaching position.

It wasn't just Curry, however. When Bryant resigned after the 1982 season, then died little more than a month later, he left a void that was going to be impossible to fill. The first to try was former Alabama player Ray Perkins, who left a head coaching position with the NFL's New York Giants to follow Bryant.

Perkins was moderately successful, but he turned off many Alabama fans with the cold, businesslike approach he took in trying to move Alabama past the Bryant era.

Discontent had turned to open sniping between 'Bama fans by Curry's final year, and despite winning the Tide's only SEC title of the 1980s, the news of Curry's leaving was received with great joy by many in the Alabama camp.

What Alabama needed was a man with Bryant ties, who wasn't afraid of walking in Bryant's shadow.

Stallings fit that bill perfectly. On the one hand, he had played for Bryant at Texas A&M, and upon graduation immediately joined Bryant's staff at A&M, then at Alabama from 1958 to 1964. Stallings was perceived as one of Bryant's favorites, almost like a son to the legendary Bear. In 1960, Stallings wrote *Bear Bryant On Winning Football,* a technical book about Bryant's coaching philosophies. And, indeed, by the time Stallings returned to the Tuscaloosa campus, people were drawing comparisons between the way he and Bryant looked and talked.

On the other hand, Stallings was not afraid of the legend of Bryant. For one thing, Stallings knew Bryant and knew him well, probably better than the majority of those people who thought they were Bryant's close friends. Having known the man that well, he was not in awe of him. For another, Stallings had developed another mentor in Landry, the legendary head coach of America's Team, the Dallas Cowboys. If there was a coach that Stallings wanted to emulate, it was Landry, not Bryant.

The entire process took two days. Ingram called Stallings one day and asked if he was interested. Ingram and university president E. Roger Sayers were in Texas the next day interviewing Stallings. Later that afternoon, they offered him the job.

It didn't take Stallings long to accept the offer. This was the one job he had coveted most of his life. Plus, he was not in a position to be choosy.

"I might have called them," Stallings said. "I didn't know if I'd have to spur Hootie on or not."

There was some outrage, of course. Both Perkins and Curry had come to Alabama with losing records as head coaches, and many Tide fans felt they deserved better.

But besides hiring Stallings, Ingram was already laying the ground work for Stallings' staff.

At Clemson, head coach Danny Ford had been forced to resign, leaving secondary coach "Brother" Bill Oliver without a job. Oliver was a former Alabama player under Bryant, a defensive back whose college position coach had been Stallings. He had coached the Tide secondary during the decade of the 1970s, when Alabama was winning more football games than any other team before or since.

At Tampa Bay, defensive line coach Mike Dubose could see the end coming for Perkins, who had taken over as head coach of the Bucs after leaving Alabama. Dubose, a former Alabama defensive lineman during the 1970s and Perkins's defensive line coach at Alabama in the '80s, had gotten his first coaching job at the University of Tennessee at Chattanooga under then-head coach Bill Oliver.

Bryant's offensive coordinator, Mal Moore, who had been fired by Perkins, had gone first to Notre Dame before joining Stallings's staff in the NFL. When Stallings was let go by the Cardinals, that meant Moore was looking for work, too.

And then there was offensive line coach Jim Fuller, another former Bryant player at Alabama. Fuller had resigned as head coach at Jacksonville State University to join Perkins's staff at Alabama, and never left. Fuller was named interim head coach after Perkins resigned, and hoped to get the job on a permanent basis but was passed over by then-university president Joab Thomas for Curry.

When Curry left, Fuller stayed on, again being named interim head. Once again, he hoped he would be named head coach, but this time he would not campaign for the job, feeling as though Ingram knew where to find him if he wanted him.

Once again, Fuller was passed over, this time when 'Bama hired Stallings. But again, Fuller stayed on to join the staff of the new head coach.

It didn't take long for Stallings to put together what some might have considered an all-star cast of former Alabama coaches — Oliver and Dubose on defense, Moore and Fuller on offense.

He filled out that first staff with his line coach from the Cardinals, Mike Solari, who had gotten his start in the profession working for the legendary George Allen when Allen returned to college coaching at Long Beach State.

From Clemson came wide receivers coach Woody McCorvey, a Montgomery native who had played college ball at Alabama A & M. From Pittsburgh came running back coach Larry Kirksey, who had been on the staff at Florida under Charlie Pell and then Galen Hall.

Rounding out the defensive side were outside linebacker coach Ellis Johnson, who had been defensive coordinator at Southern Miss, and inside linebacker coach Lance Van Zant, who had coached at just about every level in just about every part of the country over the past 30 years.

After that first season, Van Zant would be let go and replaced by Jeff Rouzie, another former Alabama player, who had coached linebackers on the Tide's 1978 and '79 national championship teams. And after the second season, Solari would leave to return to the NFL and his native California, with the San Francisco 49ers, allowing Stallings to promote a graduate assistant, Danny Pearman, to full-time status.

But the bottom line was that whatever disappointments had been created by Ingram among Alabama fans with the hiring of Stallings were nearly erased when the names Oliver, Dubose, Moore, and Fuller were added to the staff.

And how bad could it be? Stallings inherited an Alabama offense that led the SEC and set numerous school records in 1989, an offense that no defense seemed able to stop that year, an offense that returned practically intact for a senior season of 1990.

The defense would need to be rebuilt, but defense had been the weakness of that 1989 team. And Alabama fans had complete trust in Oliver, the architect of so many great defenses in the past.

The first year was a struggle, as the new coaches got to know each other. Stallings kept his hand in everything, which kept the assistants from feeling comfortable doing their jobs. An 0-3 start was brightened by a victory over Vanderbilt and built up to what may have been the turning point of the program: Auburn.

There is nothing more important in the State of Alabama than the Alabama-Auburn football game. And if there was one thing that most of Stallings's new assistant coaches knew, it was not only how important the Auburn game was but also how to win it.

Particularly on defense, the coaches decided before the Auburn game of the 1990 season that they didn't care what Stallings did, they knew how to win the Auburn game and they were going to do what they knew would work. It was a subtle rebellion, one that was in a sense aided by Stallings, who needed to find out just how good his staff was.

When Alabama ended a four-year losing skid to Auburn on December 1, 1990, with a 16-7 victory, it meant that the defensive coaches felt comfortable coaching the way they knew best. And, more important, Stallings let them.

In looking back at that year, one defensive assistant said the key to Alabama's future success was laid when Stallings proved willing to let his coaches coach.

"He really surprised me," said the assistant, in an off-the-record conversation. "He's changed and let us coach the way we know how, instead of trying to make us do it his way, and it's made all the difference in the world."

Offensively, it would take two more years for Alabama to find itself.

That first season, Stallings tried to install the same offense he used with the Cardinals, patterned after Landry's Dallas Cowboy offense, which featured a lot of movement and change of formation before the snap of the ball. The theory was that good defense is based on formation recognition, and if you change your offensive formation enough, the defense won't know what's coming.

But in the week before the first game of the 1990 season, Stallings realized that the difference in the NFL play clock (45 seconds) and the college clock (25 seconds) didn't allow a college team to do as much moving as the pro teams could do. So all of that work on formations and movement was wasted.

The next spring, Stallings decided to go to the option and had his offensive coaches work the entire spring and fall on putting the option into the offense. The only trouble was he had two inexperienced quarterbacks — Danny Woodson and Jay Barker — and neither could run the option. After a six-fumble fiasco that resulted in a 35-0 loss at Florida in the second game of the season, the option was junked — another entire spring and fall's work wasted.

The decision then was made to go with a solid pro-style offense, mixing the pass and the run, and during the spring practice of 1992 and the fall prior to the 1992 season, the offensive staff worked long and hard on the passing game, with Barker as quarterback.

What they found was that no matter how hard they worked, the passing game would be, at best, erratic. Barker often made the simplest of throws an adventure, bouncing screen passes and sailing the ball over the heads of wide-open receivers.

But the ground game was there. And, as in 1991, when Alabama led the Southeastern Conference in rushing and never lost again after the Florida game, Stallings knew this team would rely on defense and the running game until a passing game developed — if it ever developed.

As it turned out, the offense would enter the 1992 season with more problems than an erratic passer for a quarterback.

It started in June, when sophomore David Palmer was involved in a traffic accident in Shelby County, just south of Birmingham. Palmer, who as a freshman had been the Tide's most potent offensive weapon and was already being touted as a Heisman Trophy candidate going into the 1992 season, was driving a car at 85 m.p.h. when he collided into the back end of a truck, which was going 45 m.p.h. in the same direction. Tests showed Palmer's blood-alcohol level was 0.236, more than twice the legal limit of 0.10 percent. He was arrested and charged with driving while intoxicated.

Some demanded Stallings suspend Palmer for the season. Others said the incident occurred in the off-season, and Stallings couldn't be responsible for every minute of every player's life.

The first group came back and claimed Palmer would get special treatment because he was an Alabama football player. The second group said Palmer was likely to get a harsher sentence because he was a high-profile player and there would be so much publicity.

And all the while, the man with the ultimate decision was keeping his thoughts to himself. Stallings would wait to see how Palmer's day in court went before deciding if "The Deuce," as Palmer was known, deserved any punishment from the football team.

It was an incident that would haunt Palmer and the Alabama program all year.

And everyone wanted to know what Stallings would decide.

But that decision could wait. What couldn't wait was fall practice, getting a team that was picked to win the SEC Western Division to live up to its preseason potential.

Most football coaches poor-mouth their teams in July, believing, as Georgia coach Ray Goff said, "It's easy to be good in July. It's harder to be good in November.

"I can't afford to overload my butt here in July and then get some guys hurt and suddenly we're not any good. Then, I'm in trouble."

Stallings has never been that kind of coach.

"I expect to be picked high," he said before the season began. "And it doesn't worry me.

"What worries me as a coach is having a team that people pick to finish real high that you don't think is quite good enough.

I'd rather be picked high. I'd rather be picked to win every game. That means you must have a good team."

The concerns going into fall practice were the offensive line and quarterback.

The line returned five starters from the 11-1 team of 1992, although Jon Stevenson, who started as right tackle as a freshman, would be moved to his natural position of right guard and Roosevelt Patterson, who backed up Stevenson, would take over at right tackle.

But it was an offensive line that, despite Alabama's leading the conference in rushing the year before, was not a dominant offensive line.

"The last couple of years, we've pushed and shoved when what we wanted to do was be able to knock people out of there," said offensive line coach Jimmy Fuller. "Now, I think we're close to being able to do that. At least, we're headed in the right direction."

At quarterback, sophomore Jay Barker replaced senior Danny Woodson midway through the 1991 season, and went undefeated as a starting quarterback over the last five games.

But Barker had not played quarterback for very long. He had been a defensive back until his senior year at Birmingham's Hewitt-Trussville High School, when he took over as the starting quarterback in a wishbone attack.

Barker was not even recruited by Alabama until Curry's staff left and Stallings came in. Then he was signed, along with Jason Jack of Anniston and Steve Christopher of Oxford, simply because Alabama needed quarterbacks.

Redshirted as a freshman, Barker showed he had good speed and a strong arm, but was starting almost at ground level as a quarterback.

Thrown in as the starter as a redshirt freshman when Woodson was suspended from the team, Barker completed 33 of 67 passes, 49.3 percent, for 554 yards, one touchdown, and three interceptions.

Behind him was redshirt freshman Brian Burgdorf of Cedartown, Georgia, one of the top quarterback prospects in the South as a high school senior. Burgdorf had been a quarterback his entire life and was much more advanced in the fundamentals of playing the position. He was also a faster runner than Barker.

But Burgdorf did not have as strong an arm as Barker, and he had not played a down of college football. That made Mal Moore, the Tide's quarterback coach, nervous.

Then there was Palmer.

Palmer had played everywhere in high school — quarterback, running back, wide receiver, and defensive back. During his senior year at Birmingham's Jackson-Olin High, Palmer rushed for 2,001 yards and scored 26 touchdowns, and passed for another 1,232 yards and 16 touchdowns, leading Jackson-Olin to a 9-2 record.

As a freshman he lined up at quarterback and scored the only touchdown of the game in Alabama's 13-6 victory over Auburn.

Palmer had the best arm of any quarterback on the team, and everyone knew he was fast and elusive as a runner. But he was only 5-foot-9, and for Alabama to go with Palmer at quarterback, the Tide would almost be forced to run an option offense, something they had proven to be not very good at the year before.

Still, Palmer went into the season as the No. 3 quarterback and worked every practice at that position. Stallings conceded that if Palmer had to play quarterback, it meant the offense would have to be revamped. And, indeed, he installed a special, limited offense built around Palmer at quarterback.

But the decision early on was made to go with Barker first, and hope either he or Burgdorf proved capable so that Palmer could be left at his more natural position, wide receiver.

Freshmen reported for fall practice on August 5, with the varsity coming in five days later. While it was a good freshman class for Alabama, Stallings didn't expect to have to count on the newcomers as he had in 1991, when 11 freshmen stepped in and played major roles on the team.

The one freshman who was expected to contribute was kicker Michael Proctor of Pelham, Alabama. Considered the nation's top placekicking prospect by some recruiting analysts, Proctor set a state record with a 60-yard field goal and had made nine field goals of 50 yards or more. He also set a state record for extra points, converting 53 of 53 in his career.

Proctor was practically handed the position from the first day. The previous season, Alabama's placekicking chores had been shared by Matt Wethington, Hamp Greene, and Jimmy

Tuley. They combined to make 12 of 22 field goals and 34 of 37 extra points, well below the standard set over the previous four years by Philip Doyle, who rewrote the school record books for placekicking in his career.

But what most people were waiting for was the upperclassmen, who came in on August 11.

More specifically, they were waiting to see the return of David Palmer, whose future with the team was still up in the air as his court date got pushed back to August 31.

"I'm not too worried about it," Palmer said. "I don't think it will be a problem for me this fall. I just want to get it behind me and go on with football.

"I worked hard over the summer to improve, and I think it paid off. I just wanted to get faster and stronger, and I think it was a good summer."

Despite the uncertainty of his upcoming court case, Palmer entered the season as a celebrated, potential Heisman Trophy winner. As a freshman, Palmer set school season records for most punts returned for touchdowns (three), and most punt-return yards in a season (409). His touchdown returns covered 56, 69, and 90 yards, the 90 yarder the fourth-longest in school history.

Palmer had 171 yards of total offense (rushing and receiving), 1,113 all-purpose yards (rushing, receiving, and kick returns), and was the team's fourth-leading scorer with 36 points. Palmer had earned the Most Valuable Player award in Alabama's 30-25 victory over Colorado in the Blockbuster Bowl, where he returned the first punt of the game 52 yards for a touchdown and went on to rush six times for 21 yards, catch two passes for 14 yards and a touchdown, and return six kicks for 74 yards and one touchdown.

"It's too early to talk about that (Heisman) stuff," Palmer said. "I'm keeping a level head and just going on about my business.

"There will be a lot of pressure on me this year. Everyone will be looking for me now, where last year maybe other teams didn't know about me. They'll be concentrating on shutting me down.

"On the other hand, I know what to expect. So maybe it will be easier on me this time around."

The best story of early fall belonged to junior offensive lineman Dennis Deason, who signed to play with Auburn out of high school, went there for a year, then left and went to junior college, where he called Jim Fuller and told him he wanted to come to Alabama.

During his year at junior college, he came home to Birmingham to see the Alabama-Auburn football game and went out afterwards with some friends.

"I was out in a bar and this lady recognized me and hollered, 'You're one of those no-good Auburn players,'" Deason said. "I said, 'I was, but I'm transferring to Alabama.' She said, 'If you played at Auburn, we don't want you.'

"Then she bent over and 'mooned' me, and she had 'BAMA' written across her butt.

"It was a big 'ol butt. In fact, I remember thinking, 'That's a big ol' butt.'

"People that know me know I always wanted to play here. People that don't know me may think it's strange that I left Auburn to come here. But I don't care."

Deason picked a bad time to come to Alabama, a time when the Tide was loaded with as many good offensive linemen as it had had in a decade. But Deason, like most kids who grew up in the State of Alabama, didn't care. He wanted to play at Alabama, to wear the crimson jersey, and he was going to do it, no matter the odds.

"That's what kept me going," Deason said. "Whenever I got tired or discouraged, I'd picture myself running out onto that field against Vanderbilt, wearing the Alabama uniform in front of 60,000 screaming fans.

"Even now, thinking about that gives me chills. That's what keeps me going."

That dream, common to all of these players, was sorely tested during the two-a-day drills of August.

There was one thing noticeable about this team from the first day the upperclassmen showed up on the practice field: confidence.

It was manifested in the attitude displayed by the freshmen while working with the upperclassmen.

"There is a big difference between this year's freshman class and last year's freshman class," said fifth-year senior Martin Houston, a starting fullback. "Last year's class didn't look or act like freshmen. They were not intimidated by the upperclassmen.

"But this class is. They probably came in here having read so much about this team all summer, hearing that they didn't have much chance to break into the lineup. Last year's freshmen came in here thinking they could play."

The 1991 freshmen had good reason to feel that way. They did play. Eleven true freshmen saw considerable playing time, "and more could have played if we had needed them," Houston said.

But this freshman class joined a team that went 11-1 and ranked No. 5 in the nation in the final Associated Press Top 25 poll, a team that was expected to compete for the SEC championship this fall.

So there was a different attitude.

"I like to see a freshman's bubble burst," said senior wide receiver Prince Wimbley. "They come in here on their high horse as a high school superstar. We knock them back to size and make them earn respect.

"For a freshman receiver to suddenly be going against someone like George Teague — most upperclassmen thrive on getting the freshmen out there and introducing them to what college football is all about."

"I enjoy rubbing their noses in it," said senior linebacker Antonio London. "You've got to welcome them to the SEC, because this is what they'll be seeing every Saturday from now on. They need to get ready for it now, in practice."

As practice wore on, it became obvious this team not only had talent, but it had depth.

Barker and Burgdorf distanced themselves at quarterback, establishing the order for the rest of the season.

At tailback, senior Derrick Lassic, junior Chris Anderson, and sophomore Sherman Williams were running so well that any of the three could have started.

Martin Houston was finally getting the chance to start, after playing behind Kevin Turner for four years, and was backed up by former tailback Tarrant Lynch.

The offensive line fell into place as expected, with Matt Hammond at left tackle, George Wilson at left guard, Tobie Sheils at center, Jon Stevenson at right guard, and Roosevelt Patterson and Joey Harville sharing time at right tackle.

Steve Busky was back for his senior year at tight end, backed up by sophomore Tony Johnson and true freshman Kris Mangum, younger brother of former Alabama defensive back John Mangum, who went on to play for the Chicago Bears in the NFL.

Wide receiver was loaded, a welcome change from Stallings's first year, when both starting wide receivers were injured and receivers coach Woody McCorvey was forced to move tight ends and running backs to the receiver position. This year McCorvey was working with senior Prince Wimbley, sophomore David Palmer, junior Kevin Lee, sophomore Curtis Brown (nephew of former NFL receiver Charlie Brown), sophomore Rick Brown, and a walk-on senior named Dabo Swinney, who had pushed his way into the playing rotation.

"We can easily go three deep at both wide-out positions," McCorvey said. "We've got five guys who can run any route in any situation."

The irony was that only Kevin Lee was a wide receiver in high school. Wimbley was a tailback. Palmer did a little of everything. Curtis Brown was a high school quarterback and Rick Brown was a defensive back who was not highly recruited out of high school.

Now, the big question was, would they be used as more than downfield blockers?

"I think so," McCorvey said. "With the running game we had last year, people were lining up to stop the run, bringing seven and eight people to the line of scrimmage. Our running game will open up the passing game. People won't be able to play those eight-man fronts now."

Defensively, Alabama had perhaps the two best defensive ends in college football in Eric Curry and John Copeland.

The Tide lost All-SEC noseguard Robert Stewart, but had a solid replacement in James Gregory and a good utility defensive lineman in Jeremy Nunley, who could play all three line positions.

The linebacker corps had initially looked thin. But the progress of Lemanski Hall, a converted safety, had allowed the defensive coaches to move senior Antonio London to left outside linebacker and start Hall on the right side. Another converted safety, Will Brown, would back-up Hall, while sophomore André

Royal, perhaps the most physically talented of them all, backed up London.

"André Royal can be as good as there has been around here in a long time," said outside linebacker coach Ellis Johnson. "He just has to learn the schemes and the position. He could push for a starting spot before the year is over.

"I know what London can do. And Lemanski put on 20 pounds and is doing great. I look for speed at that position, and we've got that."

Inside, Alabama returned senior Derrick Oden to play alongside sophomore Michael Rogers, another outstanding athlete who could play just about anywhere.

In the secondary, George Teague, an All-SEC second-team safety, moved to cornerback opposite sophomore Antonio Langham, who also made second-team All-SEC the year before. Sophomore Sam Shade took over one safety position, while transfer Chris Donnelly, the SEC Freshman of the Year while at Vanderbilt, started at free safety.

Sophomore Tommy Johnson would back up one corner position, while freshman Eric Turner, a converted running back, came on well enough to earn a spot as a reserve defensive back, along with sophomore Willie Gaston, who was academically ineligible as a freshman.

The defense was so strong in August that after one scrimmage in which the quarterbacks were sacked 11 times and intercepted four times, offensive line coach Jimmy Fuller came up with a solution many teams down the road would consider: "Don't throw the ball."

The end of two-a-days signaled the beginning of the season. Alabama would open on September 5 in an SEC game, against Vanderbilt, and the team was ready.

Except for one thing: What to do about David Palmer?

The unquestioned star of this team had gone through all the August workouts, awaiting an August 31 court date.

Then two days before he was to appear in court, the 19-year-old Palmer was granted youthful offender status, which means just that: All Palmer was guilty of was being what the courts call a youthful offender. As a youthful offender, the records on the case are sealed, just as if Palmer were a juvenile, and whatever justice had been meted out, whatever punishment Palmer would serve would never be known.

"In a broad sense, youthful offender is nothing more than a fresh start as far as a criminal history is concerned," said Shelby County district attorney Mike Campbell. "It is not a probation. He was charged with being a youthful offender. It is sort of a hybrid, the last bite of the apple of youth for a person charged with a crime.

"The youthful offender status fills the gap between a person too old to be treated as a juvenile and someone who is not a self-supporting adult. It's usually for people ages 18 to 21."

And as the first week of the regular season began, Gene Stallings was facing the same question he was when fall practice began: What would he do about David Palmer?

Everyone wanted to know.

CHAPTER

2

A Short Celebration

A ll week, Gene Stallings was asked the question, "What about Palmer?"

And all week, Stallings's answer was that whatever he decided to do, it would be between him and Palmer, and the rest of the world might never know.

Which sounded like Palmer was going to play, right? Except that Stallings would neither confirm nor deny, leaving it up to a week's worth of speculation.

"I've talked to David several times," Stallings said. "That's all I'm going to say."

Speculation was even more rampant than before. The City of Birmingham is either blessed or cursed, depending on your point of view, with three evening sports call-in shows, and, at least during the fall of 1992, another three morning sports call-in shows. And the number one topic of conversation on all of them was whether or not Palmer should, or would, play.

At one point, Palmer was asked who he thought the most well-known people in the State of Alabama were.

Palmer sighed, looked away for a minute, then said, "The governor, Pat Dye, Gene Stallings, and, I guess, me."

There were those who looked way back, to 1964, when, on the eve of the Sugar Bowl, Alabama quarterback Joe Namath had been caught drinking, a violation of team rules. Head coach Paul Bryant called his staff together to decide what punishment to mete out to Namath.

The story goes that everyone was in favor of a slap on the wrist — everyone but one, that is. Gene Stallings voted for a suspension, and Bryant went along. But others said that was then, and this is now. Football was different in 1964 than in 1992. Stallings was different, after having spent 18 years in the professional ranks, where punishment usually meant a fine.

Indeed, those around Stallings knew he wanted to help David Palmer more than punish him, that since the incident occurred in June, it was not a violation of team rules, so why was a team punishment necessary?

"I'm concerned about the effect of all this on David," Stallings said. "I'm concerned about the effect on me. I've spent a lot of time worrying about this, too."

But public opinion demanded satisfaction. Drunk driving was a serious problem, one that the courts were beginning to get tough on. Stallings knew he would have to do something.

Still, he said nothing. David Palmer, if he knew what awaited him, said nothing and continued to practice with the team just as he had all fall. Very little was different.

Palmer said there was no reason to worry about what went on in the past.

"It's all behind me," he said. "I'm not distracted by it. I'm really glad it's over. I'm ready to start playing."

Indeed, while off the field Palmer had become more quiet and reclusive, on the field he showed every sign of being the same old "Deuce," laughing and joking with teammates, amazing everyone with spectacular catches or runs or passes.

"Football is my escape," Palmer said. "That's where I can go and have fun and get away from everything that's happened. Playing the game is my reward for all the hard work.

"From one standpoint, I'm surprised by all the attention (surrounding his arrest). From another standpoint, I understand. Because I'm an athlete, I guess that's why I got so much attention. I did a good job last year, so that's why there was a lot of hype over the incident."

Meanwhile, the coaches went about trying to prepare Alabama for a Vanderbilt team that, in head coach Gerry DiNardo's first season, had won four of its last five games and returned eight starters on offense and nine on defense.

The Commodores ran the triple option out of the 'I'-bone that DiNardo had helped develop while offensive coordinator at Colorado from 1982 to 1990. And he had a dangerous option quarterback running the show in senior Marcus Wilson, who, after taking over in the last eight games of the season, wound up as the second-leading scorer in the conference with 68 points (11 touchdowns and one two-point conversion).

It was also a big game for Chris Donnelly, a junior who would be making his first start at free safety for Alabama against Vanderbilt.

Just two years before, Donnelly had been the starting free safety for the Commodores, and even earned SEC Freshman of the Year honors after his first season in 1989.

But at the end of that second season, despite being a two-year starter, Donnelly decided Vanderbilt just wasn't where he wanted to be.

'It wasn't any one thing that made me leave Vanderbilt," said Donnelly, a 6-foot former All-State selection at Germantown (Tennessee) High School. "It wasn't just football. It wasn't just the school. It was a combination of things.

"And when the coaching change came (Watson Brown was fired and DiNardo hired), I knew if I was going to leave, that was the time to do it, a time to break away and make a clean start."

Donnelly was a welcome addition to the Alabama defense. Even though he practiced on the scout team in 1991, sitting out the season as required by NCAA rules, defensive backfield coach Bill Oliver knew Donnelly would be his starter at free safety the moment Donnelly became eligible.

It was an addition that made all the pieces of the Alabama secondary fall into place. Donnelly at free safety allowed George Teague, a second-team All-SEC selection at free safety in 1991, to move to cornerback, his more natural position. Sophomore Sam Shade, who had worked at both cornerback and safety as a freshman, could then move into the strong safety position, while Antonio Langham remained at corner.

And in nickel-and-dime packages, Willie Gaston, Tommy Johnson, and Eric Turner could all come in as an experienced players who could call signals like Teague. Teague would just move back to safety, with either Shade or Donnelly coming out.

But even though Donnelly had already proven himself in the SEC, he was anxious to prove himself to his new teammates.

"You have to step your game up another level here," Donnelly said. "We had good athletes at Vanderbilt. And I was playing against top-notch athletes, and that helped me. I had two years of playing in the SEC, so I know what to expect.

"But when you are surrounded by this many good people, it picks up your game. It makes you better. It has to. And now I'm anxious to see just how much I've improved. I really do feel like I can contribute to this team."

Of course, the irony was not lost on Donnelly that his first game in a crimson uniform should come against his old team, Vanderbilt.

"Since I left Vandy, I have not missed it once," he said. "But I'm sure it will hit me when we're out there warming up and I look at the other end of the field and see the Vanderbilt players. It's really ironic.

"It's been six or seven months since I've talked to anyone up there, and I won't talk to anyone until after this game. I'm still friends with those guys, but I just didn't want to talk to them until this weekend is over. I've never looked forward to a game like I have this one."

The Vanderbilt Donnelly would be facing was much different from the one he had played for, however. In the past, the Commodores had relied on offense, and so the best players had always been put on offense, and whatever was left over was sent to the defensive side of the ball.

But under DiNardo, and new defensive coordinator Carl Reese, that was changing. Defense often got first pick of the best athletes, as DiNardo realized that to compete in the SEC, you had to be able to play defense.

And while Vanderbilt was not much improved statistically on defense in 1991, the Commodores did return nine starters on defense. The Alabama offensive coaches spent the week preparing for Vandy's 3-4 defense, going over film of the last few games of the 1991 season, when the Commodores got on a roll and started winning.

Game day broke perfectly for the start of the college football season. Partly sunny, the temperature was in the mid-80s at kickoff with just a slight breeze to keep things cool as a capacity crowd of 70,123 packed Tuscaloosa's Bryant-Denny Stadium.

No. 2, The Deuce, was in uniform as the team warmed up. That was the first thing everyone looked for.

But fans would have to wait before seeing if Palmer would play or not. Vanderbilt won the coin toss and elected to receive to start the game. That meant the first play of the 1992 season would begin with the toe of freshman kicker Michael Proctor.

And that first kickoff did exactly what Proctor was signed to do. It sailed into the end zone and was downed for a touchback.

Vanderbilt threatened on that first drive of the season, running the option right for six yards, up the middle for eight, left for seven, and left again for six yards.

Then the Alabama defense warmed to the task, and two plays netted nothing. On third-and-10, Vandy quarterback Marcus Wilson was introduced not to Curry or Copeland, but to reserve defensive lineman Jeremy Nunley, a pass-rush specialist who came in on third and long, allowing Copeland to move to nose guard, replacing James Gregory. Nunley came up the left side and dropped Wilson for a five-yard loss.

Fourth-and-15, a punting situation. Now would come the answer to the question of David Palmer. All eyes were on the sophomore as he stood on the sideline, in uniform, wearing a crimson Alabama baseball cap.

The answer came when Chris Anderson ran out on the field as the deep man on the punt, and Palmer never left the end of the sideline where he stood, watching.

Palmer had been suspended.

But Anderson never got the chance to return the kick. In punt formation, Vandy flanked men out to either side of the line of scrimmage, and Alabama forgot to cover them. Punter David Lawrence took the snap, threw right to Robert Davis, a cornerback lined up at receiver, and Davis went from the Vandy 42-yard line to the Alabama 17 before being brought down.

It would not be the last error by the Alabama special teams. Mistakes like that would haunt the Tide all year and make every kickoff and punt coverage an adventure.

But just as it would be all year long, the Alabama defense was there to save the day. On first-and-10, Vandy fullback Carlos Thomas was hit by Copeland and fumbled. Outside linebacker Lemanski Hall recovered, and Alabama had the ball.

The Tide's first offensive drive carried them 57 yards to the Vandy 29-yard line. Tailback Derrick Lassic, on the first offensive play of the season, went 34 yards to the Alabama 49. Quarterback Jay Barker completed his first two passes of the season, nine yards to Prince Wimbley and 11 yards to Kevin Lee.

But inside the Vandy 30-yard line, the drive stalled. Lassic was stopped for a loss of three, and Barker was incomplete on two pass attempts, setting up fourth down and 13 from the 29-yard line.

Proctor came on and sent his first collegiate kick through the uprights for a 46-yard field goal, a kick that sent a roar of approval through the crowd.

The crowd would see plenty of Proctor this day, as the first half turned into a defensive struggle.

Vanderbilt completely fooled the Alabama offense. The Commodores did not come out in the expected 3-4 defense, but junked last year's plan for a 4-3 defense designed to stop the run and work to confuse Barker.

"We knew the times Alabama struggled were the times people ganged up on them to stop the run," said Vandy defensive coordinator Carl Reese. "We figured they really worked on the passing game in the off-season, to be ready if someone stacked it up on them again.

"So we went to a defense we picked up from the University of Washington, a 4-3 front (four down linemen, three linebackers), with a lot of activity by our linebackers and defensive backs, jumping in and out of blitzes, trying to give them a lot of different looks.

"We wanted to take the decisions out of the hands of the coaches in the press box and put them in the hands of the kid at quarterback (Barker)."

While it did not keep Alabama from moving the ball, it did keep the Tide out of the end zone for most of the first half.

The game was coming down to Proctor's right foot, with the freshman from Pelham kicking three first-quarter field goals, covering 46, 43, and 42 yards.

Alabama's special teams squad made up for its earlier error in the second quarter, when on fourth-and-17 from the Vanderbilt six-yard line, Tide defensive back George Teague got through the 'Dores' blocking scheme and pressured the punter, forcing Lawrence to run.

The end result was no gain, with Alabama taking over on the six. Two plays later Lassic ran for a four-yard touchdown, and Alabama led, 16-0.

At halftime, the Alabama offensive coaches threw out the game plan to adjust to Vandy's defense.

"We had to prepare for what we had seen Vandy do last year," said Alabama offensive assistant Mal Moore, who calls offensive plays for the Tide. "What we expected was a 3-4 scheme. What we got was completely different.

"We came in with too much offense, anyway. We reduced a lot at halftime, to get down to what the defense dictated."

The plan in the second half was to take advantage of Vandy's two-deep coverage by throwing to the tight end down the middle or to the backs coming out of the backfield.

Except that Reese, who has a college degree in mathematics, was one step ahead of Alabama.

"In the second half, Vandy jammed the tight end coming off the line of scrimmage to keep him from getting open," said Alabama receivers coach Woody McCorvey. "So we had to start throwing to the backs."

Before that could happen, there was confusion over Alabama's choice to start the second half. The Tide could have received the ball, but there was confusion between the captains and the coaches, and Alabama was forced to kick off, just as it had to start the game.

And this time, Proctor's kick was returned 46 yards to the Commodores' 47-yard line. Fourteen plays later, freshman fullback Royce Love ran five yards up the heart of the 'Bama defense for a touchdown, and sophomore tailback Eric Lewis ran in for the two-point conversion.

That put Vandy within a touchdown, trailing 16-8 with nearly an entire half to play.

"The coaches got on us after that," said Hall. "Vandy was taking the game right at us, on our field. We had to turn things around."

They did. Alabama's defense allowed only two first downs the rest of the game. Proctor kicked another field goal, and then the defense put the finishing touches on the game when inside linebacker Michael Rogers intercepted a Wilson pass, and saw nothing but the Vandy quarterback between him and the end zone, 36 yards away.

Rogers could have outrun Wilson. He probably could have run over him. Instead, he slowed up, allowing Hall to get in front of him and execute a perfect pancake block on the Vandy quarterback, knocking Wilson backwards a good five yards as Rogers sailed in for the touchdown and a 25-8 victory.

"That closed it out," Teague said.

It was victory No. 1, but in no way did Alabama show signs of being a championship team just yet.

The offense could not sustain a drive long enough to find the end zone. And while Barker completed 14 of 27 passes for 185 yards, he was intercepted once, and too often overthrew wide-open receivers.

"Jay was a little off at times," Stallings said. "But not near as off as he used to be. For a first game, he did fine."

The offense converted only three of 13 third-down attempts and rushed for only 104 yards.

"The running game has got to be better," Stallings said. "And what really bothers me is that we forced five turnovers and only got 16 points. We should have had more points than that."

The good news was Proctor, who kicked four of five field goals, missing from 52 yards.

"I thought I would be nervous," Proctor said. "But it didn't affect me. I felt like I do at practice."

"Kickers are weird, and Michael fits that," said Jeff Wall, a senior who had held on placement kicks for Philip Doyle's last two seasons, through the kicking rotation of 1991, and now was Proctor's holder.

"Michael is in his own world. I hosted him on his recruiting visit and didn't get three words out of him from Friday until Saturday. Nothing bothers Michael Proctor. He's the same every time, and that's good in a kicker."

But Proctor does have his own way of doing things. For instance, he is not much for practicing.

"I don't really think a lot of reps (repetitions) are necessary," he said. "I think you need to kick a few, to get into a groove. But that's about it."

A prime example came early in the year, before practice one day, when the rest of the team was stretching and warming up.

"We were goofing around, throwing and kicking before practice," said freshman tight end Kris Mangum. "Michael walks over, stretches a little, and says, 'I think maybe I'll kick today.' So he gets someone to hold the ball for him, and the first one he kicks is a 60 yarder.

"It was not only good, it was halfway up the posts. Then he said, 'That's enough,' and walked off."

Once the game starts, Proctor is more of a fan than a player.

"I try to stand off to the side and watch the game like a fan, like I would do if I was in the stands," Proctor said. "I find someone else who isn't playing, and talk to him like you would the guy next to you in the stands. That way, when you do run out there to kick, you're not all worked up over the game. You go out there, and then the adrenaline starts and you just do it. I don't like to get too excited about what's going on."

Even the adjustment most kickers say they have trouble with, going from kicking off a tee in high school to kicking off the ground in college, didn't seem to bother Proctor.

"The ground is not well kept at most high schools, so you need the tee," he said. "Here, the ground is so well kept and level, it's just like kicking off a tee."

Weird? "Everyone says I am," Proctor said. "But maybe they're different and I'm the one that's normal."

Despite the shaky start by the offense, everyone felt the problems would be resolved with the return of Palmer. After the game, Stallings said the decision to suspend Palmer was made Friday, the day before the game. He did not tell either Palmer or his assistant coaches until Friday evening. And it was a one-game suspension. Alabama fans went to bed Saturday night celebrating.

The celebration did not last long.

CHAPTER

3

The Deuce

Just outside the city limits of Tuscaloosa, down Highway 11, beyond the J & J Bait Shop and row after row of cotton field, stands a cinder block building surrounded by a gravel-and-clay parking lot. The fading lettering on the side tells you this is "YOUR CLUB FOR BOOGIE" and "OPEN 6 DAYS."

A five-dollar cover charge gets you a red ticket stub and entrance into The Citizens' Club, also known locally as the "black" nightclub. This has long been the place the University of Alabama's black athletes have gone to relax and unwind, to celebrate victories or forget defeats.

It has become famous in Crimson Tide football folklore. In 1988, tailback Bobby Humphrey and linebacker Vantreise Davis were attacked in the parking lot of The Citizens' Club. Humphrey had a broken jaw and Davis suffered a minor stab wound in his shoulder.

In 1990, running back Siran Stacy was arrested outside the club, taken to jail, and charged with creating a disturbance.

Former head coach Bill Curry toyed with the idea of making The Citizens' Club off-limits to his football players, as had been done with Harry's Bar, where white players traditionally hung out and often busted a few bottles in the wee hours of the morning. This is the place Curry was talking about when he said, "There are some places you don't go at two in the morning."

This is where a number of Alabama football players headed the evening after the season-opening victory over Vanderbilt.

"We were all out," said wide receiver Kevin Lee. "We were having fun and dancing."

David Palmer was there, too, out with the mother of his two children, who had come down from Birmingham to see him. Palmer is 19 years old. The legal drinking age in Alabama is 21.

According to players who were there, Palmer stayed pretty much to himself, at a table with his friend, and seemed to be having a quiet evening.

There is no curfew for the football team on Saturday after a game. Sunday is a day off for the players, the mandatory day off now required by the NCAA.

Still, when the crowd started coming in after midnight, most of the players started to leave, not wishing to get caught up in that.

Sometime after 2 a.m., Palmer left, too. The difference was that around 2:30 a.m., he was pulled over at mile marker 74, near the bait shop, for speeding. According to Alabama state trooper spokesman Capt. Roy Smith, Palmer was driving a Honda Civic 75 m.p.h. in a 55 m.p.h. zone. The trooper who stopped him observed that Palmer was under the influence of alcohol and took him to Metro Jail, where the wide receiver refused a blood-alcohol test and was automatically charged with speeding and driving under the influence.

Sunday morning, the story hit Bryant Hall, where the football team lives.

"I thought everyone was kidding," said tailback Derrick Lassic. "I thought everyone was fooling around."

But it was no joke. Less than 12 hours after sitting out a one-game suspension for the incident that occurred barely 10 weeks before in Shelby County, Palmer was in jail again.

He was booked at 2:55 a.m. According to a jail employee quoted in the *Tuscaloosa News,* six hours after being booked Palmer's blood-alcohol level registered 0.104 percent, still above the legal limit of 0.10.

At 1:13 Sunday afternoon, Palmer's blood alcohol level was low enough for him to be released, and he got out on a $300 bond.

The coaches, his teammates, and football fans were shocked.

When Alabama head coach Gene Stallings heard the news, "It made me sick to my stomach," he said.

"Everybody thought David could handle himself," said team captain Prince Wimbley, a wide receiver. "We felt like with the incident that happened before, no one thought that we needed to baby-sit him."

"I thought people learned from their mistakes," said Lee. "After the one-game suspension, you figured he'd learned his lesson.

"When Prince told me, I said, 'Stop playing with me.' When he said he was serious, I had to put my head down. I was hurt. David is a good teammate and a good friend off the field."

Because Palmer had been granted youthful offender status for his arrest in June, legally this would be his first DUI. The penalty for a first offense of a DUI ranges from a fine of $250 up to $1,000, with a maximum of a year in jail.

Palmer could apply for and receive youthful offender status in Tuscaloosa, as he had in Shelby County, and avoid being charged with a DUI at all.

What complicated the matter was that in getting youthful offender status in Shelby County, Palmer received probation. And while no one but the judge, Palmer, and Palmer's attorney knew the terms of the probation, if the Shelby County judge felt Palmer had violated the terms of the probation, Palmer could be facing more severe penalties back in Shelby County.

"Make no mistake," said Shelby County district attorney Mike Campbell, "David Palmer did not get some slap-on-the-wrist probation here. There are some aspects to the sentencing he received which, depending on the outcome of the case in Tuscaloosa, might require that we have some further activities here."

Yet there were bigger worries than just the legalities.

"I am concerned for David," Stallings said. "I really am, because I think he has a problem somewhere that we need to help him overcome."

It didn't take long for the jokes to start. "The Deuce" was now commonly referred to as "The Juice," and the same people who cheered him as a freshman were talking about the embarrassment Palmer had become to the Alabama program.

Did Palmer have an alcohol dependency?

"I don't know," Stallings said. "I wish I could answer that. I know his judgment has not been very good."

Everyone looked for reasons. Everyone had theories and offered solutions.

But the truth is, Palmer is just like too many kids who grow up in a single-parent home in the inner city.

No one seems to know much about Palmer's father. Friends of the family describe his upbringing as typical. His mother, Peggy Palmer, was not much more than a child herself when she had two sons, Robert and David.

By most accounts, the two boys were raised by their grandmother, Annie Pearl Johnson, until her death in 1988. Maurice Ford, who claims to be Palmer's uncle, says he raised the boy, and indeed, Ford is credited by some for the care he took in looking after Palmer. Others refer to Ford as Palmer's "agent," and say he was just riding a talented athlete for as long and for as much as he could.

In a 1988 story in the *Birmingham Post-Herald*, Robert Palmer, nicknamed Jaybird, described himself as a "thug."

"I let some older guys lead me in the wrong direction," he said. "I was using drugs, smoking and drinking. I was in different gangs and clubs."

David Palmer is three years younger than his brother and, like most younger brothers, wanted to hang out with Jaybird.

"When I told him I was going to go out with the guys, David wanted to come," Robert said. "But I told him no. I didn't want him getting involved with gangs. I told him clubs are not the thing to be in. The only thing he would end up doing is fighting."

Robert changed his ways when he went out for the football team at Jackson-Olin High School as a junior, and David followed. As a senior, Robert rushed for more than 1,000 yards and scored 11 touchdowns as the Mustangs made the Class 6A playoffs.

Willie Ray was an assistant football coach at Jackson-Olin at the time, and Robert credits Ray with helping get him off the streets.

"Jaybird wasn't a thug," Ray said. "He just wouldn't listen.

He was truly a good guy. We tried to get him into a junior college, but he decided to go his own way.

"We got David when he was younger, and he was closer to us than Jaybird was. After Jaybird went on his own, he made a turn for the worse and got back with the wrong people. He got some girls pregnant and had some babies. But he was a man then. It was a different ball-game."

The coaches and teachers at Jackson-Olin, like those at many city schools, are used to being the father figure for so many of their students and athletes. Too many kids come to them without a real father figure in the house, a role Jackson-Olin head coach Earl Cheatum has filled for hundreds of boys over the years.

"Coach Cheatum could get things out of David no one else could," Ray said. "Coach Cheatum just laid things on the line. I remember we had to sit David down for one ball game one time. David got to 'smelling himself,' thinking he was a little better than everyone else, and Coach Cheatum put him in his place.

"Sitting out that game really opened David's eyes."

While in high school, David Palmer became a father.

"David had problems with lady friends," Ray said. "I know two of his children are living with his mother. At one time, the children and their mom were living with David's mom, but now I don't know."

Former Jackson-Olin principal Charles Townsend, now retired, said teenage pregnancy is a problem everywhere, not just in Ensley, the Birmingham neighborhood where Palmer grew up, or at Jackson-Olin.

"Children having children is one of the great problems of society now," Townsend said.

Maurice Ford said that the fact that David has children is not an issue.

"It happens every day," he said. "It's unfortunate. David had sex, and he got caught. Kids have sex. It's a going thing. Some get caught, some don't. David got caught several times. That's life.

"But his mom takes care of those kids. They're at his house now. It's not like he had them and turned his back on them and no one is taking care of them. You know, the mother of two of his children was in the car with him (when Palmer was arrested in Tuscaloosa), so he still has a relationship there."

David Palmer grew up in a house where people came and went all the time — family members, cousins, uncles, friends who were without a place to stay for a while.

"His mom was a single parent trying to raise him and Jaybird and a couple more people in that house," Ford said. "He had to go without what other kids had. And he was always smaller than everyone else, so they picked on him.

"But that made him tough. And once people saw they couldn't rile him or rattle him, they started to respect him. And he always had talent. That made him stand out."

That talent was evident from the earliest days in a neighborhood where baseball was the game everyone played.

"We thrived on playing baseball," Ford said. "You had to play sports to be accepted, and David, when he was eight years old, he was the starting second baseman on a team with 12-year-olds. It was a league for 12- to 15-year-olds, and David was starting. He was small, but he stood out. We knew he would be good. Everyone pushed him to be good."

If there has been a dominant male figure in Palmer's life, it has been Ford. He coached Palmer in youth league games. He dealt with the coaches who came to recruit Palmer out of high school.

"Maurice really reared David," said Ray, now vice-principal at Ensley High School. "From the time David was born, all the way through now. He was with him through metro football, metro baseball, metro basketball. Maurice and David are real close."

After the first arrest that summer, Ford felt David was being crucified by the same people who had made him a star.

"At first, it might have been bad judgment," Ford said. "Now, I think he needs help. Whether it's bad judgment or alcohol, he needs counseling to get his head on straight. There is so much pressure on him, and he's only a kid.

"I appreciate what Coach Stallings is doing, keeping him on the team. Without football, David might do himself more harm. If he kicked David off the team, David might leave.

"But if he gets back on that field, you wait. He'll come back and people will be supporting him again. And he'll be OK."

Ford doesn't like what he sees as the fickleness of fans, but at the same time, he realizes those fans are the reason Palmer might be able to escape life in the west end of Birmingham and make a better life for himself and his family.

"They cheer him when he scores a touchdown," Ford said. "Now he's in trouble and they say he got what he deserves.

"I've told David that one day, that 'Deuce' comes off his back and he has to be able to deal with life. Right now, he understands that. He just has to get his life going straight.

"Once he does that, the Deuce will get loose again. And then you'll hear people cheer."

But it would be a while before David Palmer heard those cheers. Saying that his star player needed Alabama, Stallings decided to suspend The Deuce indefinitely.

"I really think that in David's career right now, he needs us," Stallings said. "I think he needs me. And I'm not going to turn my back on him.

"It's a very difficult decision, but at the same time it's a responsibility we need to address and he needs to address, and that's the way we are going to handle it.

"In all my coaching career, I don't believe I have ever had a player quite as gifted and talented as David. But I am going to suspend him indefinitely, until further time when the counselors or the judges or the probation people say they feel everything is going fine for him. It may be three weeks or it may be three months. I really don't know. I want to do everything I can to help him become a better individual. That's what my aims are."

Palmer would be allowed to stay in the athletic dorm and be a part of the team, Stallings said. Palmer would be seeing counselors on a regular basis while the legal process ran its course.

"He will be sort of like a redshirt player until I make the decision otherwise," Stallings said.

Because Palmer played as a true freshman and was suspended from the first game, he would be eligible to be redshirted, which is the term for an NCAA rule that allows a player to practice with the team for one year, not play in any games, and retain that year of eligibility for later use.

But more important, according to Stallings, was that David get help.

"The bottom line is that David has got to help David," he said. "He's got to realize the consequences. He's got to realize the probation he's under, and he needs to honor those particular requirements."

It was a minor blip on the screen when compared to the David Palmer situation, but there was another distraction that week.

In a story in the *Atlanta Journal-Constitution*, University of Georgia defensive back Ralph Thompson accused Alabama football coaches of offering him illegal inducements to go to Tuscaloosa and play for the Crimson Tide.

Thompson was sitting out the season in his hometown of Nashville, Tennessee, after a University of Georgia Student Review Board suspended him for twice being charged with drunken driving.

In the *Journal-Constitution* story, Thompson was quoted as saying: "I was offered a car" by the Alabama coaches recruiting him.

Stallings said the allegations caught him by surprise.

"It was a shock to me," he said. "I went back to check my (recruiting) notes. I didn't really remember Ralph, to tell you the truth.

"I did not offer (Thompson a scholarship), and I'm the guy that does it. You've got to realize this was two years ago. I had his name written in my (recruiting) book, but I don't remember offering him a scholarship."

But the next day, when the story hit the wire, Georgia head coach Ray Goff said Thompson called him to deny the story.

"Ralph called me," Goff said. "I asked Ralph if it was true, and he assured me it was not. I said, 'Ralph, the gentleman that interviewed you has it on tape.' And he said, 'Coach, it's not true.'

"So I called Coach Stallings and apologized to him for what one of my players said. I don't even know if Alabama offered Ralph a scholarship, to be truthful."

Stallings was appreciative of Goff's clearing the matter up immediately.

"Sometimes, for whatever reason, a player gets carried away," Stallings said. "I appreciate his honesty, coming back and saying there was nothing to it. And I appreciate Coach Goff calling me."

Asked whether something like this could damage Alabama's reputation, Stallings said, "I would hope the reputation was a little stronger than a false accusation. Anyone can say anything. It's got to be substantiated. I have no idea why it was said. I know it's not true. And I appreciate the player coming back and saying it."

It was a blip that went away as fast as it appeared, but it would prove to be a harbinger of more trouble. Alabama, a school that has never been investigated by the NCAA and never been handed any kind of penalty, would have its reputation smeared again before the season was over.

But for now, the Thompson story was over. David Palmer's story would have to wait for the legal system and his counselors to clear him to play.

And just when it looked as if nothing more could happen in one week, it did. On Thursday, starting offensive guard Jon Stevenson got word that his older brother, Robert Stevenson, a U.S. Air Force pilot, had been killed in a crash of his military plane Wednesday night.

Stevenson returned to his family in Memphis, where they all flew to his brother's memorial service at Lemoore (California) Air Naval Station. Robert Stevenson, 28, was survived by his widow, who was pregnant with the couple's third child.

Understandably, Jon Stevenson would not play in the upcoming game.

Again, Saturday was a perfect day for football. The game kicked off a little after 4 p.m., with a capacity crowd at Birmingham's Legion Field enjoying the 84-degree temperature and partly cloudy skies.

The Tide was ranked No. 8 in the country going into a non-conference game against Southern Mississippi, a team that had gone 4-7 the year before, the Golden Eagles' first under head coach Jeff Bower.

A good indication of how the game would go was the first two offensive possessions.

Alabama kicked off and Southern Miss lost seven yards on three plays before punting on fourth down.

On the other hand, the Crimson Tide took over and managed to gain two yards on three plays, with a fumble and incomplete pass.

The difference was that on fourth down, Alabama lined up in punt formation, with defensive back Tommy Johnson flanked out wide to get a jump on the downfield coverage. And when no Southern Miss player lined up out there to cover Johnson, Tide punter Bryne Diehl, a former high school quarterback, took the snap and threw to Johnson, who raced 73 yards for a touchdown.

It was the same play Vanderbilt had pulled on Alabama the week before, and a dream come true for Diehl.

"You don't grow up dreaming of being the punter at Alabama," said Diehl, a native of Oakman, a town on the Tuscaloosa side of Birmingham.

"You always dream of doing bigger things. But you do what you can do. My dream was to always play here. This is how it happened."

In his senior season at Oakman, the 6-foot-3, 200-pound Diehl quarterbacked his team to its first undefeated regular season. He completed 46 of 79 passes for 915 yards and 15 touchdowns.

"But when I turned slow, I knew I couldn't be the quarterback at Alabama," Diehl said. "And I turned slow the summer before the 10th grade. Bad slow.

"When I was little, I was fast. But suddenly, I knew I was too slow to play quarterback at this level. So I started punting."

By his junior year in high school, Diehl realized he had a chance to punt at the major-college level, even if he couldn't play quarterback. And while he had offers to play quarterback at smaller schools, once Alabama invited him to walk on as a punter, Diehl knew what he was going to do.

It took two years before Diehl got the chance to punt in college.

"There is only one punter," Diehl said. "You either make the trip as the punter or you don't. There isn't a backup who might see playing time, like at other positions. Either you're it, or you're not.

"There isn't much time to learn the position, either. We have a specialty period before practice, and then we punt at the end of practice, during punt protection or punt return. So it's a short time to impress the coaches."

What finally impressed the coaches about Diehl was not only that he got good distance on his kicks (he averaged 43.3 yards per kick in high school) but that he got his kicks off more quickly than anyone else.

"I went from a three-step to a two-step (punter) to a one-and-a-half step," Diehl said. "It made my operation time quicker."

In his first game, Diehl averaged 36.3 yards per punt, with a long kick of 47 yards.

But how did he find out he was going to be the team's punter?

"When my name showed up on the travel list," Diehl said. "We have a depth chart posted every day, and I saw I was on top of the depth chart the whole fall. But no one ever told me I was the punter, and you can never tell."

The Alabama coaches had put the fake punt in that week, after getting burned by Vandy the week before.

"It (the touchdown pass) was only the second time I'd ever thrown that pass," Diehl said. "My only concern was to get the ball out there.

"Tommy was so wide open, I had to look twice to be sure. Then I was trying to hurry the snap so Southern Miss wouldn't have time to see him and adjust. The coaches told me if he was open, throw the ball. Tommy was wide open. I just threw it. It was a great run by Tommy."

That would be the most exciting offensive play of the day, at least until the fourth quarter. Because defense dominated this game.

The Alabama defenders continued to impress, this time holding the Golden Eagles to just three first downs (two by rushing, one by penalty), 28 yards rushing on 27 attempts, 26 yards passing on seven completions out of 19 attempts.

But the Tide offense kept it close. Southern Miss defensive back Bobby Hamilton intercepted Jay Barker and returned the pass 18 yards for a touchdown.

On Alabama's first play following that touchdown, tailback Derrick Lassic fumbled, and Southern Miss recovered at the Alabama 18-yard line. Three plays netted four yards, and Lance Nations kicked a 33-yard field goal to put the Golden Eagles in front, 10-7.

The Tide special teams got Alabama back in the game, when three possessions later Diehl punted and Southern Miss's Perry Carter fumbled the kick and Tommy Johnson recovered for Alabama at the Southern Miss 20.

Four plays later Michael Proctor kicked a 25-yard field goal to tie the score at 10 going into the fourth quarter.

And then the offense came alive. Starting at its own 38, Alabama put together a 10-play, 63-yard drive that was a model of what this offense wanted to be.

Fullback Martin Houston carried for three yards up the middle, followed by tailback Chris Anderson going wide right for 16. Tarrant Lynch came in at fullback and went up the middle for six yards, then Anderson went wide left for two. Lynch went back up the middle for five yards and the first down.

Having drawn the defense in, Barker then ran a play-action pass and hit Curtis Brown for 17 yards. Anderson lost a yard on a sweep around right end, and Barker threw again, incomplete to Brown, on second and 11 — except that Southern Miss was flagged for pass interference, giving Alabama a first down at the Southern Miss two-yard line.

Anderson went up the middle for one, then off right tackle into a pile, and rolled across the goal line for the touchdown.

"I think I was under the pile," Anderson said. "I just kept driving my legs. I saw the end zone and it was close. I was just putting a little extra effort into it."

That 17-10 lead would not be safe until cornerback Antonio Langham intercepted a pass with a minute left, enabling the Tide to run out the clock.

'We had way too many penalties (nine for 78 yards)," said Stallings. "We kept beating ourselves over and over and over. We fumbled the ball too many times.

"But our defense played pretty well. I think it would have taken them a while to score. The name of the game is winning, and I'm glad we won."

Besides the nine penalties, Alabama fumbled the ball six times, losing two, and had the one interception.

But on defense, Eric Curry had four of the team's six quarterback sacks, came close four more times, and recorded five individual tackles.

"Southern Miss had more of a scrambling quarterback, which is better for me because of my speed," Curry said.

"When they kept running toward Eric, I just laughed," said defensive end John Copeland, who had four tackles, one sack, and two pressures. "I knew they were in trouble."

It was ugly, but all that mattered was that it was win No. 2, a win Stallings would gladly take, given the events of the week.

"We had a lot of distractions," Stallings said. "It's hard for the general public to realize. I know it affected me.

"A lot of things bothered us. Penalties really hurt. But the best thing is, we won."

CHAPTER

4

A Spirit of Power

The Tide was now 2-0 and ranked No. 9 in the country. But still, there was an uneasy feeling about this team.

No one doubted the defense. Though the season was only two weeks old, the defense was stifling, led by the "Bookends," defensive ends Eric Curry and John Copeland.

But offense was a different matter, and no one believed a team could compete for the national championship without some semblance of an offense.

Despite the Tide coaches' dedication to working on the passing game in practice, quarterback Jay Barker was still so inconsistent that quarterback coach Mal Moore was leery of calling pass plays. In the Southern Miss game, for example, the offense was basically a run-oriented attack — of 73 offensive plays, 50 involved either the tailback or fullback.

Alabama had converted only one of 12 third-down situations against Southern Miss, and was flagged nine times, turned the ball over three times, and fumbled six times, losing two.

And the results were as frustrating to the coaches as they were to the fans.

"We're not an inexperienced offense," Moore said. "This offensive line returns from last year. We're not young, except maybe at quarterback, and quarterback has not done that badly."

Even with so many starters back from a year ago — virtually the entire offense — Alabama was acting like a group that had only just begun playing together.

"We're too experienced on offense to be beating ourselves," said receivers coach Woody McCorvey. "The defense puts us in a position to do something. We've got to get the ball in the end zone."

The offense was becoming predictable, just as it had been the year before.

Of course, being predictable isn't always bad.

"We have been predictable," Moore said, after the Southern Miss game. "We were predictable last year, too, particularly in the running game. Yet we led the conference in rushing.

"That's something we're trying to get back to, to do what we really do well. Being mistake-free is the key to our offense."

And the first place the coaches pointed to when talking about mistakes was the quarterback position, blaming Barker's inexperience as the reason for the inefficiency.

While Barker was relatively new to the position, by the start of the 1992 season he had played his senior year of high school, worked a freshman year at Alabama as a redshirt, and been the primary backup most of his second year until taking over for Danny Woodson as starter for the final four games of the 1991 season.

"In a sense, it is getting old," Barker said, of hearing himself constantly referred to as inexperienced. "But I've only played six games, so in a sense I am inexperienced.

"But I've got six games, and that's enough to get better and understand the game and how it's played. I see a lot more this year. I feel more comfortable, recognizing defenses. I'm making better decisions on the field."

"For God did not give us the spirit of fear, but a spirit of power..."

That verse of scripture, from the first chapter of II Timothy, verse seven, was one that Barker repeated to himself often in getting ready for this season.

He recognized that last year he played with a spirit of fear. "You want people to believe in you," Barker said. "You want people to respect you.

"But I wasn't highly recruited as a quarterback. I'd only played the position one year in high school, where most guys had been playing it all their lives. I still wasn't sure about the position, and I'd tell other guys that I had only played quarterback for one year, and I could tell it changed the way they looked at me. It hurt their confidence."

And confidence is one characteristic a quarterback, any quarterback, has to have.

Instead, Barker played with that spirit of fear, a fear of failure. No one wanted to prove himself worthy more than Barker, but at times it seemed the harder he tried, the more he failed — passes thrown in the dirt, passes thrown over receivers' heads, fumbled snaps, interceptions thrown into the heart of the coverage.

Those mistakes caused the offensive coaches to have doubts about their quarterback, to get conservative because they were not sure what Barker would do under pressure.

"I just didn't want to make a mistake," Barker said. "I was so intense I couldn't relax. Coach Stallings wanted me to push for the job (in 1991), but I wasn't ready. I lacked maturity.

"Last year, there were times it was a guessing game. I'd drop back and frantically try to find the open receiver and not understand the scheme or know what the defense was doing."

But as the 1991 season unfolded and Barker was thrust into the starting role for the final four games, he started gaining experience.

More important to him, he turned to his faith in God and believed in that God.

"Football has to be something that is fun to do," he said. "If it's not, there is no reason to play.

"It's an opportunity the Lord has given me to do something I love. When I'm on the field, to me it's a way to worship the Lord. My objective is to play for the Lord, to praise Him, to win for Him. The other stuff will take care of itself."

Barker was one of the more outspoken Christians on the Alabama football team, and he knew some people rolled their eyes when he started talking about God and quoting the Bible. He saw reporters turn off cameras or put down their pens when he talked about the things that are more important to him.

But the truth is, for Barker to talk about God is as natural for him as it is for other players to talk about their love of hitting people or their desire to one day play in the NFL.

His Christianity did not make Barker meek. In fact, it was Barker's competitive nature that caught the eye of the coaches and made them feel as if he had something to offer.

"I hate to lose," Barker said. "We all do. Even playing cards around the dorm, people get mad around here when they lose. Whoever said, 'winning isn't everything' didn't win very much.

"The Lord wants us to win. The Lord wants us to take charge."

That was where the "spirit of power" came in. Barker replaced that sense of fear with a sense of strength as he moved into his second season as Alabama's quarterback.

"I gained so much confidence in the Auburn game last year, and in the Blockbuster Bowl game against Colorado," Barker said. "When the last game was over, I wanted to keep playing. Everything was starting to fall into place for me."

Against Colorado, Barker completed 12 of 16 passes for 154 yards and three touchdowns in the Tide's 30-25 victory.

"I knew I had to be an effective leader on the field," Barker said. "But until you prove yourself, no one will listen to you. I know the quarterback has to be like a coach on the field, but I also knew I couldn't do that until I had played a few games and had some success.

"Those last two games of last year gave my teammates confidence in me. A lot of times in the course of a game there is bickering in the huddle as you get tired and things don't go your way. You have to have a guy who is there to reassure them, to quiet them down. That's the quarterback's job. I can do that now."

Indeed, despite Barker's erratic play through the first two games of the season, there is no doubt the players followed him. If nothing else, they knew he had never lost a game as a starting quarterback, a streak that reached six after the Southern Miss game. Even if he didn't execute, maybe it was just that he was a winner.

"There is another verse, Philipians 4:13, that says, 'I can do all things through Christ...'" Barker said. "I realize that, and that takes the pressure off."

The coaches were taking a hand in relieving some of that pressure, too. Before the Southern Miss game, they had decided to start cutting back on the offensive game plan.

Some saw it as a sign they were losing confidence in Barker.

"I don't think that's the case," Barker said. "I hope they have confidence in me. We've been effective throwing the ball, except on third down. At times I've overthrown receivers, and sometimes the ball has just been dropped. There is no question we have to get better.

"But the plan is there to be effective."

Still, asked to play the role of defensive coordinator getting ready to play Alabama, Barker admitted it didn't seem like much of a challenge.

"I think we are predictable," he said. "If I was going against us, I'd expect us to run on first and second down and throw on third and long. It's something we've got to get better at."

One way to eliminate mistakes was to simplify the offense. It was becoming increasingly evident to many of the offensive coaches that it was time to start tearing pages out of that playbook, to start going into game day with just a handful of plays that everyone felt comfortable with.

"It's frustrating," Moore said. "To have this happen, after all the work we've done, is a shock and disappointment. And it has to be corrected. We don't have any excuses. We just have to correct it."

At least this time there was more controversy on the other side than in Alabama's camp.

The third game of the season would take the Tide to Little Rock, to play one of the Southeastern Conference's two newest members, the University of Arkansas.

But the Razorbacks made an inauspicious debut as members of the SEC, losing to The Citadel, a Division 1-AA school, 10-3, in the season opener.

Arkansas athletic director Frank Broyles was so embarrassed that he immediately fired the head coach, Jack Crowe, and made defensive coordinator Joe Kines interim head coach.

It made it interesting for Alabama, because Crowe was a native of Birmingham, a graduate of the University of Alabama in Birmingham, and had begun his coaching career in high schools around the city.

Crowe had later gone on to be offensive coordinator at Auburn under former head coach Pat Dye while that program was being rebuilt, and after being fired by Dye, took a similar position at Clemson University under head coach Danny Ford.

Crowe left Clemson to take the coordinator's job at Arkansas under Ken Hatfield, and when Ford was forced to resign at Clemson, Crowe's former employer hired Hatfield away from Arkansas.

But while Crowe was at the airport getting ready to move to Clemson with Hatfield's staff, Broyles offered him the job as head coach at Arkansas, an opportunity Crowe could not turn down.

In two years at Arkansas, Crowe's teams had gone 3-8, then 6-6, and he was looking forward to competing in the SEC against people he knew. Crowe thought he had recruited well, particularly at quarterback, and even though he had hired a new offensive staff at Broyles' bidding, Crowe liked his team's chances of being competitive and going to its second straight bowl game.

Then came the unforgivable loss to The Citadel, in front of the home folks on the university campus in Fayetteville.

The next day, Crowe was let go and Kines promoted.

"Coach Broyles came in and said he wanted to speak with us (the staff)," said Kines, describing how he got the job. "Then he called me in and offered me the position and obviously I accepted."

Just to finish the wild and twisted story of Arkansas, eventually Broyles would bring in Danny Ford, the former Clemson coach, as a special assistant to Kines. And to no one's surprise, when the season ended, Kines lost the interim head coaching title and Ford was named the next head coach at Arkansas.

But for this week, it was like a homecoming between Arkansas and Alabama. Kines was in his second year at Arkansas, having left the staff of former Alabama head coach Ray

Perkins at Tampa Bay of the NFL. Before that, Kines had been Perkins' defensive coordinator at Alabama from 1985 to 1986.

Kines had played college football at Jacksonville (Alabama) State University, so he knew Alabama well, as did his secondary coach, Louis Campbell, who held the same position at Alabama from 1975 to 1976 and 1980 to 1984.

In his first game as head coach, Arkansas went out and beat the SEC's other newest member, South Carolina, 45-7.

But Kines knew that beating South Carolina and playing Alabama were two different levels entirely.

"Alabama is a football team that's based on tradition and plays with determination," the 48-year-old Kines said. "They just want to win and get back on the bus and go home."

Kines wasn't quite right. Alabama wanted to do more than just win this game. The Crimson Tide wanted to make a statement.

And following the calmest week of practice yet, the Alabama offense went out and cut loose on the hapless Hogs.

Everything Alabama had not been able to do in the first two weeks of the season, it did against Arkansas.

Tailback Derrick Lassic rushed for 112 yards and one touchdown. Barker completed 14 of 17 passes for 192 yards and three touchdowns. The offense converted nine of 15 third-down attempts and, more important, scored five touchdowns in a 38-11 victory.

"Jay Barker made more big plays in this game than he had in the past six or seven games he's played in," Stallings said afterward.

Alabama scored quickly, with Lassic going 33 yards for a touchdown on the Tide's first offensive play.

Alabama scored slowly, driving 99 yards in 15 plays, taking seven minutes, 40 seconds before Barker hit Chris Anderson with a shovel pass that went 22 yards for a touchdown.

And the defense was its usual dominating self, setting up the offense's first touchdown by holding Arkansas to minus-five yards on its first three plays and forcing a punt.

Anderson returned the punt 21 yards to the Arkansas 33, and Alabama came out in a three-wide receiver, no-tight end set, spreading the Razorback defense. The play was a draw, with Lassic going up the middle for the touchdown — right through the hole cleared out by guard Jon Stevenson, who in his first game after the death of his brother was playing like a man on a mission.

The loss of any brother is painful. But Jon Stevenson had always looked up to Robert, a 28-year-old Navy lieutenant, the way the youngest of four brothers would always look up to the oldest.

Football was the center of Jon's life. Robert did his best to remind him there was more to life than scoring touchdowns.

"He tried to keep me down to earth," Stevenson said. "We really never talked much about football, per se. He never saw me play in person, although he caught some games on TV.

"But he was always supportive of my career. He always wanted to give me advice on what to do. He made sure I never got down on myself. We didn't talk about football. It was the other things."

Stevenson admits that for the longest time, he didn't have much time for the "other things." Playing football was the center of his life, and it paid off as the Memphis native evolved into a prep All-America at Christian Brothers High School.

A natural guard, Stevenson started as a freshman at tackle for Alabama, because that was where the biggest need was, and Stevenson was so far advanced in terms of technique and strength that the coaches knew he could play anywhere on the line.

His first year just intensified Stevenson's reputation as a hard-driving, serious athlete who attacked football with conviction and determination. Fun was not part of the equation.

Alabama had developed enough linemen to enable the coaches to move Stevenson back to guard his sophomore year, and the 6-foot-2, 275-pounder blossomed.

But the death of Robert, whose plane disintegrated during a training mission over the Nevada desert, deeply affected Jon. And when he returned for the Arkansas game, he came back with pain and anger.

"Lots of times, I was trying to kill the guy (across from me during the Arkansas game)," Stevenson said. "I shouldn't have done that. I should have been more focused on doing my job. I should have taken my frustrations out at practice."

But the game worked as a catharsis, and the deeply religious Stevenson saw that all the things he and Robert had talked about, the "other things" in life, were more real than this game played by overgrown boys.

Stevenson said he had to put his life in a different perspective.

"Football is a big part of my life," Stevenson said. "And it helps pay for my scholarship. But there are more important things than football. My teammates and coaches are important to me, and now I've got something more to play for."

Stevenson assumed responsibility for his brother's widow, Lee Ann, and her soon-to-be three children.

"I want to keep a male figure in their life and keep in touch so they'll remember who I am," Stevenson said. "If they ever need any help, I'll provide that.

"I'm practicing harder than I used to and playing harder than I used to. If I get a chance to play pro ball, that would be an easy way to help them, but there's not much likelihood of that. So I've got to study and get more into my books.

"I will never be the way I was before, but that's fine. That's the way it's supposed to be."

Arkansas had only three first downs by halftime, with two yards net rushing. The Tide defense had picked off three passes, which was as many as the Arkansas offense had completed in two quarters of play, and Alabama led, 28-0.

It got worse for the home team, which was being watched from a second-row seat by Arkansas governor and future president of the United States, Bill Clinton.

"The biggest difference in the game was speed," Kines said. "This game was played at a faster pace than our first two. Alabama has great speed, and that's what we'll face in the SEC."

Cornerback George Teague blocked an Arkansas punt to set up a one-yard touchdown by Sherman Williams. Sam Shade picked off two passes and Antonio Langham one. Lemanski Hall had seven tackles, Michael Rogers six, and four players recovered four fumbles for Alabama.

"I never played against a rush like that," said Arkansas

starting quarterback Jason Allen. "Their quickness threw us off early in the game. They're just a very, very quick team."

But this game belonged to the offense, and they knew it. As the game wound down to the final minutes, wide receiver Kevin Lee was going to each of his offensive teammates and brushing off their shoulder pads.

"What are you doing?" said tackle Roosevelt Patterson.

"Getting the media off our backs," said Lee.

The victory was accomplished using a reduced playbook, as the coaches went with plays they knew the offense could execute.

"We cut back a lot," said wide receiver coach Woody McCorvey. "We cut down a lot of our running plays and passing game. That allowed us to get in more repetitions in practice and made us better.

"For example, usually we go into a game with 12 or 13 running plays. But you can't rep that many in practice. So we went into this game with six running plays, but we ran them from out of a lot of different formations."

And it left everyone feeling good. "Everything was clicking," said Barker.

As one observer in the press box said during the game, "There were two surprise guests at the game tonight: Governor Bill Clinton and the Alabama offense."

There was one bad note. Defensive end Eric Curry broke a small bone in his hand and would be lost for two to three weeks.

But on the other hand, Arkansas' Kines turned prophetic afterwards when he said, "We may have just seen the national championship team."

Stallings would not go quite so far, but even he knew his team was suddenly looking like a contender.

"We still have a lot to work on," he said. "But if we can carry the same intensity in the coming weeks, we have a chance to make some things happen."

CHAPTER

5

"Defense is a Way of Life at Alabama"

The offense captured the imagination of the Alabama fans for one game, but the Crimson Tide defense had the whole country talking.

Anchored by defensive ends Eric Curry and John Copeland, through three games Alabama ranked first in the Southeastern Conference in total defense, scoring defense, fewest first downs allowed, third-down conversions, sacks, and turnovers.

In a quirk of statistics, the Tide ranked second in the conference in pass defense, which the SEC ranked by yards allowed per game, but first in the country in the NCAA's pass defense statistics, which are based on passing-efficiency ratings. Alabama was allowing only 3.8 yards per pass attempt, and only 9.36 yards per pass completion.

The Tide ranked first in the country in total defense, fourth in scoring defense, and fifth in rushing defense, and as the season wore on, those numbers would only get better.

"I say, thank God I don't have to play against our defense," said Alabama tailback Derrick Lassic. "They come after you.

They hit you. I believe every member of our defense would hit their own mother if she had the ball. Family, friend — that's all forgotten if you've got the ball. It's frightening."

Southern Miss managed only three first downs for the entire game against Alabama, and only one first down — by penalty — in the second half.

Arkansas did not get its first first down until nine minutes remained in the first half. One of the most amazing statistics was that the Razorbacks gained two yards rushing on their first offensive play, then finished the first quarter with minus-1 yard in total offense.

That was in keeping with the Tide defensive philosophy, as defined by secondary coach Bill Oliver.

"Our No. 1 objective is stop the run," Oliver said. "Stop the run and give them only one way to go. Make them throw. Don't let them have balance.

"It's no secret. That's the way good defense has been played for years and years."

But statistics are not important to Oliver. What matters most is winning, something he had a lot of experience in with four national championship rings from his days as either a player or coach at Alabama.

"Defense is a way of life at Alabama," said Arkansas interim head coach Joe Kines. "They play the way all defensive teams strive to play. They are as well coached as any defense playing football on Saturday or Sunday."

The key, according to defensive line coach Mike Dubose, is that the Alabama staff kept up with the changes in the game over the years. Yes, most of them had an Alabama background. But they also got out and coached at other places, learned, and brought it back to the university on what was, for most of them, a second go-around.

"This staff has a lot of experience at a lot of different places," Dubose said. "This staff understands the game and has kept up with the changes in the game over the years."

The quality of players these coaches were working with didn't hurt, either.

This defense was built around players who could run; and speed makes up for many mistakes in football. It is no accident that defensive linemen like Curry and Jeremy Nunley were high school linebackers; that linebackers Lemanski Hall, Derrick Oden, and André Royal were high school defensive backs, and that linebacker Antonio London also returned punts for his high school.

Dubose said the Alabama staff looks for good athletes who can run and can think, and then finds a place for them.

"To do what we do, you have to understand the game as well as have athleticism," Dubose said. "If you don't understand football, you can't do it. You have to understand why a defense is called and how it matches up from an offensive standpoint.

"If they do that, then we've got 11 coaches on the field and our job is easier."

Unlike many staffs that start simple and add as the season goes along, Oliver believes in throwing everything at his defense early, teaching them a little bit about everything so they will be ready for anything.

"Our philosophy is teach a lot of stuff in spring and fall, but we don't perfect much of it," said linebacker coach Ellis Johnson. "You can't survive with just a little bit of scheme. We throw it all at them, and then as the season goes along and we need it, they have a chance to perfect it.

"But we also throw a lot at them we never use. Still, at least if we run across something in a game we didn't practice for that week, odds are our guys have seen it somewhere along the way."

Safety Sam Shade is typical of the Alabama defensive player. He was an outstanding running back in high school, and winner of the Bryant-Jordan Scholar-Athlete Award, a scholarship given by the Alabama Sports Hall of Fame to a high school athlete who has excelled on the playing field and in the classroom.

"We take a lot of pride in recognizing different formations and the plays that are run off those formations," Shade said. "We watch a lot of film, and we depend on recognition. Plus, we play every play in practice like it's a game, so we have a feel for what it will be like."

And that is what the defensive coaches like best about this defense.

"These guys have fun," Oliver said. "We practice hard. Some people don't, out of fear of getting someone hurt. If we did that, our players might play that way. So the approach we take is ornery in every drill, whether it's 11 on 11 or one on one. That's the way it's been done here for years."

Oliver would know as well as anyone how things were done at Alabama. The 53-year-old native of Epps, a small town just outside Tuscaloosa, played for Paul "Bear" Bryant in the early 1960s; then, after stops at the high school level and at Auburn, he was hired by Bryant to coach the Tide's secondary from 1971 through 1979, a decade Alabama dominated as no other college team had before or since.

"We won a lot of football games in the 1970s," Oliver said. "That spoils you."

Strangely enough, Oliver wasn't one of those guys who grew up wanting to be a coach. He always expected to graduate from college and go back to raising cattle on his father's farm.

But two months of working cattle and an offer to coach high school ball in Georgia were enough to convince Oliver his future lay elsewhere, and it was a decision he has never regretted.

In 1965, legendary Auburn head coach Ralph "Shug" Jordan hired Oliver to coach his secondary, and during the next five years, Auburn went to three bowl games. The 1969 defense set a school record for interceptions, with 34.

In 1971, Bryant offered him the same position at Alabama, and Oliver jumped at the chance.

"Coach Bryant, Ken Donahue (former Alabama defensive coordinator) — those people had a major impact on me," Oliver said. "Just to be around them and see how it was done, that shaped me."

But along the way, the game changed. Defenses were so dominating that the rules were changed to open up the passing game, and offensive linemen gradually began to be able to hold, legally.

"I can still remember Coach Bryant walking in the office one day and saying, 'Men, they just took the first step in ruining football when they permitted offensive linemen to hold. They just took the fun out of defensive football,'" Oliver said. "I remember the moment. It was the biggest change in the history of the game."

Oliver began to shape his own philosophies in the 1980s, when the passing game really came into its own. After a brief stint as head coach at Tennessee–Chattanooga, he became secondary coach of the Memphis Showboats of the United States Football League, facing such wide-open offenses as the run-and-shoot of the Jim Kelly-led Houston Gamblers and the Bandit Ball offense of the Steve Spurrier-coached Tampa Bay Bandits. When the USFL shut down in 1985, Oliver landed in Clemson with another ex-Tider, Danny Ford, from 1986 to 1989.

"The game changed so much," Oliver said. "It spread out. It changed the way you think on defense.

"It became more of a team concept for me. At Auburn, if we'd led the nation in pass defense, I'd have been ecstatic. Now, our philosophy is to eliminate the run and make it a one-way street for the offense. Give them one way to go, through the air, and someone once said that three things can happen if you have to put the ball in the air, and two of them are bad."

So Oliver began to coach in ways that often put one part of the defense in jeopardy on any given week. But he worked with coaches who understood that even though statistically their particular responsibility might come out looking bad, it was for the greater good of the team.

But the bottom line was still the things he learned as a freshman player on Bryant's first Alabama football team.

"Sometimes as a coach, you have a tendency to get too fancy," Oliver said. "You lose sight of the things that are part of your foundation. You can't leave your foundation. You can't leave good, basic football. The best way to win is don't get too complicated.

"The only thing I've ever done is, wherever I've been, I've tried to do what I was supposed to."

Usually, that was to stop opposing teams from scoring more than his own teams. And more often than not, Oliver did just that.

Gene Stallings livened up what otherwise might have been a dull week by hinting early on that suspended wide receiver David Palmer could be back in action for the Louisiana Tech game.

"There are doctors and counselors to be consulted," Stallings said. "We just have to wait and see.

"David has handled himself well under tough conditions. It's a growing up and learning process, and we're trying to help him do that."

That was Monday. Every Thursday during the season, Stallings has a breakfast meeting with the seniors on the team at Bryant Hall. This Thursday, he told them he had decided to bring Palmer back to the team for the Louisiana Tech game.

After practice on Thursday, the last day practice is open to the media at Alabama, Stallings publicly announced Palmer's return.

"I have had conversations with two doctors and one nationally known expert on behavioral problems and it was their consensus that in David's best interest, he be allowed to continue with his normal activities," Stallings said, in a prepared statement.

"At this time in my career, I'd rather win the player than the game. Simply put, I'm trying to help David make the right decisions and I feel at this time it is in his best interest to get David back on the playing field. David has expressed to me his regrets over the earlier incidents and indicated as a result, he felt fortunate to be receiving good advice and counsel from professional people who will give him an opportunity to overcome some mistakes. I raised five children of my own and have coached thousands more during my coaching career and have helped them adjust to the changing pressures of everyday life. I informed our seniors of this decision at our weekly breakfast meeting this morning and they were all in agreement."

Palmer had met with Shelby County officials, site of his first arrest, and had retained his youthful offender status.

His court date in Tuscaloosa for the arrest after the Vanderbilt game had been pushed back, from October 8 to "the end of October or the first of November," said Tuscaloosa district attorney Charley Freeman.

While Stallings's decision was widely criticized, especially by the local chapter of Mothers Against Drunk Driving (MADD), he had made up his mind.

"The reason I let him come back is not because he's a good football player," Stallings said. "That has nothing to do with it. Obviously he's a good player. But we're 3-0 without him."

Palmer's position coach, Woody McCorvey, was as close to David as anyone on the staff.

"David understands what he's done," McCorvey said. "Some people will say he's not paid the price.

"David is a good person, no matter what anyone says. He regrets what he did. He's embarrassed by what he did. I don't care what the public thinks. I know David, and he's hurting a lot more than people think."

While there were supporters, as well as cynics, who regarded Stallings's decision to be one based on a struggling offense, there is no question Alabama fans were glad to see Palmer back in the fold.

Even Mal Moore, who calls the offensive plays for Alabama, admitted having Palmer back in the game plan opened up a lot of options for the Crimson Tide.

"David is unique in his ability," Moore said. "He has the ability to turn an average play into an outstanding play. There is no question we entered every game with certain things where we featured him, that were designed for him. Things that give us more punch and explosiveness. And that was obviously lost (by Palmer's suspension)."

That explosiveness would be evident that very Saturday, when Alabama took on lightly regarded Louisiana Tech at Legion Field.

It was a cold and cloudy day, with a fog that shrouded Legion Field so that the old stadium seemed lost in time.

The game itself was reminiscent of football from another era, a defensive struggle that the Alabama players would talk about long after the regular season was over.

The Tide kicked off to the Bulldogs to start the game, and neither team managed a first down through three changes of possession.

Then Alabama took over on its own 22-yard line, and put together an impressive 59-yard drive that was centered around tailback Derrick Lassic and fullback Martin Houston.

Lassic carried four times for 14 yards, Houston three times for nine, and Palmer caught two passes for 24 yards.

But the drive stalled at the Tech 19-yard line, and Michael Proctor came on to kick a 37-yard field goal.

Proctor added a 35-yard field goal to start the second quarter, and Tide fans were just waiting for the offensive explosion.

Instead, that was all the scoring in the first half. The Louisiana Tech defense was stifling the Alabama offense, limiting the Tide to 17 yards rushing in the first half, and sacking Barker twice.

In addition, Alabama was flagged three times in the half, and seemed to shoot itself in the foot every time the offense appeared ready to start rolling.

The Bulldogs got a big break early in the second half when confusion in the Tide secondary allowed quarterback Sam Hughes to connect with wide receiver John Henry, and Henry raced 61 yards to the Alabama nine before Tommy Johnson knocked him out of bounds.

"It was a misunderstanding in the secondary," Johnson said. "Me and the safety (in this case, George Teague) had a misunderstanding. I thought I had a little help inside and he thought it was man-to-man." Matters were further complicated when the Alabama defense jumped off side, giving Tech a first down from the 4-yard line.

However, on first down, Tide linemen Jeremy Nunley and James Gregory stuffed the run for no gain.

On second down, Hughes's pass was broken up by Sam Shade.

Linebacker Lemanski Hall and cornerback Tommy Johnson pressured Hughes into hurrying a pass on third down that fell incomplete.

And on fourth down, Chris Boniol's 22-yard field goal attempt was wide left.

"We had a lot of pressure up the middle," said Alabama defensive back George Teague. "If he had kicked it right, we might have blocked it.

"There was no way we were going to let them score. The intensity in the huddle was unreal. There hasn't been that much emotion on the field all year."

It would be Tech's best chance all day. Take away that 61-yard pass play, and the Bulldogs netted only four yards passing and minus-four yards rushing in the second half.

For the game, Louisiana Tech had minus-eight yards rushing and 125 yards passing, with just five first downs, an average gain per play of .79 yard, only one third-down conversion in 16 tries. And their quarterback was sacked five times.

But none of the sacks was by Eric Curry, a testimony to the tenacious play of Louisiana Tech offensive tackle Willie Roaf. It was one of Curry's worst days of the season, with no tackles credited to him when it was all over.

Curry's day was epitomized by one third-down play, where a fired-up Roaf ripped Curry's helmet off and threw it through the end zone.

"We were backed up to our own goal line," the 6-foot-4, 300-pound Roaf said. "I was kind of ticked off. We hadn't been able to get anything going all day.

"We tried a pass on third down. I kind of got him on the outside. My hand slipped up under his facemask, and when it did, I just decided to rip it on off and throw it into the end zone. Then I looked at him and said, 'Curry, you're going to have to deal with this for the next eight or nine years.'

"He looked at me like I was crazy. But he realized I'm a ball player. That's how you earn respect. You've got to go out there and do your best and dominate."

It was just another lineman trying to prove himself against one of the best defensive linemen in the game, the kind of battle Curry had to face every week.

In fact, Roaf credits that game with making him one of the top linemen drafted in the following spring's NFL draft.

"Before the Alabama game, not too many people knew about me," Roaf said. "In the preseason magazines, I was nowhere to be found.

"That (Alabama) game was my money game. I knew if I played well against Curry, it would get me noticed. I knew it was a game people would use to judge me. I went out there to dominate him, and I think I did a pretty good job of it."

It was about the only battle the Louisiana Tech offense won, however.

The problem for Alabama was that its own offense was just about as futile, gaining only 67 yards on the ground and an even 100 passing. The Tide converted on only four of 15 third-down attempts, had five penalties, and surrendered five sacks.

"There were two great defenses out there playing today," said Louisiana Tech coach Joe Raymond Peace. "I said going in I had never been so impressed with a defense as I was Alabama's. After playing them, I feel the same way.

"We had our chances. We had a first-and-four to go ahead, or at least get some points, that could have changed the complexion of the game. We just couldn't do it. We didn't execute offensively all day." And yet the Bulldogs were never more than one mistake, one long pass away from possibly winning, until Palmer gave the fans what they had been waiting for in the fourth quarter.

Every time Palmer took the field, the air was filled with calls of "Deuce! Deuce!" Every time he touched the ball, you could almost feel the excitement generated by the possibilities.

Finally, with just over eight minutes left to play, Palmer lined up around his own 37-yard line to return a Louisiana Tech punt in a steady rain.

Palmer dodged the first tackler, broke into the clear, and did not stop until he had crossed the goal line 63 yards later.

"All day we had returned to the left," Palmer said. "We changed it to return right and it resulted in a touchdown. The other 10 guys went to the wide side of the field. It was kind of wet out there. I couldn't make a quick move, so I slowed down and made them hesitate."

His first game, and it looked like The Deuce had never been away.

"I hate that he returned a punt on us," Peace said after the 13-0 loss. "But he sure is exciting to watch."

It was the best medicine in the world for Palmer, who admitted he had been depressed at times during the previous three weeks, times when he thought he might never play football for Alabama again.

"I wanted to be on the field, making a difference," Palmer said. "I was down.

"So it was nice to hit the end zone. Knowing I was back, it was exciting. I was just trying to help the team anyway I could — catch, run, block, just do something."

Palmer said the hardest part of the past three weeks was just not feeling as if he was part of the team.

"Nobody knows how hard it was, sitting on the sidelines watching my teammates and knowing I wasn't going to play," he said. "I knew what I loved to do was taken away from me. But I think I dealt with it pretty well.

"I tried to be positive and keep my head up."

And that, Palmer said, was just what he intended to keep doing.

"I felt I made a mistake," he said. "But I'm not taking a backseat and being a second-class citizen. Everyone makes mistakes. I can bounce back from this one.

"I don't know how long I'll be meeting with the counselors. Long enough for me to change my situation, I know. But I don't know how long that will take.

"I just go and talk with the man. He wants to see how I feel about everything, see how I really feel about all the attention and the criticism. I think the treatment is to show me how to cope with all the things that are going on. I don't think I have an alcohol problem."

Palmer also firmly believed he was back for good.

"I'm sure I'll play the rest of the season," he said. "We haven't discussed anything else. I'm back on the team."

CHAPTER

6

One to Enjoy

The Southeastern Conference went into week five of the 1993 season with five teams ranked in the Associated Press Top 25 poll: No. 7 Tennessee, No. 9 Alabama, No. 13 Florida, No. 16 Georgia, and No. 24 Mississippi State.

Eleven of the SEC's 12 teams were ranked in the NCAA's top 50 in total defense, with Alabama leading the nation. The only team not ranked in the top 50 was LSU.

Around the SEC, Arkansas hired former Clemson head coach Danny Ford as a "special assistant. " Ford began working at no salary, since he was in the final season of being paid by Clemson for not coaching.

It didn't take a real insider to sense that the hiring of Ford was a move designed to lock up the most successful head coach prospect currently not coaching, with an eye toward the future.

Already in Columbia, South Carolina, where Sparky Woods' South Carolina team was off to an 0-4 start, there was sentiment to hire Ford, who still lived on his ranch in South Carolina.

In fact, the most popular bumper sticker seen in the state read: "You have to drive a Ford to get out of the Woods."

Arkansas interim head coach Joe Kines said not to read anything into the hiring of Ford.

"With Coach (Jack) Crowe's resignation, we've been one coach short," Kines said. "The thing we wanted to do was what would give this program the best chance to improve. I always felt Danny was one of the best teachers of football in the country. We had a position to fill, and you try to fill it with the best possible man, so why not the best?

"I've had a lot of advice as to whether this was good, bad, or indifferent. The only two people who don't seem concerned about it are Danny and I. It's not as big a deal as everyone makes it out to be, other than he's a national championship coach and now he's an assistant. But it's not a problem here."

The problems this week were in South Carolina, home of the SEC's other new member. The Gamecocks were 0-4 and getting ready to face Alabama on the road in Tuscaloosa's Bryant-Denny Stadium.

As if it wasn't enough that South Carolina was winless in its past nine games, dating back to the 1991 season, starting quarterback Wright Mitchell quit the team the Monday after being replaced in a 13-9 loss at Kentucky.

"I'd rather play just about anyone in the country than Alabama," said Gamecocks coach Sparky Woods. "Especially starting a new quarterback. We did not want Wright to quit. We felt we could use him as the year went on. It will be difficult to go with freshmen against that Alabama defense.

"But I guess he felt that if we weren't making progress with him as the starter, he'd been a backup long enough. This was the decision he felt he had to make."

Wright, a fifth-year senior, could have graduated the year before, but chose to remain in school simply to get the chance to be the starting quarterback. After four games, he ranked 10th in the conference in passing, and South Carolina was last in total offense and scoring offense.

"After evaluating our season, the staff had some strong opinions as to the direction we needed to go," Woods said. "We studied our preparation and our plan, and then we began to look at personnel. It's not the quarterback's fault that we're not putting points on the board, but the best place to start with the evaluation of your players is with the quarterback. He's the guy that handles the ball on every play."

Mitchell was benched in the Kentucky game in favor of redshirt freshman Blake Williamson, who completed six of 17 passes with one touchdown and one interception.

"What we are looking for at quarterback is some kind of energy that will convert plays we are not converting right now," Woods said. "Certainly, changing quarterbacks against Alabama won't fix everything. It's a difficult role to put anyone in. But the objective is to upset the University of Alabama, so we've got to do everything we can to make that happen."

Meanwhile, at Alabama, the heat was being turned up again on the Alabama offense.

Penalties, fumbles, lining up in wrong formations, "We just keep shooting ourselves in the foot," said Alabama quarterback Jay Barker.

And limping to a perfect 4-0 record.

"We are 4-0, and it feels like we're losing," Barker said. "Everyone is so critical of the offense. And in a sense, we deserve it. But it's not like we're not trying. We're just killing ourselves.

"We're not out there trying to kill the point spread."

The previous week's 13-0 victory over Louisiana Tech was a giant step backwards for the Tide offense. A week after it looked like the problems were solved, the offense went back to being offensive.

No touchdowns. Only 67 yards rushing. An average of 2.49 yards per play. Four conversions in 15 third-down attempts. Five quarterback sacks.

Even more disturbing were the errors by the offensive staff. Quarterback coach Mal Moore admitted after the game that he did not do a good job of preparing Barker.

"Louisiana Tech blitzed us more than we were prepared for," Moore said. "It was stuff we hadn't seen, and we didn't adjust. They really brought the pressure on us."

But the pressure was aided by Alabama trying to run plays out of the wrong formation. Once, a reverse was called to one direction, but the formation was for a different direction, and the confusion resulted in a loss of yardage.

Another time, the formation was supposed to be the "I," but the offense came out in a split-backs formation.

"It sounds relatively simple," Stallings said. "But when that quarterback comes out (of the huddle), now all of a sudden the play is not the way it's supposed to be, so you have a misplay.

"And that happens two or three times. In the heat of battle you call the formation the wrong way — it happens more than you probably think. Sometimes an experienced player will make the adjustment on his own because he knows in order to run a certain play, it's got to line up a certain way."

In short, it was just poor communication between the quarterback and the rest of the team.

"Confusion going into the huddle," Barker said. "Maybe we were a little rushed in calling the play, and when we went to the line of scrimmage I was looking at the defense and not our formation. I've got to make sure we're lined up right. But that's something that should be easy to fix."

The lack of a running game and poor pass protection point to something else.

"We're not making good decisions offensively," Stallings said.

"I have no problem with the effort. We're just not getting the production we need in some areas we need to get it in."

It was certainly a point of concern for assistant coach Jim Fuller, who was responsible for the center and guard positions.

"I'm real close to playing other people, and I don't think that's unfair," Fuller said. "We're at a point where I'd like the three starters to have a great game. But if they don't, I'm giving other people the opportunity. I've got to."

The three starters Fuller was concerned with were guards George Wilson and Jon Stevenson and center Tobie Shiels.

Meanwhile, assistant coach Danny Pearman was responsible for the tackle positions and had resigned himself to the fact that Roosevelt Patterson, Matt Hammond, and Joey Harville were the best he had.

"It's not that our guys don't give good effort," Pearman said. "But sometimes we're getting whipped or we're blowing assignments. These guys are the best I've got and I've got to make it work.

"If a guy gives you all he's got and it's not good enough, well, that's all you can ask."

However, Fuller believed he had other options.

"Don't get me wrong," he said. "I'm not laying it all on my three starters. I share responsibility because I'm the coach. And there are breakdowns at other positions that have hurt the offense too.

"But if you give a guy the opportunity to produce and he doesn't, you've got to make a decision."

The most frustrating part is that all five starters returned from the 1991 season, in which they had helped Alabama lead the SEC in rushing. But after four games of the 1992 season, Alabama was eighth in rushing, averaging 148.5 yards per game.

"It's like, I call George Wilson in after the Southern Miss game," Fuller said. "I graded him at 52 percent. He said he thought I was grading him too strict. I asked him how he'd grade himself, and he said he thought he graded out about 60 percent.

"I said, 'OK, I'll give you 60 percent. But that still means you're getting beat 40 percent of the time. Is that want you want? Is that good enough?'

"That's the reason Coach Stallings has told us if we want to get other people in the game, get them in. I made the mistake this past week of not putting other guys in the game. It won't happen again."

The good news was that the breakdowns weren't happening a lot.

"We average four breakdowns per 60 offensive plays at the center-guard position," Fuller said. "But couple that with mistakes other offensive players are making, and even if it's only two mistakes per player, that's 22 mistakes in a 60-play game.

"A month ago, we were talking about playing two offensive lines. Now, we're struggling to find one."

As it turned out, South Carolina proved to be everything a good homecoming foe is supposed to be, providing an opportunity to showcase the best of this Alabama football team.

South Carolina kicked off to the Crimson Tide to start the game, and David Palmer caught the ball at the two-yard line, returning it 21 yards to the 23. But a holding call pushed Alabama back to the 13, where the offense took over for its first series.

On first down, tailback Derrick Lassic went around left end for 10 yards and a first down. Barker then threw a screen pass to Lassic to the left side for 15 yards and another first down. The next play was Lassic up the middle for 22 yards and a third first down. Then came a fake to Lassic and a reverse to Palmer, who went 39 yards to the South Carolina one-yard line and a fourth first down. Lassic went behind George Wilson at left guard for the touchdown, and in a matter of one minute, 20 seconds, and five plays, Alabama led the Gamecocks, 7-0.

Alabama kicked off and South Carolina took over at the Gamecock 21-yard line. Three plays netted a minus-6 yards, with redshirt freshman quarterback Blake Williamson getting sacked by Lemanski Hall while running away from Eric Curry for a loss of seven on third down.

On fourth down, Carolina punted, and the tempo of the game had been established.

Palmer returned a punt 24 yards to set up a three-play drive by the Tide for a second touchdown. This time it was Sherman Williams at tailback, gaining 30 yards on two plays and scoring on a 14-yard run for a 14-0 lead.

The Tide kicked off again, and on second down and 10, James Gregory caused a fumble that Bryan Thornton recovered at the Carolina 14. Alabama tailback Chris Anderson covered those 14 yards in two plays for the third touchdown of the game and a 21-0 lead.

By halftime Alabama would lead 38-0, and eventually would win its fifth game of the season, 48-7. The Tide offense produced 485 yards of total offense, including 356 yards rushing; averaged 6.3 yards per play; converted six of 13 third-down situations; and picked up 29 first downs.

Individually, Lassic rushed for an even 100 yards on 13 carries with one touchdown. Anderson finished with 120 yards on 13 carries and two touchdowns. David Palmer had 118 all-purpose yards.

Barker completed five of 11 passes for 69 yards, with one interception and one touchdown.

But perhaps more important, backup quarterback Brian Burgdorf saw his first considerable amount of playing time, and hit six of 11 passes for 60 yards.

Burgdorf provided one of the funniest moments of the season when he ran out on the field on first-and-10 at the Alabama 22 with six seconds remaining in the half.

Everyone was expecting Burgdorf to just fall on the ball, but when he got in the huddle, he called, "Diamond formation, trips right, hail Mary." In other words, Burgdorf called for a bomb.

"You should have seen the other players' eyes light up," Burgdorf said. "The linemen were asking about the pocket, what kind of protection. The receivers just looked stunned.

"Finally, I told them I was just kidding. I took the snap and fell on the ball."

Brian Burgdorf was a redshirt freshman from Cedartown, Georgia, the third-rated quarterback prospect in the South his senior year, behind Eric Zeier, who went to Georgia, and Heath Shuler, who went to Tennessee. Unlike Barker, Burgdorf has always been a quarterback, and it showed in practices, where he was consistently the more polished of the two players competing for the position.

In fact, in practice, the only real edge Barker seemed to have on Burgdorf was arm strength. Where Barker could cock his wrist and send the ball deep, Burgdorf had to step into his throw to get it downfield.

"But I don't think a strong arm is everything people say it is," Burgdorf said. "It may be to the coaches, but it's not to me. I think anticipation is important. I don't throw as hard, but you don't have to throw hard every time. I remember they said (former BYU quarterback and Heisman Trophy winner) Ty Detmer didn't have a very strong arm, and he did all right."

Where Burgdorf seemed to have the edge was in accuracy and consistency. Burgdorf consistently put the ball where his intended receivers could catch it and then run with it.

"I think making the good throw is what is important," he said. "Not leading your receiver too much, not overthrowing him. You want to get it where he can do something after he catches the ball."

Making the good throw is what earned Burgdorf honors as a high school quarterback. He passed for 2,274 yards and 19 touchdowns as a senior, with only three interceptions. For his career, he threw for 4,661 yards and 39 touchdowns with a total of five interceptions.

"I hate to throw interceptions more than anything," Burgdorf said. "If you do get intercepted, you have to forget it and go on. But I hate it. I'll run before I throw an interception, or throw the ball away.

"I can remember all five of the interceptions I threw in high school. My senior year was the worst, when I threw three. I don't even like to think about it."

Barker was bigger than Burgdorf, who stood 6-foot-2, 185 pounds. But Burgdorf was faster and the better scrambler.

The biggest difference was experience. Barker had not lost a game as a starter, and Burgdorf just happened to come along during that time.

"We all want to be the starting quarterback," Burgdorf said. "Jay is the starter now. But I believe we'll both play. And I want to get better. I want to try to be the No. 1 quarterback."

Stallings repeatedly said he wanted to play Burgdorf, especially at times when the offense was struggling.

"Jay is the starting quarterback," the head coach said. "But I won't have any hesitation playing Brian. I think he's going to be a good quarterback before he's through."

The only problem was, that Alabama's games were so close so much of the time, the Tide offensive coaches were hesitant to make a change. Barker did have the edge in experience, and erratic or not, at least he had not lost a game as a starter and had the confidence of his teammates. So as the year went on, Burgdorf never really got the chance to prove himself.

And while some people felt that Burgdorf was in a hopeless situation, being a redshirt freshman playing behind a sophomore, Burgdorf never saw it that way.

"I want to be the starting quarterback, no question," Burgdorf said. "But we both enjoy winning, and that's what's most important to both of us. We all want to win."

All in all, the South Carolina game was one for the starters to sit back and watch. Defensive ends Curry and Copeland played a total of 13 plays, then turned the duties over to the second defensive line.

"I think the starters enjoyed watching us play," said redshirt freshman defensive lineman Shannon Brown, who had three tackles and the first quarterback sack of his college career. "They got a kick out of it. They were joking with us. But they were also trying to coach us.

"Coach Dubose told us to play like there were two goose eggs (zeros) on the scoreboard, and that's what we tried to do. But there was a lot of leeway on the sideline."

It didn't matter who was playing defense, as long as they wore a crimson jersey. South Carolina did not get its initial first down until its last possession of the first half. The Gamecocks did not convert a third-down situation until second-string quarterback Steve Taneyhill scrambled for 10 yards on third-and-five with two minutes left in the half.

Carolina did not score until the fourth quarter, one play after an offside call negated a fumble the Tide forced and recovered at its own two-yard line.

"Their defense was just too much," said South Carolina lineman Ernest Dixon. "We came out in the first series and they just controlled the line."

It was absolute joy to be a defensive player at Alabama on this homecoming day.

"Sometimes you see that look in a quarterback's eyes, where he's scared and confused," said linebacker Derrick Oden. "When that happens, we just try to make him feel even worse."

Perhaps the best quote came from Stallings, when he was asked how he would go about attacking the Alabama defense.

"That's somebody else's problem," Stallings said with a smile.

It did not take Woods, the South Carolina coach, long to make a change at quarterback again. In the second quarter, he benched Williamson and went with true freshman Steve Taneyhill, who turned in a respectable performance, completing 10 of 17 passes for 135 yards with no interceptions, and led the Gamecocks to their only touchdown of the day, in the fourth quarter.

It was bittersweet for Tide fans. Taneyhill was a quarterback Alabama had watched and been after since he was a sophomore at Altoona, Pennsylvania, High School. In fact, it came down to Alabama and South Carolina for the 6-foot-5, 200-pound Taneyhill.

Taneyhill had attended South Carolina's spring game and announced that he would be the starting quarterback before the season was over, and he proved correct.

Woods turned the offense over to Taneyhill the week after the Alabama game, and South Carolina won five of its next six games.

That was a reflection of Taneyhill's confidence in himself.

"He has always had that ability to get other people to play at the top of their game," said his mother, Susan Taneyhill. "He was so confident (in high school), he made everybody around him that way."

When Taneyhill visited Alabama, some people were surprised at his long hair, which he often wore pulled back in a ponytail, and his earring. When a reporter jokingly told Tide assistant Mal Moore that the school didn't need any long-haired, earring-wearing quarterbacks, Moore smiled and said, "We could make an exception for him."

Tanneyhill heard from the Alabama fans after the victory over South Carolina.

"A lot of people said I went to the wrong school," Taneyhill said. "They were yelling at me. I told them to wait until next year."

Next year? How about next week?

Taneyhill became the starter the next week against Mississippi State and led the Gamecocks to their first victory of the season, causing South Carolina wide receiver Asim Penny to say about the freshman quarterback, "I don't care if he wears a dress, as long as he keeps getting the ball to the receivers and making touchdowns."

Woods, whose team walked out on him after the Alabama game but eventually returned, was thankful for the freshman.

"He brings enthusiasm and confidence and big plays to the game," Woods said. "And that's something we have not had much of in the past. He made plays that turned into points for us."

And while some people tried to point to the player revolt that led to the turnaround in South Carolina's football fortunes, Woods was more realistic.

The reason for the turnaround, Woods believed, was "great leadership by our seniors, the development of our younger players, and the addition of a quarterback by the name of Steve Taneyhill."

Alabama fans were doing just fine with Barker. But still, many couldn't help but look at Taneyhill and wonder, "What if . . . ?"

CHAPTER

7

The Second Saturday in October

The third weekend in October is a legendary time for Alabama football, because it is traditionally the Saturday of the Alabama-Tennessee football game.

But just as much a part of that tradition, although not something Tide fans talk about, is the second weekend in October — not because of any great rivalry that occurs then, but rather because it is the one weekend Alabama fans can count on seeing a marshmallow on the schedule.

Going back to 1958, Alabama has won 27 games, lost six, and tied one on the Saturday before the Tennessee game. Usually, that Saturday was reserved for the likes of Furman and Tennessee–Chattanooga and Vanderbilt and Tulane.

"I know when I was here before at Alabama (as an assistant from 1958 to 1964), we would schedule a game before we played Tennessee that we thought we could win," Stallings said. "And we would spend about two weeks getting ready for that single wing (Tennessee's offense of that era)."

It led to some very forgettable games, such as defeats of Furman, 29-6; or Chattanooga, 13-0; or Vanderbilt, 21-0. They weren't blowouts, because the Tide was focusing on the Tennessee game coming up the next week. But they were games Alabama could win without having to really put forth the effort.

Those kinds of matchups continued for Stallings this time around at Alabama. In 1990, he coached the Tide to a 25-6 victory over Southwest Louisiana before playing Tennessee, and in 1991 it was a 62-0 victory over Tulane.

The record shows that it is not a good thing to get too ambitious the week before the Tennessee game. Former Alabama coach Ray Perkins played Penn State three years in a row on the second weekend of October and went 1-2. He also was 0-3 versus the Vols in those years.

Bill Curry, who replaced Perkins, was a coach who got caught looking ahead when it came to October. His teams were 1-2 on the second week of October, losing to Memphis State and Ole Miss. But when it came time to play the Volunteers, Curry's teams were 3-0.

The patsy this week was Tulane again, but instead of playing the Green Wave in Tuscaloosa or Birmingham, Alabama had agreed to go on the road and meet Tulane in the New Orleans Superdome.

Stallings played the role of the good football coach who takes every game "one at a time," as the cliché goes. Asked if his team was looking ahead to Tennessee, Stallings said, "Absolutely not. I'm concerned about Tulane. That's the only one I'm concerned with. Last week I was only concerned about South Carolina. Different people do it different ways, but this is the way I approach it. I think one of the bad things you can do is lose a game you are supposed to win. I want to win games we're supposed to win. I don't think, in this day and time, you can overlook anybody."

Second-string tailback Chris Anderson was a player who felt he had been overlooked.

In 1990, Anderson walked right off the campus of Huntsville High School and into the starting lineup at the University of Alabama, leading the Tide in rushing as a freshman. He had consecutive 100-yard rushing days, followed by a 95-yard effort, and Anderson appeared to be the rising star at tailback.

When spring practice rolled around in 1991, Anderson was No. 1 on the depth chart. The climb had been so fast that he decided to skip spring practice to play baseball.

"It was a bad decision on my part," Anderson said. "I went in as the starting tailback and came out No. 3. Looking back now, I should have been out there for football instead of playing baseball."

Almost forgotten as a sophomore, Anderson had only 26 carries for the season, for 213 yards. It was as if the coaches had written him off, as if he had chosen baseball over football.

"I don't know that I blame them," said Anderson. "You've got to go with the backs you're looking at every day, and I wasn't there. Siran (Stacy) and Derrick (Lassic) were."

Still, there were days. Against Temple, Anderson set a school record with a 96-yard touchdown run. He averaged 8.2 yards per carry.

But he learned his lesson. When spring practice rolled around in 1992, Anderson forgot about baseball and made sure he was on the practice field.

Even though Lassic, the senior, emerged as the No. 1 tailback, Anderson was in the playing rotation, and through the first five games of the season, had 38 carries for 381 yards and three touchdowns.

Against South Carolina, he had the best game of his career, picking up 120 yards and two touchdowns.

"That was a real confidence builder for me," said Anderson, who modeled men's clothes while he was in high school. "I worked hard all summer to be the No. 1 tailback. I understand Derrick is a senior, and has earned the right to be the starter. But I also know I'm in the (playing) rotation, and when I'm in there, I'm trying to make something happen.

"My goal is to rush for 100 yards every game. If I only get five carries, then I'm trying to get that done in five carries."

At 5-9 and 180 pounds, Anderson doesn't look durable enough to take the pounding of a starting tailback. But his strength is surprising. He got a lot stronger in the weight room without losing any speed.

"I can run with authority," he said. "One guy is not going to bring me down with one arm anymore. I think I'm a lot harder to bring down.

"I couldn't run any better than I did Saturday. I hope it carries over. This whole offense is just so close to busting out. It's almost there. If we can perform well again this week, the confidence will be high as it needs to be going into the last half of the season."

Alabama fans flocked to New Orleans for the Tulane game, many using the trip to go ahead and order Sugar Bowl tickets, convinced the Tide would be there on New Year's Day.

So many Alabama fans came that Tulane officials had to start selling tickets in the upper deck at the Superdome, something not usually done for Green Wave games. Roughly 17,000 tickets were sold through the Alabama ticket office, and Tulane officials reported selling another 8,000 to Tide fans through their office.

As it turned out, the game drew 50,240 fans, the biggest home crowd at a Tulane game in five years. And the crowd advantage definitely belonged to Alabama.

It wasn't that anyone expected that good of a game from Tulane. The Green Wave was ranked No. 105 in the nation in the *USA Today* computer ranking, behind South Carolina (102), Division II Jacksonville State (103), and Division I-AA Samford (104).

Many people felt that it was just another case of Alabama playing one of the easiest schedules in the nation, a criticism that didn't bother Stallings.

"It really doesn't make any difference," he said. "If you could have guaranteed me that we'd be 5-0 with tougher opponents . . . the only thing about it is, even though you might play a little bit better opponents, you may be more bruised up, too."

Bourbon Street was a sea of crimson the Saturday of the game, and fans flocked to the Superdome to buy tickets at the gate for the game. It gave Alabama a near-home field advantage that Saturday night as the Tide faithful arrived early, took over quickly, and stayed late — or at least until they couldn't resist the lure of the French Quarter any longer.

What they saw in the first half may have made many of the Alabama fans wonder if they would be able to unload those recently purchased Sugar Bowl tickets.

After 30 minutes of play, the Tide was holding onto a 6-0 lead, thanks to two Michael Proctor field goals of 42 and 39 yards.

All the progress Jay Barker had been making in the previous weeks went out the window as he continually killed Alabama drives with incomplete passes. Through the first quarter, Barker had completed only one of six attempts, and that on a simple three-step drop to Prince Wimbley. His other five passes were low to Wimbley, high to David Palmer, a drop by Kevin Lee, an overthrow to a wide-open tight end Steve Busky down the middle on third down, and a drop by the usually sure-handed Curtis Brown.

On top of that, he was sacked twice and forced to run once out of the shotgun on a missed handoff that resulted in a loss of six yards.

When Alabama stayed on the ground, the Tide proved it could move the ball. Tailback Derrick Lassic was on his way to a big game in the first half, with 94 yards rushing through two quarters. But when it counted, the offense could not convert on third down.

The six-point lead almost went up in smoke on the last play of the first half when Tulane, on first-and-10 from the Tide 21, executed a near-perfect "fumble-rooski" on the Alabama defense.

Quarterback Shawn Meadows took the snap, then laid the ball down next to his left guard, Andy Abramowitz. Meadows then rolled right, as if running a sweep, and the entire Tide defense went with him.

After covering the ball on the ground, Abramowitz picked it up and rambled 21 yards untouched into the end zone for an apparent touchdown.   Only an alert line judge saw what no one else in the Superdome saw — that when Abramowitz went to cover the ball, he put his knee on the ground and so was down. Instead of a 21-yard touchdown, the play officially became a fumble by Meadows, recovered by Abramowitz for no gain.

Needless to say, it was an unhappy locker room at halftime for the Tide. Lassic asked the coaches to leave the dressing room so the seniors could address the team.

"The coaches are always talking to us," Lassic said. "But this is our team. Someone had to step forward and be a leader.

"I'm not a speaker, but I felt somebody had to say something. I don't like making speeches. I'd rather just lead by example. But we walked in there at halftime with our heads down, like we were whipped. Somebody had to say something."

So Lassic did. He told his teammates to get their heads up, to start playing like a top-five team. He told them to pick up the pace, that it was time to get serious about what they were doing.

"I told them if we want to be a championship team, we have to score points when we're in the red zone (inside the opponent's 20-yard line)," Lassic said. "We weren't getting it done. When you get inside the 20- or 25-yard line, you have to score. I used Tennessee as an example, because when they get it in there, they almost always score."

Barker, for one, took the speech to heart.

"Derrick really got us hyped," he said.

Then a few other seniors said a few things that might have blistered the paint off the Superdome walls.

"I think that's good," said Stallings, talking about being asked to leave the team at halftime. "Sometimes the players need to be alone. The players got themselves ready to play in the second half. They talked as a group and I like that."

Lassic went out in the second half and made sure to everyone he backed up what he said. The senior rushed for over 100 yards in the final two quarters to finish with 188 yards in the game, with one touchdown on a five-yard run.

Proctor tacked on another field goal, and Anderson added two touchdowns on 84 yards rushing in seven carries.

Barker, who was four of 12 in the first half, threw only four times in the second half, completing two — a four yarder to Wimbley and a 20-yard screen to Anderson in the fourth quarter.

Burgdorf came in in the fourth quarter and completed two of three passes for 65 yards, and the Tide scored two more touchdowns, one a four-yard run by Sherman Williams one play after Burgdorf connected with Tarrant Lynch for 51 yards to the Tulane four-yard line.

Burgdorf hit David Palmer for a 14 yarder on the next Tide scoring drive, then Anderson took the pitch and went wide left for 57 yards and the final points in a 37-0 victory.

And fullback Martin Houston was quietly becoming everything the Tide coaches wanted at fullback. The 5-10, 245-pound senior from Centre, Alabama, rushed for 65 yards on nine carries, but more important to Stallings, he was even more effective as a blocker.

A fifth-year senior, Houston had worked hard for four years, making the transition from high school tailback, where he was the Alabama Class 4A "Player of the Year," to college fullback after bulking up during his first year.

During his redshirt freshman season, the Tide offense, under former offensive coordinator Homer Smith, became a pass-oriented attack, and Houston, after dropping passes in preseason practices, got labeled as having bad hands.

So he spent that year as Kevin Turner's backup, coming in on short-yardage situations, most often as an extra back for blocking purposes.

Turner was so effective that year as both a receiver and a runner that Houston seemed destined to remain a second-string fullback for his whole career.

His playing time increased under Stallings, who moved the offense back to a run-first philosophy, and thus wanted a big fullback who could block as well as run. Stallings wasn't so concerned with the fullback being able to catch balls on routes out of the backfield.

When Turner's eligibility was up, Houston inherited the fullback position and was determined to make the most of his senior year.

"I'm as tired as I've been in five years here," Houston said one day toward the end of preseason practices. "But I'd rather be tired from running with the first team than tired from wanting to.

"For the last four years, 'first team' has meant someone else. I always wanted to start before now, but with Kevin Turner in front of me, I had to be patient and wait my turn and hope it paid off in the long run."

Houston didn't sit around wasting time those first four years. He got married, had a son, Xavier, and graduated in four years with a degree in human resources management.

"Before I got married, if things didn't go well for me I'd go back to my room and sit and think about it," Houston said. "Now, I have a wife to go home to, and a little boy. That makes me tend to leave football at the football complex.

"And now that I'm in graduate school, I have a class that meets only once a week. My other two classes are independent studies, so I set the time I meet with my professors."

It never occurred to him not to come back to play football this final season.

"I didn't even think about the fact that I was that close to graduating," Houston said. "I never thought about not coming back. At least, not until two-a-days. That was when I wondered why I was doing this when I didn't have to. But most of us wonder that every year during two-a-days."

Besides, not coming back would have meant not proving himself as a fullback.

"I just want to pick up where Kevin Turner left off," Houston said.

Running back coach Larry Kirksey said that, like the offense as a whole, Houston really came on as the season went along.

"Martin started out just average," Kirksey said. "But by the end of the year, he was outstanding."

Alabama's 24 first downs, 435 yards rushing, 573 yards of total offense, and nine of 17 conversions on third down against Tulane almost overshadowed another defensive performance that was becoming routine in its dominance:

- Alabama held the Green Wave to 58 yards rushing, the fifth consecutive week opponents had been held to under 100 yards rushing against the Tide.
- Alabama picked off four Tulane passes, with Willie Gaston, Chris Donnelly, Antonio Langham, and George Teague getting one each.
- Tulane converted only three of 14 third-down attempts.
- And the shutout, the third of the season, meant Alabama had held opponents scoreless in 19 of 24 quarters through six games of the 1992 season.

The game was significant for one other reason, one of a personal nature to Stallings.

He reached the .500 mark for his career as a college coach. After being 18 games under the break-even mark (27-45-1) for his six seasons at Texas A&M, he was 51-51 after two-and-a-half seasons (24-6) at Alabama.

CHAPTER

8

"Bring on Tennessee"

While Alabama was in New Orleans, whomping up on Tulane, the Tennessee Volunteers were falling victim to the rejuvenated Arkansas Razorbacks, 25-24, where it was hard to tell just who was the head coach, Joe Kines or Danny Ford.

Both stalked the sideline like head coaches. But it was starting to appear as if Kines was turning to Ford for the kind of game decisions a head coach is supposed to make. During the victory over Tennessee, a television audience watched as Ford stopped Kines from celebrating a touchdown, grabbing him by the wrist and pulling him down the sideline where a decision had to be made on whether or not to go for two.

There was also beginning to be some question in Knoxville as to who should be the head coach of the Vols. Johnny Majors was not on the sideline for the first three victories of the season, over Southwestern Louisiana, Georgia, and Florida; he was recovering from heart surgery he had undergone before the start of the season. Majors named longtime assistant Philip Fulmer as acting head coach, and a Tennessee team that was not expected to finish any higher than third in the SEC's Eastern Division was off to a 3-0 start and—after upsetting Georgia and Florida—was ranked as high as No. 8 in the nation.

Since Georgia and Florida were the preseason favorites to win the SEC Eastern Division, Tennessee suddenly found itself in the driver's seat for one side of the field in the inaugural SEC Championship Game in Birmingham in December.

Some said that fast start also hastened Majors's exit from the hospital. Fickle Tennessee fans were so enamored of Fulmer, now that he was getting the praise for what Majors saw as his team.

"My doctors are very pleased with my progress," Majors said, when announcing his decision to get back to coaching. "I did not twist any arms. The decision was made before the Florida game. The doctors just asked me not to try to be a hero, to use common sense.

"I'm the man who will be calling the shots with the football team right now. I'll make the final decisions."

Majors's first game back was against Cincinnati; he watched from the press box, since the doctors were not sure he was spry enough to be roaming the sideline during a game. But the next week, Majors put himself back in the headset for Tennessee's game with LSU, as the Vols improved to 5-0 and a No. 4 national ranking going into what looked like a pushover game with Arkansas.

Still, there were rumblings from inside the Tennessee program.

After the victory over Florida, Vols fullback Mario Brunson talked about the difference between playing for Fulmer and Majors.

"There were games in the past where we were real tight in the locker room," he said. "Maybe it was due to the youth of this team (that Tennessee wasn't tight against Georgia or Florida). There was no pressure on us. We weren't expected to win those games."

But pressure is one thing Tennessee fans felt Majors didn't handle well, in spite of his outstanding record as head coach of his alma mater. The bigger the game, the more Majors tended to rant and scream at his assistants and players during practice.

Majors was asked if he thought his return would be a distraction to his team, which was off to such a fine start.

"As long as they do well and hustle hard in practice, they'll get along with me just fine," Majors said. "Just like they always have."

Auburn coach Pat Dye knows something about coming back from surgery. He had undergone surgery over the summer to correct a condition where he had too much iron in his blood, and Dye went into great detail explaining what the doctors did and what was wrong during the SEC football media days in July.

Sportswriters, obviously impressed with Dye's knowledge of medicine, asked the Auburn head coach if he was surprised by Majors' quick return from open-heart surgery.

"How would I know how soon Johnny could come back?" Dye said. "I don't know anything about heart transplants or operations or whatever he had. I think Johnny and his doctors know more than I do about that."

Now, if you want to talk about livers and blood.

It was Tennessee that everyone was expecting to give Alabama the kind of test that would prove whether the Crimson Tide was for real or not. The critics who talked about Alabama's weak schedule had said all along that the second half of that schedule would determine Alabama's true worth, and that second half started with Tennessee.

However, it looked as though the Tide was getting another break when the Vols were upset by Arkansas — a three touchdown underdog going into the game — in Knoxville's Neyland Stadium on the second weekend in October.

That loss dropped Tennessee to No. 13 in the Associated Press Top 25, and left Alabama as one of only six undefeated teams in the country, led by Washington and Miami, two teams that went back and forth as No. 1 in the polls. The only other undefeated team that stood between Alabama and the top of the poll was Michigan. The Tide was ranked No. 4, just ahead of No. 5 Texas A&M, Florida State, which had lost to Miami again; and an undefeated Colorado.

But while some of the glitter may have disappeared nationally in the Tennessee-Alabama game, nothing was diminished as far as the two schools and their fans were concerned.

The rivalry went back almost as long as the two schools had fielded football teams, and it was legendary Tennessee coach Gen. Bob Neyland who once said, "You never know what you're made of until you play Alabama." For years, when Alabama was beating cross-state rival Auburn with regularity, it was the Tennessee game that Tide fans worried about.

That this Alabama team felt it was ready for Tennessee, however, was evident when the players walked off the Superdome playing surface Saturday night, only minutes after the Tulane game.

"Bring on Tennessee" was the attitude of more than one player.

The Tide had watched the Vols fall to Arkansas earlier that afternoon, sitting in their hotel rooms waiting for their evening encounter with the Green Wave.

"I think watching Tennessee probably helped us," Lassic said. "Tennessee was probably looking past Arkansas. Their losing made us realize we couldn't look past Tulane."

And so, even though it struggled, Alabama completed the first half of its schedule right on track, a perfect 6-0, the only undefeated team left in the Southeastern Conference.

"We know the first half of our schedule was kind of weak," Lassic said. "And the second half will be tougher.

"But the progress we made in those first six games will help us now. We know what we have to work on, and what we can do well. We understand ourselves better now."

It took Derrick Lassic a long time to understand himself, and what a boy from Haverstraw, New York, was doing in the Deep South.

Recruited by former Alabama head coach Bill Curry, Lassic was the "Player of the Year" for the State of New York after rushing for 1,787 yards and scoring 31 touchdowns during his senior season at North Rockland High School.

But being Player of the Year in New York didn't mean much to people in Alabama. And Lassic would never forget that he was part of a recruiting class that many Tide fans labeled "the worst in school history."

Lassic went south to play in a warm-weather climate, but once he got to Tuscaloosa he wasn't sure it was the place for him.

Several times that freshman season he convinced himself he'd made a mistake and packed his bags to go home. The closest may have been when starting tailback Bobby Humphrey broke his foot in the second game of the season and Lassic, who was being redshirted by Curry, wanted to play.

Curry said no, and Lassic decided to quit.

"I was all set to go," Lassic said. "I had the bags packed. About eight of them."

However, when he told his father what his plans were, Lassic didn't get the sympathetic ear he was hoping for. Instead, Preston Lassic told his son in no uncertain terms, "As soon as you get home, you are to get a job. You aren't staying at your mother's place unless you pay some rent."

Lassic decided rent-free Tuscaloosa was slightly more comfortable than it had seemed.

Then there were the injuries. Because of his hard style of running, Lassic always seemed to be getting banged up. And he didn't know how to play with pain.

Even as he began his senior season, Lassic admitted he heard the question, "When are you going to get hurt?" more often than he cared to remember.

He saw limited playing time as a redshirt freshman, and then personal tragedy and injuries took him out of almost the entire 1990 season, a year the tailback job was wide open and freshman Chris Anderson wound up leading the team in rushing.

On March 20, 1990, while sitting in his dorm room watching the NCAA basketball tournament, Lassic got a telephone call.

He thought it might be his girlfriend, Cherlintha Miles, who was driving up to see him from Montgomery. Instead, it was a woman from a nearby hospital.

"She said, 'Your friend was in an accident. Why don't you come over,'" Lassic said. "I was thinking something happened to the car and that maybe she needed a ride home."

He was not prepared for what they told him when he got to the hospital. Miles, 20, had been killed in a one-car crash.

Lassic did not leave his room for a week, not even to eat meals, and lost 20 pounds. Three days after Miles's funeral, which he could not attend, his bags were packed again.

This time his father was more sympathetic, but still convinced Lassic to stay in school.

Stallings, who had replaced Curry as head coach that January, and his assistant coaches kept coming back to Lassic's room to talk to him.

"Derrick just wanted to lie there in bed," Stallings said. "He didn't care about anything."

Lassic did come out for spring football, but his heart wasn't in it. That fall, he came back out and started to show some promise.

Playing behind Siran Stacy, Lassic played in every game and rushed 70 times for 368 yards with two touchdowns. For the first time, he was injury free.

"I was able to play that whole year, every game, even when I got a hip-pointer late in the season," Lassic said. "That showed me I had learned how to play with pain. If I'd gotten that hip-pointer my sophomore year, I'd have been out for one or two games."

Going into his senior season, Lassic had finally earned the chance to start. His speed (4.4 seconds in the 40-yard dash) got him to the hole quicker than any back at Alabama in a long time, and once there, his strength (330-pound bench press) allowed him to punish tacklers.

And this season, he had the haircut, too — dreadlocks.

"I can't cut my hair," Lassic said before the first game. "There's a reason, but I can't tell you until after the season."

It was superstition. Lassic stayed healthy throughout the 1991 season and never cut his hair. Taking a cue from Samson, he decided not to cut his hair until his luck ran out.

"I had a good year with all that hair," he said. "So I'm not going to cut it. I'm not superstitious, but it's like Coach Stallings says, if it ain't broke, don't fix it."

Lassic laughed at himself, knowing how silly he was sounding.

"Still," he added, "You never know."

Someone asked the 5-foot-10, 200-pounder why he didn't just change his running style a little to protect himself. Lassic was the hardest runner on the team, a back who hit full speed in two strides and, when he saw that getting tackled was inevitable, did his best to dish out more punishment to the tackler than he got.

"The running style is a reflection of my personality," Lassic said. "I go all out all the time. I hate losing at anything. So I run with aggressiveness. I try to win each battle, giving everything I've got."

The hair did get cut, though. After fumbling four times against Southern Miss, Lassic was benched by running backs coach Larry Kirksey.

The next week, the hair came off. Lassic felt it was time to do something to change his luck. The most obvious place to start was at the top.

After that, he broke loose for 100 yards rushing against Arkansas, South Carolina, and Tulane.

"It's a great feeling to have guys pat you on the back for a change," Lassic said. "After those fumbles against Southern Miss, I came to the sideline and asked Coach Kirksey what I was doing wrong. I had both hands on the ball. He said it was just one of those things.

"So I prayed that it wouldn't happen again. Fumbling bothers me. There is no excuse for fumbling. The punishment (getting benched) fit. I'd have done the same thing if I was the coach."

But then Lassic had to worry about being labeled a "fumbler" in the minds of the coaches.

"That's the worst thing that can happen to a running back," he said. "Then, in pressure situations, the coach is reluctant to go with you. That's why I'm glad I got their confidence back."

After the Southern Miss game, Lassic didn't think of going home. This time he called home for help.

"I asked my high school coach what I was doing, and he said he didn't know, because I didn't fumble at all in high school," Lassic said. "He said, `You know what you've got to do now?' I said, `No.' And he said, `Forget about it.'

"So I did. When I got the ball again the next week against Arkansas, I knew the coaches had forgotten, too."

Even so, Lassic shared time with the Tide's other two tailbacks, Anderson and Sherman Williams. It was often a three-pronged attack, with Lassic softening up the defense in the first two quarters, Anderson coming in fresh for the third, and Williams finishing off the Razorbacks in the fourth.

Lassic missed a 1,000-yard season by only 95 yards. He had 178 carries for 905 yards rushing and 10 touchdowns, but Stallings said Alabama fans haven't seen the last of Lassic.

"He can play pro," Stallings said. "You haven't seen his last game."

Even if Lassic doesn't get the chance, Stallings paid him perhaps the ultimate Alabama compliment when, after Lassic rushed for 135 yards on 28 carries and earned the Most Valuable Player award in the Sugar Bowl, Stallings was asked what Bear Bryant would have liked best about the game.

"He would have enjoyed watching Derrick Lassic run," Stallings said.

Something else Bryant would have enjoyed: Alabama had taken six games in a row from the Vols, going back to Ray Perkins's last season, through all three seasons under Bill Curry, to the heart-stopping 9-6 and 24-19 victories the Tide had enjoyed the past two seasons under Stallings.

But this series had always been a series of streaks. Before the current six-game winning streak, Tennessee had won the previous four in a row, going back to Bryant's last season.

Bryant had beaten Tennessee 10 times in a row in the 1970s, but then, his Alabama teams were beating just about everybody in that decade. The Vols had won three in a row before that.

And so it went. Tennessee had managed to go six years without losing to Alabama, from 1955 to 1960, with a 7-7 tie in 1959 keeping the Vols from winning six in a row.

But ancient history meant nothing as much as what had happened lately, and what had happened lately was best summed up by former Tide center Roger Shultz who, walking off the turf of Neyland Stadium after a 9-6 victory his senior season, pointed over his shoulder and said, "They ought to make us pay property taxes here because we own Tennessee."

Indeed, Tennessee senior defensive back J. J. McClusky put it in perspective for Vols fans when he said, "The last time Tennessee beat Alabama I was 15 years old. That's a long time ago."

Even Majors, the former Tennessee All American who returned home as head coach, admitted the Alabama game was special to him.

"It might not look like it the past six years," Majors said. "But, yes, it's a big game."

Coaches talk about treating each game the same and taking them one at a time, but both schools had their traditions when it came to the third Saturday in October.

At Alabama, that meant a tape of "Rocky Top," the Tennessee fight song, being played over and over and over and over all day, every day in the football building the week of the game. It meant managers wearing orange jerseys and Tennessee caps all week at practice. It meant the scout team coming out in orange, when normally the scout team just wore either crimson (on defense) or white (on offense).

And in Knoxville . . .

"I remember before two-a-days," said Tennessee freshman Jason Parker. "The first practice when the older guys came in, Coach Majors said to practice like Alabama was the next game.

"I said, 'I guess beating Alabama means a lot around here.'"

Junior running back Charlie Garner, a junior college signee, said he was told the day he signed that he was being brought in to beat Alabama.

Majors was 4-11 as a head coach against Alabama, and the Big Orange fans never let him forget it. He was second-guessed more than usual the week of this game, and the theory was that Majors was so uptight the week of the Alabama game, he made his players uptight, too.

"Second guessing and looking back is always easier," Majors said. "In virtually every game we lose, I go back and say, 'We shouldn't have done this.' That's human nature.

"I look back at the Arkansas game and we should have thrown the ball more. We'd be 6-0 right now and happier today."

Alabama linebacker Antonio London understands what this week means. London was raised in Tullahoma, Tennessee, and was the top prospect in his home state after his senior year in high school.

"There was a lot of pressure on me to stay and go to Tennessee," London said. "I really thought after I made up my mind (to go to Alabama) that people would accept it and support me. But then I started getting hate mail, people saying I'd never make it at Alabama, that I'd never amount to anything because I'd left the state.

"I had to grow to understand the rivalry between Alabama and Auburn. But I always understood the rivalry with Tennessee."

A senior, London was signed by Bill Curry to replace former Alabama linebacker Derrick Thomas, who finished his Crimson Tide career by winning the Butkus Award as the best linebacker in college football.

When London signed, he was told he would get No. 89, the number he wore in high school. Instead, he found out he had been given 55.

"That was Derrick Thomas's number," London said. "I didn't think there was any way I could live up to that."

For that matter, London wasn't sure he could even play at this level, despite being the top prospect in his home state.

"The first person I saw when I got to Alabama was (former line-backer) Spencer Hammond, who weighed about 230 pounds," London said. "The second was (former linebacker) Keith McCants, who weighed about 260. I weighed about 190 pounds, and I remember thinking, 'These are linebackers. I play the same position they do. Something is wrong.'"

But Curry convinced London to keep No. 55, and four years later, London proved worthy.

From his first season to his last, London lived up to his billing as a big playmaker who could easily fill his own 30-minute highlight tape, if he wished.

His freshman season, he recorded three tackles, caused a fumble, and recovered a fumble against Miami in the Sugar Bowl.

As a sophomore, a broken bone in his cheek limited his playing time, but he blocked a field goal attempt in the Fiesta Bowl, broke up a pass play, and recorded a quarterback sack for an 11-yard loss.

As a junior, his first full season as a starter at outside linebacker, London blocked field goal attempts in three consecutive games, the last preserving a 20-17 victory over LSU.

Going into the Tennessee game, the 6-foot-2, 235-pound London — he bulked up considerably from his freshman year — was second on the team in tackles with 33, with one sack, five quarterback pressures, and a caused fumble.

"Antonio makes big plays because he's smart and he can run," said outside linebacker coach Ellis Johnson. "He's been labeled as a freelancer, but a lot of the things he's doing are things we teach, and he's just reacting to what he sees.

"He is as much of an effort player as anybody I've ever coached. Even when Antonio is not having a good game, he's still giving 100 percent. And guys like that usually end up with the fumble or the blocked kick just because he's always giving the effort."

London has known little other than success as an athlete. It seems that from the first time he got into a game, he was making big plays.

London led the state of Tennessee in receptions as a junior wide receiver, and led his district in punt returns as a senior. He played basketball and holds the state record in the high jump, having cleared six feet, 10 inches.

"I wish I had stayed competitive in track," London said. "I will always wonder if I could have been a world-class high jumper.

"But I couldn't do both. I weighed 180 pounds when I was high jumping in high school. A year ago they had a high jump pit set up in the coliseum and I had to try. I knew I was too heavy, at 220 pounds. But I cleared 5-10. I was afraid to try any higher."

London got up to over 240 pounds before his senior year, but plays better at 235. Once known strictly as a finesse player, the added muscle turned him into a respected hitter as well as a big playmaker.

"I don't think I've lost any speed," said London. "I've always had the mentality that I am fast enough to get there and make the play. I'm not concerned with things like my time in the 40, probably because I'm afraid I'd do bad. The last time I ran the 40 for time, I did it in 4.65 seconds.

"As for the big plays, I like to think of myself as a person that plays hard and goes 100 percent. Some people say I'm just in the right place at the right time, but I study a lot of film and work hard to try to be in the right place. And I have good players around me, because usually if someone makes a big play, it's because someone else did something to cause it."

Even with all the big plays, one big one stands out in London's mind.

"I got to sack (former Tennessee quarterback) Andy Kelly twice and blocked a field goal (against the Vols)," London said. "To do that against my home team made it special.

"Because for me, it's a matter of being able to go home. Even though I'm 3-0 against Tennessee, when I go home all I hear is, 'Wait 'til next year.' They really believe this is the year they'll finally beat Alabama. I've been hearing from people up there since Tennessee beat Florida. So it's bragging rights for me, so I can go home again."

There were a number of players who wanted to be able to go home to Tennessee again.

Second-string guard John Clay was from Nashville, and played his high school ball at a prep school in Chattanooga. Safety Chris Donnelly was from Germantown, a suburb of Memphis, and signed out of high school with Vanderbilt, where the big game every year was with the cross-state Vols.

Defensive lineman Jeremy Nunley was from Winchester, Tennessee, a town so close to the Alabama state line that he said when anybody wanted to go to town, they went south to Huntsville. So they felt more like a part of Alabama than Tennessee.

And starting right guard Jon Stevenson was a former All-State lineman from Memphis.

They had personal reasons for looking forward to the Tennessee game. But so did the rest of the team. This was the big test, the one where everyone in the nation — the game was being televised by ABC-TV — found out if the Alabama defense was as good as it seemed, and if the offense was better than it appeared.

CHAPTER

9

"I Guess You Do Own Tennessee"

The comparisons were inevitable.

Jay Barker knew that when Alabama traveled to Knoxville to play Tennessee, many Alabama fans would be measuring the quarterback they had—Barker—against the quarterback they almost had, Tennessee sophomore Heath Shuler.

"I'm not interested in comparisons," Barker said. "I'm just being myself. I want to be Jay Barker and play my game."

In the recruiting wars of 1991, Shuler and Eric Zeier were everyone's first choices at quarterback. Zeier, from Marietta, Georgia, committed to the University of Georgia early, and even graduated high school early to take part in the Bulldogs spring practice. He was the starting quarterback by that fall.

It took Shuler a little longer, because Tennessee had a senior, Andy Kelly, who had been successful at quarterback for the Vols. But in his second season, Shuler was the starter and clearly, along with Zeier, a rising star at the position in the SEC.

Barker, of course, was a desperation signee who few big schools wanted at quarterback. In his signing class were two other quarterbacks, Steve Christopher of Anniston and Jason

Jack of Oxford, Alabama, who had led their teams to state titles. Barker was the least publicized of the three.

But Jack was an option quarterback, and Christopher did not qualify academically, and eventually transferred. Barker wound up the starter, almost by default.

So by almost any measure, Barker knew he would lose in a comparison with Shuler. Shuler went into the game as the second-rated passer in the conference, 21st in the nation. Barker was fifth in the SEC and not listed among the top 50 in NCAA statistics.

Shuler was second in the SEC in rushing touchdowns with eight. Barker had none.

Shuler had completed 56.8 percent of his passes, with two interceptions and five touchdowns. Barker had completed 54.7 percent, with four interceptions and four touchdowns.

"But the key is winning," Barker said. "If you contribute to doing that, that's what's important. Just winning. If people want to talk about what I've done, I'd just point to the won-lost column.

"I'm lucky to have not lost a game as a starting quarterback. I know it's not just because of me. Our defense has had a lot to do with it, and the people around me on offense. But still, we're getting the job done and we've won. I can say I've led this team to a 10-0 record as a starter, and that's something to be proud about."

Barker didn't care that he would never be mentioned in the same breath as Shuler, Zeier, or Florida's Shane Matthews, when it came to talking about the league's best quarterbacks.

"The difference between us?" Barker said. "I don't know. I think they've played the position longer than I have.

"I know I'm not a great quarterback. And I've got to continue to work to get better. The guys around me help a lot."

It is easy to point to the mistakes Barker had made, the overthrown or underthrown passes, the throws into coverage. Even in the victory against Tulane, after calling an audible at the line of scrimmage, Barker went the opposite way from the rest of the team and ended up being dropped for a loss.

But the coaches also were beginning to see things that Barker was doing better. On first down, his completion percentage was 56 percent. On second and long, he was hitting 61 percent.

The result?

"We're not seeing the eight- and nine-man fronts like we did last year," said Alabama assistant Woody McCorvey, who views the game from the coaches' box on Saturdays, helping Mal Moore call plays.

"People are more apprehensive about putting all their people up front now. We don't have the greatest passing game in the world, but people have to respect it. Last year, they didn't."

Barker also had improved in his ability to read defenses and call plays at the line of scrimmage.

"Jay is confident this year," McCorvey said. "He's not hesitant about checking off when the defense gives him another look. And he's not missing many. He's checking to the right call, and at least getting us out of a potentially bad play."

The struggles have come in passing situations, third-and-long, when everyone in the stadium knows Alabama has to pass. In those situations, third down and six yards or more, Barker had completed just 16 percent of his passes.

But the bottom line is winning. And while Barker admits the offense has struggled at times, he also thinks he may know the reason.

"In a sense, the better the competition, the better this team plays," Barker said. "And this team seems to enjoy playing on the road. The more hostile the environment, the more we seem to like it.

"We talk quite a bit about the 16-game winning streak. This team hates to lose. We want to keep that streak going. It's something to be proud of."

Ultimately, Barker was looking to get the last laugh on his detractors if, on the evening of December 5, he was walking out as the starting quarterback in the SEC championship game.

"I don't think 'the last laugh' is the right phrase," Barker said. "But what people say of me won't matter if we can say we did it. All I want to be able to say is that I made a difference to Alabama winning."

Alabama fans could compare Barker to Shuler all they wanted. The real comparison, the Tide coaches felt, was the Tennessee offense versus the Alabama defense.

"No question, this will be the best offense we've faced," said Alabama linebacker coach Ellis Johnson. "Add it up: talent, scheme, and team speed, and they put pressure on you in a lot of different ways.

"We've been under pressure before, so I don't think our players are not used to it. But our guys may be put in situations they have not seen before this season, and it will be interesting to see how they react."

The starting point for that pressure was, of course, Shuler, who many considered the best athlete playing quarterback in the conference.

"Shuler complicates things," Johnson said. "He's a good passer, so he can stay in the pocket and hurt you. But he's also mobile enough to get out of the pocket and get away from you.

"He can throw or run off their sprint-out and bootleg options, so you've got to stay safe on the backside. And they run the option with him, so you've got to be concerned with that.

"The only thing Shuler lacks is experience, and he's getting more of that every day."

On the other hand, the Alabama defense had been particularly unkind to quarterbacks so far this season. The Tide led the SEC in quarterback sacks with 25 and ranked second in interceptions with 11.

Defensive end Eric Curry led the team at the halfway point of the season with six and a half sacks and 14 quarterback pressures. He would be playing against Tennessee without a cast on his hand for the first time since breaking his hand against Arkansas.

Antonio Langham led the conference in interceptions with four, and would be healthy after playing the last two games on a sprained ankle. The defense led the nation in total defense, rushing defense, and scoring defense, and ranked second in pass defense.

"But it is ridiculous to think we can play Tennessee and expect them not to score on us or beat us on a big play or go ahead at some point in the game," Johnson said. "And those are things that haven't happened to us this year. So we've got to see how we react to that."

Shuler's ability to make plays on his own was bound to put pressure on the Tide defense at every level.

"There will be a lot of emphasis on containment," said free safety Chris Donnelly. "If he gets out of the pocket, then the defensive backs don't know whether to stay back and guard against the pass or come up to support the run. It's a tough choice."

The outside linebackers, in particular, were going to play an important role in this game.

"With a guy like Shuler, you have to be alert for everything," said right outside linebacker Lemanski Hall. "You've got to make decisions whether to come out of coverage or stay in coverage. He keeps you alert the whole time.

"I think if we can get to him early and confuse him, we can shake him up a little bit. But I know he's a good athlete. We've just got to put pressure on him."

But there were no tricks planned by the Alabama defensive staff.

"You can't do anything special," Johnson said. "They're too balanced for that. What we have to do is contain him by playing extremely smart.

"Shuler will fool somebody at some point of the game. But if everyone is scrambling to get to the ball, I think we've got enough team speed to get to him."

In Knoxville the Friday before the game, all anyone could talk about was breaking the streak.

There were signs in every window, T-shirts, and newspaper articles looking for solutions.

On a corner of the campus near the stadium, Michael Kennedy, a student at UT, was camping out, counting down the days and hours to the Alabama game. Kennedy is the person inside the Smokey the Dog costume on Saturday afternoon.

"I don't usually camp out like this," Kennedy said. "But this is *the* game."

Dressed in his Smokey costume, Kennedy had been sleeping in a pup tent under a tree since the Wednesday before the game.

"Every time class changes, I tie a rope around a (stuffed) elephant's neck and drag him around campus," Kennedy said.

The corner is adorned with signs that read, "I am mascot, hear me roar" and "Honk if you hate 'Bama."

"They're honking," Kennedy said. "Especially about 3 a.m. They come by just to honk. I'm not getting much sleep."

But most of all, the streak nagged at the players.

"This team has accomplished so much," said Tennessee running back Aaron Hayden. "Championships, bowl games, team win totals. That (the losing streak) is probably the only blemish on the seniors' record."

Redshirt freshman George Kidd, a starter at linebacker, took the tack that he hadn't lost to Alabama yet.

"The atmosphere is different here during Alabama week," Kidd said. "But they haven't beaten me yet. Maybe we can change things around here."

Meanwhile, Kennedy kept up his vigil, trying to summon the right spell to break the jinx.

"I've never seen us beat Alabama, and I'm a senior," he said. "So it's lingering in the back of everyone's mind. This has been the most important game on the schedule since Day One.

"I was a sophomore in high school the last time Tennessee won. So it's been a while. But that's going to change. Bama's going down.

"I hope."

It was near-perfect football weather in Knoxville, as 97,388 fans, the largest crowd to ever witness an Alabama game, crowded Neyland Stadium, hard by the Tennessee River.

As the Alabama coaches were making their way to the press box, Tennessee fans were yelling at them, "Who have ya'll played? Who have ya'll played?"

Tide wide receiver coach Woody McCorvey shot back, "Well, we've played Arkansas."

The Volunteers won the toss and deferred to the second half, so Alabama took the ball. David Palmer fielded the kickoff and returned it 23 yards to the Alabama 37-yard line, and the tone of the game was established on the first play.

Alabama came out in a one-back set, Barker took the snap and pitched the ball to Lassic, who went around left end for seven yards. On second-and-three, the Tide was in an I formation, with Houston at fullback; and with the team going left, Lassic took the pitch and cut back up the middle for seven yards and a first down.

It was back to the one-back set again, but this time the toss right to Lassic netted only one yard. On second and nine, Alabama went with a split backfield, and the draw play to Lassic picked up four.

Third-and-five was a passing down. This was where Barker had come up short so many times in the past. This time, he hit wide receiver Prince Wimbley, only to have off-setting penalties — a late hit by Tennessee, an ineligible receiver downfield for Alabama — nullify the play.

Third down and five again, and it was back to the I. Barker dropped back to pass but was hit just as he let go of the ball, and it fell incomplete.

Bryne Diehl's punt carried 44 yards into the end zone, setting up the Tennessee offense at the Vols' 20. On first down, quarterback Heath Shuler dropped back, was forced to run, and London brought him down from behind after a one-yard gain.

On second down, Shuler rolled right and threw for wide receiver Kendrick Jones, but the throw was low.

On third-and-nine, Shuler passed to the left side of the field, complete to Dwayne Freeman. Tommy Johnson made the tackle after a seven-yard gain, and Tom Hutton came on to punt.

It was three downs and punt for Alabama, and then Tennessee went for field position, going nowhere on first and second down and then punting on third down. Diehl got off another good kick, this one 58 yards, and Tennessee was pinned back on its own 10-yard line.

Shuler lost two yards on first down, tackled by London again, and then missed a wide-open Kendrick Jones deep down the right side. On third-and-12, Hutton came on to punt, and the kick, while covering 44 yards, left Alabama starting on the Tennessee side of the field, at the Vols' 46-yard line.

That's what Lassic was waiting for. Alabama went to the I formation to get the extra blocker in the backfield in fullback Martin Houston, and Lassic carried three times — right, up the middle, and right again — for 24 yards and two first downs.

Lassic came out for a breather on first down from the 22, and Chris Anderson came on to continue the tailback barrage, sweeping left for one yard.

Lassic returned, took the toss going right, faked the reverse handoff to Palmer, and went 16 yards to the Tennessee five-yard line.

Lassic went four yards around the right side to the one, but on second down, right tackle Roosevelt Patterson jumped, backing Alabama up five yards.

On second-and-six, Lassic took the toss going left, cut back upfield almost immediately, and got to the one again. Then, on third down, Lassic dived over the middle for the touchdown.

The senior tailback had rushed for 50 yards on what was officially a 46-yard drive, carrying the ball seven times out of eight plays.

"My brother Nat called me before the game and told me he had a dream," Lassic would say afterward. "He said I was going to rush for 144 yards and score three touchdowns."

The game wasn't even a fourth over and Lassic was a third of the way there.

But Tennessee came back with a big play by tailback Charlie Garner, who ripped through the middle of the Alabama defense for 44 yards to the Tide 32-yard line. He picked up nine more yards on first down, but got hurt and had to leave the game.

On second down, Shuler rolled right on a play-action pass and was met by defensive end John Copeland for no gain. On third down, fullback Aaron Hayden tried the middle and was stuffed by Eric Curry for a one-yard loss.

Then the unthinkable happened. Placekicker John Becksvoort, who had gone into the game a perfect eight-for-eight on field goals and 23 of 23 on extra-point attempts, missed for the first time all year, this one a 42-yarder. The 10,000 Alabama fans went wild, and the 87,000 in orange began to wonder if the losing streak would ever end.

On the missed field goal, Alabama took over at the 25, and on second down and 10, Palmer went in motion from the left side, took the toss from Barker, and raced 30 yards to the Tennessee 45-yard line.

Immediately, Alabama came back with Palmer in motion again, taking the toss from Barker. But this time, Palmer reversed the ball to Kevin Lee coming from the other side, and Lee went 24 yards to the Tennessee 21.

Lassic picked up five yards to end the first quarter, then slipped on a toss right for a loss of two yards to start the second period. He picked up three yards on third down, bringing on Michael Proctor, who kicked a 33-yard field goal for a 10-0 lead.

It was three plays and punt for Tennessee again, setting Alabama up with a first down at the Tide 34-yard line. First down was a play-action pass from Barker to tight end Steve Busky that Busky dropped, convincing the Tide coaches to go back to the ground game.

With the offensive line blowing holes open, Lassic proceeded to carry the ball on eight of the next 10 plays, picking up 28 yards, and scoring on a one-yard run up the middle for a 17-0 lead.

Tennessee fans could not accuse Johnny Majors of being conservative, as he continued to put the ball in Shuler's hands to put in the air. Down 17-0, Shuler took the Vols 38 yards, hitting five of five passes, and Becksvoort kicked a 44-yard field goal to get Tennessee on the scoreboard before the half, 17-3.

At the half, Alabama had rushed the ball 34 times for 214 yards, with Lassic already over the 100-yard mark (115 yards on 24 carries and two touchdowns).

"We felt we could run the ball on Tennessee," Lassic said. "We challenged the offensive line this week, and they responded."

It was not expected. Alabama's offensive line had had problems with a four-man front all season, and Tennessee ran a particularly difficult four-man front for Alabama to defend because the defensive linemen were so aggressive.

"Some 4-3 teams are 'reading' teams, where they read the play at the line of scrimmage," Stallings said. "But that's not Tennessee's style. They pin back their ears and come at you. They do a lot of blitzing, with cornerbacks as well as linebackers. They throw a lot at you."

What concerned Alabama offensive line coach Jimmy Fuller the most was that the Tennessee defense was always moving.

"They move all seven of their front people (four down linemen, three linebackers)," Fuller said. "The three linebackers move from side to side, and it can confuse the people blocking up front.

"Too many times the offensive linemen will go up there and it won't be exactly the way we drew it up for them. It will be a mixture, and they'll have to think a little more than they normally do.

"If they don't recognize it, then we'll have to do what we call 'him' blocking," Fuller said. "Where one guy says, 'You block him and I'll block him.'"

It worked through the first half, especially when Alabama went back to the I formation, which gave the Tide the leverage of running the fullback, Martin Houston, out in front of the tailback to either side of the field.

But Tennessee adjusted in the second half. After a first-down pass from Barker to Palmer gained 21 yards, and Lassic and Houston combined for 10 yards on two downs for a first down at the Tennessee 15, suddenly the offense went backward. Lassic was dropped on a sweep for a four-yard loss, Barker overthrew Lassic on a screen pass to the right side, and on third-and-14, Barker was sacked trying to throw the ball.

Proctor's 45-yard field goal attempt was wide left, and Tennessee took over at its own 28-yard line.

Not that it mattered much. On first down, Tennessee lost three yards. On second down, the Vols gained nine. Third down, Shuler was sacked by Copeland for a four-yard loss, and Tennessee had to punt away.

Anderson came on at tailback for Alabama, and his first play was a toss sweep left for 12 yards, followed by a run off right tackle for three.

Palmer took the toss going left and faked the reverse to Lee, picking up four yards, then Barker ran a quarterback draw for five yards and a first down.

Anderson picked up 11 yards on first-and-10 from the Tennessee 45, followed by Houston picking up 10 with a quick pop up the middle to the 34. Houston ran a counter play off the fake to Lassic and picked up 13 to the 11; and then backup fullback Tarrant Lynch went for two, Lassic went wide right for four, Houston went to the left side for two, and Alabama was looking at fourth-and-two from the 3-yard line.

Stallings let himself be talked out of going for the field goal, and on fourth down, Lassic was dropped for a one-yard loss on a sweep right.

"I knew I should have gone for the field goal," Stallings said. "But I let the players talk me out of it. They had confidence, and wanted to go for it.

"I felt like if we knocked it in, we put them away. But it was a very unwise decision. Very dumb on my part."

Dumb, because in the fourth quarter, Diehl's 37-yard punt was caught by Shawn Summers, who pitched the ball to Nilo Silvan, who returned it 29 yards to the Alabama 42.

After an incomplete pass, Shuler hit Cory Fleming for 17 yards to the 25. Hayden carried for no gain, then Shuler threw a screen to Fleming that picked up 22 yards. The sophomore quarterback capped the drive with a three-yard pass to tight end David Horn, and suddenly the Alabama lead was just seven points, 17-10.

As had been the custom, at that point Alabama reigned in its offense and decided to grind out the clock.

But that produced three plays and a punt, sending the Tennessee offense out with a chance to tie the score with over 11 minutes left to play.

The noise was deafening when Shuler dropped back to pass. However, his throw was batted away by Tide linebacker Lemanski Hall and Shuler was decked by Copeland, a blow that forced Shuler to the sideline.

Backup quarterback Jerry Colquitt was forced to run on second down, and lost three yards. He fumbled the snap on third down, picked the ball up and fell forward for one yard, and another chance was gone.

Alabama took over and turned the game over to Lassic and Houston. Lassic went 20 yards, then Houston 13. Lassic picked up three, Houston two. Lassic gained one, Houston one.

Then on third down, Barker was sacked and fumbled, but came up with the ball. Still, Diehl came on to punt the ball away to Tennessee with almost five minutes left to play.

Shuler returned to the game with a first down at the Tennessee nine-yard line. On first down, he was forced out of the pocket and tackled by linebacker Michael Rogers for no gain. Every play seemed like life or death now for Tennessee, and on second down, Shuler hit Craig Faulkner for eight yards.

Third down, Shuler kept the ball on an option right. He got 12 yards before being tackled by Antonio Langham.

Then the defense stepped it up. Shuler was sacked by James Gregory for an eight-yard loss, then by Copeland for a loss of five. His third-down pass intended for Fleming was hurried and overthrown, leaving the Vols with no choice but to punt the ball away.

What could be safer than for Alabama to hand off to the fullback and let Houston just crash into the line? On first down, Houston gained two yards. But on second down, after picking up five yards, Houston fumbled, and after a mad scramble for the ball, Tennessee linebacker George Kidd came up with it, giving the Vols one last chance.

It was first-and-10 from midfield with one minute, 33 seconds left to play when, as secondary coach Bill Oliver said, "the defense rolled up their sleeves, used their hearts and used their brains and made the plays to win the game."

Shuler was sacked by Eric Curry on first down for a four-yard loss.

After Tennessee used its final time-out, Shuler stepped to the line of scrimmage. With 97,388 fans standing and screaming and straining for breath, Shuler dropped back to pass. He avoided the rush, saw Fleming come open down the middle of the field, stepped up, and fired the ball.

Only at that same instance, Michael Rogers jumped up, tipped the ball up in the air, and safety Chris Donnelly came down with it at the Alabama 37-yard line.

Barker fell on the ball twice, and it was over. Alabama won, 17-10, on October 17, the 17th victory in a row for the Tide, the seventh victory of the season, the seventh win in a row over Tennessee.

"I was glad to see Donnelly get it," said Houston. "I told him I loved him."

Despite the close score, Alabama dominated the game. The Tide controlled the ball for 36 minutes, 56 seconds of the 60-minute game. Alabama rolled up 355 yards of offense, 301 on the ground, with a season-high 66 rushing attempts.

"The offensive linemen were saying, 'Run it behind me, run it behind me,'" Fuller said. "We were having a rough time deciding who to run it behind."

Lassic finished the game with 142 yards on 33 carries and two touchdowns, "two yards and one touchdown short of my brother's dream," he said. "But I'll take it."

His 33 carries wore him out.

"I'm kind of numb right now," Lassic said. "That was our game plan, to run the football.

"But if that's punishment, then punish me! Punish me! I love it. You can't punish me enough."

"If you've got a workhorse, work him," Stallings said of Lassic.

Meanwhile, Shuler was held to 12 completions in 23 attempts for 116 yards, one touchdown, one interception, and was sacked five times. Tennessee managed only 78 yards rushing, seven first downs, and just three conversions in 12 third-down attempts.

"I left Tennessee to come to Alabama to play, and now I know I'll never lose to them," London said. "That's something special."

That brought out another Alabama-Tennessee tradition, cigars. After every victory over the Big Orange, the Crimson Tide lights up victory cigars, a tradition started by former Alabama assistant Dude Hennessey.

"This is an Alabama tradition, and I love it," said guard Jon Stevenson. "But I must admit I hate cigars."

But the best quote came from an unidentified Tennessee player, who caught up to defensive back Antonio Langham as Langham was walking off the field.

"Well," the dejected Vol said, "I guess you do own Tennessee."

CHAPTER

10

A Time to Pass

A few days after his seventh straight loss to Alabama, Tennessee coach Johnny Majors said, "I don't see any great teams in the SEC. Alabama has a chance to be highly ranked. The schedule is not as tough as maybe a few others in the conference. But the defense gives them a chance to play with anyone.

"There's just not a great team in this league, unless Alabama turns out to be really improved on offense."

But while Majors wasn't convinced, the rest of the Southeast was beginning to jump on the bandwagon. Talk of a national championship showdown between Miami and Alabama picked up, as the polls started to fall into place for just such a game.

The Crimson Tide was up to No. 4 in the Associated Press Top 25, behind No. 3 Michigan, No. 2 Washington, and No. 1 Miami. Because of the new bowl coalition, if the season ended with those four teams ranked exactly the same way, Miami and Alabama would meet in the Sugar Bowl while Michigan and Washington would be in the Rose Bowl.

The feeling among Alabama supporters was one of cautious optimism, as fans asked each other, "What do you think

Alabama's chances are of playing Miami for the national championship?"

With his three consecutive 100-yard rushing games and 644 yards rushing through seven games, Alabama tailback Derrick Lassic suddenly was being mentioned as a possibility for the Heisman Trophy.

That was when Lassic dropped the news that he already had a Heisman.

"The same club (New York's Downtown Athletic Club) that gives out the Heisman Trophy presents an award to the top high school players in the tri-state area every year," Lassic said. "It's a plaque, and they give you a watch that says Heisman Award and has a picture of the Heisman statue (on the face of the watch). I have it up in my room.

"It's given out the week after the Heisman Trophy, at a dinner at the Downtown Athletic Club. The Heisman winner is there, too. I met (former Notre Dame star) Tim Brown the year I won it."

The truth was, however, that Lassic thought someone was playing a practical joke on him when he was told he was mentioned in *USA Today* as a Heisman candidate.

"I'm a candidate the way Ross Perot is a candidate for president," Lassic said. "It's a long shot. The important thing is for us to keep on winning. Awards are gravy — and I love gravy on my potatoes. But the main thing is the potatoes."

Lassic was quickly establishing himself as the potatoes of the Alabama offense. His number of carries had risen gradually since the South Carolina game, from 13 against the Gamecocks to 20 against Tulane to 33 against Tennessee.

His 33 carries against the Vols were the most of his career, including high school.

"But I enjoyed every one of them," he said. "I was like a kid on Christmas morning. That's as many carries as I've had in my life, but I'm not complaining.

"After the game, I didn't feel a thing. I was feeling great."

Sunday morning, however, was a different story.

"Sunday morning I woke up feeling like someone had been beating me with a sledgehammer," Lassic said. "I was so sore. Prince (Wimbley, Lassic's roommate) looked at me and said I looked like I was 80 years old.

"But to be honest, I wouldn't mind feeling that way every week. The soreness you can get over."

And he was back to the same haircut he wore in high school.

"Am I superstitious?" Lassic said. "My mom calls it 'stupid-stitious.' I guess I am, a little."

The Heisman talk was a nice distraction for a player who was emerging as one of the real leaders on this Alabama team, despite not having been elected captain before the season began.

But Lassic said the important thing was to never lose sight of that main goal.

"I want to go out with that big ring on my finger that says, 'No. 1,'" Lassic said. "I was in Atlanta this summer, wearing my SEC championship ring (from 1989) and feeling pretty proud until I met a guy who plays at Georgia Tech, and he was wearing his national championship ring.

"Suddenly, my ring didn't look so big any more. I put my hand back in my pocket and said, 'I need one of those.'"

Talk of that 1989 SEC championship, the only one in the past 10 years for the Tide, and that Alabama was on the verge of a second, made Lassic remember what everyone said about him and his fellow freshmen from 1988.

"They said we were the worst freshman class ever to go to Alabama," Lassic said. "They said we wouldn't be around very long. We talk about that, even now. And while I'm not one to say, 'I told you so,' look at what we've done."

Indeed, look at the players who emerged from that 1988 class: Lassic, defensive end Eric Curry, fullback Martin Houston, linebacker Derrick Oden, guard George Wilson.

What that class did was go 10-2 with the SEC title in 1989; 7-5 in 1990, but only one game away from a repeat SEC title; 11-1 in 1991, and one game short of the title again; and now 7-0, the front-runners to be in Birmingham for the first SEC championship game.

"Our record shuts people up," said Busky. "It proves you can't judge people until they go on the field and play. Our class — they said Alabama would be hurting by the time we were seniors. I don't see us hurting right now."

Jeff Wall was a walk-on, but he remembers the way people talked about 1988, too.

"The worst class ever," said the player who went on to make his mark as the holder on kicks for four years. "When people say you're the worst, you hurt."

And a lot of more highly recruited players who ended up at other schools have been hurt as a result.

Team captain Prince Wimbley started wearing his 1989 SEC championship ring around campus after the Tennessee game.

"I'm going to start wearing it from now on," he said. "Hopefully, we'll get another one."

It was certainly looking that way. At 7-0 overall and 4-0 in the SEC, Alabama was clearly in control of its own future.

"I don't think anyone has a chance of catching Alabama," said Mississippi State coach Jackie Sherrill, whose team had two losses in conference play. "Anything can happen on any given day, but Alabama has distinguished itself by being a very consistent football team. They haven't won 17 football games (in a row) without being consistent."

The two Mississippi schools—Sherrill's State team and Ole Miss—both trailed Alabama in the SEC Western Division by two games, each having two losses. The Tide's next game was against Ole Miss, with Mississippi State looming ahead, the week before the regular-season finale Auburn.

"I haven't had the opportunity to play Washington or Miami," said South Carolina coach Sparky Woods. "But we were very impressed with Alabama. By the looks of their team, they have the opportunity to win every game. Certainly, defensively, they are as good as any team we faced."

"If anyone is playing better defense than Alabama right now, I don't know who it is," said Georgia coach Ray Goff. "Obviously they are competing for a national championship right now."

Vanderbilt coach Gerry DiNardo was saying the same thing.

"Alabama is a national championship contender," DiNardo

said. "Their defense has to be one of the top defenses in the country.

"The offense does what it has to do to win. They are not hung up on statistics and what it looks like and how much they run and how much they pass. They do what it takes to win and combine that with great defense and they are a national championship-caliber-type team."

But with all that recognition comes more pressure, and now that the national championship talk had started, it just meant every game was more important than the one before.

"The good teams I've had in the past, to get depth and build depth and stay healthy is the most important thing you can have," Sherrill said. "At the end of the year, it doesn't matter what happened in the first six games. Every game you play is more important and for higher stakes as the season goes on."

While rival coaches talked about how good this Alabama team was, a good barroom argument was brewing over what would happen if this team, built around great defense, played the Tide's last championship team, that 1989 team that was built around great offense.

"That's a tough question," said Alabama wide receiver Prince Wimbley, a member of both. "It'd be a toss-up. You couldn't lose with either one. Put it like that."

"I'd like to see that game," said Jeff Wall. "It'd be a great match. It would probably come down to who played the best on that day.

"It'd be two great coordinators — ('89 offensive coordinator) Homer Smith and (current secondary coach) Bill Oliver. It'd be a sellout, that's for sure."

The 1989 team was led by quarterback Gary Hollingsworth, backs Siran Stacy and Kevin Turner, and tight end Lamonde Russell. It averaged 30.18 points, 193 yards rushing, and 241.26 yards passing per game, an average of 434.26 total yards per game.

That team set records for most offensive plays in a season, most pass attempts and completions, and most field goals in a season. The names of Hollingsworth, Stacy, Russell, Turner, and kicker Phillip Doyle litter the records section of the Alabama media guide.

This 1992 defense had several games to play, but it could prove to be one of the best of all time. Led by defensive ends John Copeland and Eric Curry, the 7-0 Tide led the nation in total defense (160.43 yards per game) and rushing defense (52.14 yards), was second in passing defense (108.29 yards), first in scoring defense (6.57 points), and eighth in turnover ratio (24 forced turnovers).

"I'm a defensive player," said linebacker Antonio London, who was a freshman on that '89 team. "This is the No. 1 defense in the nation. I definitely think we'd shut them down."

Fullback Martin Houston, another veteran from that '89 team, isn't so sure.

"Our defense this year is very aggressive," he said. "That was a finesse offense. It took advantage of aggressive defenses. We were suited to play this kind of defense. I'd love to see it."

At this point, however, such arguments were premature. All this team had done was put itself in a position to do the things that '89 team did.

"I came here to win a national championship," Wimbley said. "We're sitting in the right position to do that. It's in reach again. There is so much to look forward to. I don't have much time to think about the past."

The more successful this Alabama team had become, the more it had concentrated on the run.

In the four games that tailback Derrick Lassic had rushed for 100 yards or more, the Tide averaged 46.6 points. In the other three games, Alabama averaged only 18.3 points.

For the season, Alabama had a 69-31 run-pass ratio. Over the last three games, that ratio was 76-24.

"You're running too good," Wimbley told his roommate, Lassic. "You're taking away from my catches."   Lassic laughed.

"He doesn't really mind," Lassic said. "He's unselfish. As long as we're winning. That's all that matters."

Wimbley agreed.

"Hey, if people can't stop the run, we'll win every game," he said. "We're a 'run first, pass second' offense. Our running game is so good, it's not giving our passing game a chance to shine.

"But if people start to concentrate on stopping the run, we'll be ready. I still feel like we can throw on anybody. If we have to, we can throw. We can throw anytime."

Lassic laughingly called the Alabama receivers "the best downfield blockers in the country." That's not what wide receivers want to be known for.

"That would be frustrating if we were losing," Wimbley said. "But we're winning. We're not selfish. We like 17 wins in a row and the high ranking."

About this time a year ago, teams started playing eight-and nine-man fronts against Alabama, determined to stop the best running game in the conference.

Eight-man fronts mean man-on-man coverage of wide receivers. Last year, that was enough. This year, the players think loading up to stop the run will only play into their hands.

"If I was a gambling man, in man coverage I'll take our receivers against any DB (defensive back) in the country," Lassic said.

Lassic was going to get the chance to take that bet this Saturday. Ole Miss was a team that lived by the blitz and blitzed from a variety of formations.

The Rebels line up with anywhere from two down linemen on defense to six. They might bring one linebacker or six. A safety might rush alone or with other defensive backs.

"The blitz from practically every alignment, every play," Stallings said. "Whether or not you call it a 4-3 defense or a 3-2 or two linemen and six linebackers, whatever, they come from lots of different angles."

How serious were the Rebels about blitzing?

Out of 200 plays the Alabama offensive staff studied of the Ole Miss defense to get ready for this game, the Rebels ran some kind of blitz 104 times. They used some form of stunt — variations of defensive linemen rushing — 65 times.

It sounded crazy, but it worked. Ole Miss ranked third in the SEC in total defense and second in rushing defense. The Rebels were third in fewest first downs allowed per game and fourth in third-down conversion defense. Ole Miss was fourth in turnover ratio, and the team's 10 interceptions ranked third in the conference.

The madman behind this attack was Ole Miss defensive coordinator Joe Lee Dunn. Alabama got a firsthand lesson in Dunn's defense the year before, when Dunn was at Memphis State. After scoring 10 first-half points, the Tide never scored again on the Tigers and held on through three quarters to win, 10-7.

"Joe Lee is peculiar," said Ole Miss head coach Billy Brewer. "He comes to work at 4 a.m., and when the other coaches come in around 7, he's done. He puts it all to memory, and then does it all.

"He calls all the plays, calls all the substitutions. On game day, the other coaches might as well be sitting in Section C, because Joe Lee does it all. He never talks to the press box."

Someone asked Brewer when he found out what the defensive scheme of the week was.

"About noon on Saturday," Brewer said.

Asked what Brewer says to Dunn, the Ole Miss head coach said, "Good luck, Joe. I hope it works. 'Cause we're going to talk from time to time if it doesn't."

All that blitzing is designed to confuse and frustrate an offense. Alabama assistant Danny Pearman remembered the time he was a player at Clemson and faced Dunn's South Carolina defense.

"They beat us, 27-7," Pearman said. "There was just a lot we tried to do against that defense that didn't work. We didn't have any patience and got frustrated. Nothing worked for us."

Patience, Pearman said, is the key.

"It helps to understand what they are doing," he said. "But the best thing is to make it as simple as you can. If you can get the ball in the hands of the guys who can make you successful, you're better off. The offensive line just has to give the quarterback time to get the ball into those hands.

"They can frustrate you. But you can also burn them quick. And if you can do that, it builds confidence that if you've done it once, you can do it again."

But the Rebels were confident, too. Ole Miss was on a two-game winning streak.

"I feel good about the way we are playing," Brewer said.

"Certainly one of the strong points of our team is our defense. We have to play exceptionally well on offense against Alabama."

Brewer had every right to feel good about his defense. In the final game in Tuscaloosa for the Tide, the Rebels did everything conventional wisdom said a team had to do to beat Alabama.

They loaded up on the line of scrimmage and stopped the run, holding the Tide to 83 yards rushing, 157 yards below their per-game average of 240.

It was a gambling defense, with Ole Miss using two down linemen and five linebackers for much of the game. Those linebackers swarmed into the Alabama backfield, looking for anyone holding the ball — quarterback or running back.

The only way to get the ball out of the backfield was going to be to throw it over the top of the oncoming defense, and no one, not even the Alabama coaches, knew for sure just how successful quarterback Jay Barker would be doing that.

On the first play of the game, Alabama went to the air, with Barker throwing a quick sideline pass to flanker David Palmer. However, Ole Miss was there, and Palmer got nothing to show for the reception.

Then came the Tide's first look at the Ole Miss 2-5 defense, and Lassic got the call. The senior tailback went off the left side for four yards.

On third down, seeing that 2-5 defense again, Barker called time out, and when play resumed, he overthrew Prince Wimbley on a deep route.

That was pretty much how the first quarter went for both teams. Ole Miss was showing a variety of defensive fronts, from a 2-5 to a 3-4 to a 2-4 to even a 2-6.

And at the end of the first 15 minutes of play, not only was there no score, but Alabama had only one first down and 19 yards of total offense. Lassic had five carries for six yards, and while Barker had completed three of six passes, the passing game accounted for only 12 yards of offense.

So once again, the Tide defense decided to take matters into its own hands.

'Bama punter Bryne Diehl got off a 57-yard kick that rolled dead at the Ole Miss 2-yard line. On first down, Rebel running back Cory Philpot was met behind the line of scrimmage by John Copeland for a loss of one.

On second down, Ole Miss quarterback Russ Shows completed his second pass of the game — only it was to Alabama cornerback George Teague at the nine-yard line. Teague cut back across field and was tackled at the 13, but the Alabama offense had its best field position of the day.

And almost blew it.

On first down, Ole Miss blitzed and dropped fullback Martin Houston for a two-yard loss. On second down, the Rebels brought five linebackers, and Barker was sacked for a loss of seven, setting up third-and-20 at the Ole Miss 23.

The blitz came again on an obvious passing down, but this time Alabama was ready. Barker rolled back and threw for the front left corner of the end zone, where David Palmer had outrun free safety Tony Collier. The pass was a little too far in front of Palmer, but "The Deuce" simply did what he has always had the knack for doing: He stretched himself as if he were a rubber band and caught the ball on his fingertips for a touchdown.

"All I did was just throw it up toward David," Barker said. "It's one of those things David can do better than anyone else."

Once the ice had been broken, the Alabama offense got rolling. On the Tide's next possession, Barker guided them 77 yards in 11 plays. A flanker toss sweep netted Wimbley five yards, then Barker hit Palmer for 24 to midfield. After Houston picked up one yard running, Barker hit Palmer again on a quick throw to the left for eight yards.

Chris Anderson picked up five yards down the middle, then Barker hit Kevin Lee twice, once to the left side for 13 yards and once to the right side for eight.

That set up second-and-two from the five-yard line, and Barker tried the fade route to Palmer in the end zone again, but this time over-threw him too much. On third down, Anderson's toss sweep to the left netted three yards and a first down at the Ole Miss two-yard line.

And on first down, Lassic practically walked through the middle of the Ole Miss defense for the touchdown and a 14-0 lead.

It looked as if Alabama would go in at half holding a 14-0 lead, until the unthinkable happened — the Tide secondary got beat deep.

On first-and-10 from the 47, Rebel wide receiver Eddie Small slipped past Teague, and Shows hung it up there for him, resulting in a 53-yard touchdown pass. After Michael Proctor's 28-yard field goal with six seconds left on the clock, the half ended with Alabama leading 17-7.

Still, this was one time the defense didn't have to worry. After the poor first quarter, the Alabama offensive coaches figured out the Rebel defense and got them just where they wanted them.

"We tried to go on the first sound early, to try to catch the Ole Miss defense before it had a chance to set up," said Alabama receivers coach Woody McCorvey. "But that ended up just hurting us. So we went with a long snap count, and they started jumping off sides.

"Plus, it gave our linemen a chance to see where the blitz was coming from and be ready to pick it up."

To help pick up the blitz, Alabama did two things. One was to stay with a two-back offensive set, to keep the extra blockers in to protect Barker.

The other was to go with quick drops, three- or five-step drops, and then throw either right or left, to Lee or Palmer or Wimbley or Curtis Brown.

"They really kept our defense running sideline to sideline with those quick passes," said Ole Miss head coach Billy Brewer. "They had a good plan."

The second half was more of the same. Barker would throw right, then left, then right, with maybe a run up the middle just to keep the defense honest.

It wore the Ole Miss defense out.

"We got tired chasing those little receivers all over the field," said Rebel linebacker Dewayne Dotson.

Alabama's first drive went 57 yards to the Ole Miss 13, where Barker's lob to the end zone was intercepted by Rebel cornerback Dwayne Amos.

But eventually, Barker connected enough times — a personal record 25 completions on 39 attempts for 285 yards with one touchdown and one interception — to lead Alabama to the end zone two more times in the fourth quarter.

The first touchdown was set up by passes to Palmer, Lee, and consecutive passes to Curtis Brown, covering seven and 25 yards to the Ole Miss eight. Three Sherman Williams running plays resulted in a one-yard Williams touchdown run.

The last touchdown was set up by the defense again, when Copeland fell on a loose ball at the Ole Miss 19. Brian Burgdorf came on at quarterback and ran three times, gaining five, one, and 11 yards. Then Williams got his second touchdown of the day on a four-yard run around right end.

Brian Lee picked up three more points for the Rebels on a field goal, and the final was Alabama's 18th consecutive victory, eighth of the season, 31-10. David Palmer finished the day with seven receptions for 67 yards. Wimbley had three catches for 51 yards. Lee had eight for 82 yards. And all the receivers were happy.

"That's what we dream of, getting defensive backs one-on-one," Lee said. "No one can stop us man on man. Even Coach Stallings said before the game that if our offensive line gave the quarterback time, he would be able to get the ball to the receivers, because no one can beat our receivers one-on-one."

It wasn't all sideline-to-sideline stuff, either. Eventually, the Ole Miss cornerbacks would step up to take away the short pass, and then Barker would throw downfield.

"That's what was really pleasing," McCorvey said. "Jay hit guys upfield, in the seams, and deep."

Barker had complained of a sore elbow before the game.

"Afterward, all my teammates were saying they were going to get hammers and keep hitting my elbow this week," Barker said, laughing.

It was a good day to laugh.

"We didn't have anything to prove," Stallings said. "But we did have a lot to play for."

Wimbley said it sent a message to the rest of the teams on the Alabama schedule.

"They're on their heels right now," he said. "They don't know what we'll do: pass or run. Now they know we can do both. They've got to be wondering what it takes to stop us."

CHAPTER

11

Walking Through the Valley of Death

A fter wondering for so long what it took to get some respect from voters in the Associated Press poll, Alabama finally found out: a week off.

The schedule gave the Crimson Tide a much-needed week off after the Ole Miss victory. But while Alabama was resting, Michigan was struggling to a tie with Purdue, Miami let West Virginia come back in the fourth quarter to make a close score out of a game that was really a rout, and Washington, in the game of the week, beat 16th-ranked Stanford.

So when the Monday of the LSU game rolled around, Alabama suddenly found itself No. 3 in the polls, just ahead of Michigan, and right behind Miami, which had dropped behind Washington — a move that angered Hurricane coach Dennis Erickson.

Erickson accused the voters of being impressed by coaches who run up the score, instead of seeing that he had taken out his starters and West Virginia had come back against the Miami second and third strings.

His sentiments brought a wide range of reaction from SEC coaches.

"If you win by a bigger margin, it influences people that vote," said Florida head coach Steve Spurrier, who has been accused of pouring it on a weaker opponent once or twice. "That's human nature. If you're fighting for No. 1, like Miami and Washington, maybe those coaches, in the backs of their minds, have to think about that.

"But then again, I don't think either coaching staff wants to do it . . . . If we had a playoff system, we wouldn't have to worry about it."

Georgia coach Ray Goff said running up the score is something he would never do. "I've never tried to do it and never will," Goff said. "But obviously, there are some coaches that have done that. No doubt about it."

Mississippi State coach Jackie Sherrill said it isn't a matter of running up the score.

"It comes down to respect," Sherrill said. "The team that plays well against the opponent that is respected will get more sentiment than the team that plays the opponent without the same amount of respect. So the score doesn't have as much to do with it as how you perform against the really good opponents."

In short, Washington's victory over ranked Stanford was more impressive than Miami's victory over unranked West Virginia?

"Yes," Sherrill said. "If you play No. 1 vs. No. 2, the loser is not going to drop as much as if the No. 7 team played a team that wasn't ranked, or No. 4 played the No. 24 team. You get more drastic changes (in the polls) then."

Tennessee coach Johnny Majors, whose team was now 5-3 and ranked No. 16, said he was against running up the score, too.

However, "I just wish I was in the position to have to make that decision late in the game now," Majors said.

Alabama's jump to No. 3 without playing a game was greeted with appropriate good humor by head coach Gene Stallings.

"It seems the thing to do is not play," Stallings said.

The Tide's 8-0 record and No. 3 ranking was its highest since the 1989 season, when an undefeated Alabama went as high as No. 2 in the polls going into the last regular-season game, against Auburn.

And unlike so many coaches who say they don't pay attention to polls, Stallings admitted he was beginning to look at them a little more closely now.

"Yeah, I'm beginning to watch them a little bit, even though I know we've got a long way to go yet," Stallings said. "But yeah, I noticed we did move up."

Lassic said the climb was all part of the march to a national championship game.

"We're like a hungry fighter," he said. "It's been so long since we've had a championship around here, and the last one we had to share (with Auburn in 1989). We want this one."

Washington was leading an apparent resurgence of Pac-10 football. Besides the top-ranked Huskies, there were four other teams from that conference ranked in the Top 25: No. 11 Southern Cal, No. 12 Arizona, No. 21 Stanford, and No. 25 Washington State.

The SEC also had five teams ranked: No. 3 Alabama, No. 14 Florida, No. 15 Georgia, No. 19 Mississippi State, and No. 24 Tennessee.

"Is the SEC the best conference in the country this year?" said *Los Angeles Times* sportswriter Gene Wjciechowski. "No. But it's still one of the finest. The Pac-10 is No. 1, and even though I don't regard the Big East as an actual conference yet, it's hard to argue with the teams in that league right now (No. 2 Miami, No. 9 Boston College, No. 10 Syracuse).

"And the ACC (Atlantic Coast Conference) gets a lot of consideration (with No. 6 Florida State, No. 17 N.C. State, and No. 18 North Carolina, with Virginia and Georgia Tech in and out of the polls all year).

"But even with that, I still think the SEC is a tough conference, and you may very well have the national champion out of that conference. I think a good measuring point of how people think about the SEC is (Georgia running back) Garrison Hearst. His Heisman Trophy hopes are helped by the fact that he plays in the SEC, while (San Diego State running back) Marshall Faulk is in the WAC (Western Athletic Conference). I'd still put the SEC against any conference in the country and not be ashamed."

In the NCAA statistics for the week of November 2, the Pac-10 had four of its teams ranked in the top 15 in the nation in total defense, compared to three teams from the SEC.

The SEC had four teams ranked in the top 15 in scoring defense, while the Pac-10 had two.

But when winless teams such as South Carolina upset ranked teams such as Mississippi State, or Arkansas upsets Tennessee, there is a feeling that the SEC is not completely healthy.

"There is a balance to this conference that can be deceiving," said LSU head coach Curley Hallman. "On any given day, there can be an upset. I don't think there is a big change."

The excitement over expansion may have diminished somewhat, too, when the two teams brought in — Arkansas and South Carolina — wound up not being as good as everyone had hoped.

"People see that and say the SEC has diluted itself," Wjciechowski said. "A lot of people thought Florida would be the toast of the town. They kind of sagged, but they sagged to No. 14 in the nation. So it's not like they dropped off the face of the earth.

"I know Auburn has had its ups and downs, but I wouldn't want to make a living off (having to beat) Auburn. Every conference has its teams that are struggling a little."

And ultimately, Wjciechowski said, the SEC championship game would restore respect the SEC might have lost.

"I think people will watch that game because of the intriguing ramifications," he said. "That has people's interest. You have to respect the SEC for taking the gamble.

"Financially speaking, it's great. But at some point, the coaches will wonder if they've given themselves a chance to win the national championship. They beat up on each other so much, but then, that's why the SEC is still tough.

"Tough enough to try something like the championship game. That carries a lot of weight."

Alabama would carry a lot of weight into Baton Rouge to play LSU this Saturday afternoon.

It was more than the undefeated season, the winning

streak, and the No. 3 ranking. While Tiger fans prided themselves on "Death Valley's" reputation as one of the toughest places to play in college football, it had little effect over the years on the teams from Tuscaloosa.

Alabama had not lost a game in Baton Rouge since 1969, going 10-0-1, beginning with a 14-7 victory in 1971. Over that same time span, the Tide had outscored the Tigers 229-117. Since 1964, the two teams had played each other every year, alternating home and home, and the Tide's record in the Tigers' stadium during that time was 12-1-1.

The oddity of the series was that in home games, the Tide had not fared so well. Alabama held a slim 6-5 edge over LSU in games played since 1969.

"Baton Rouge is a great place to play," said offensive guard George Wilson. "If you don't do what you're supposed to, it can be a tough place to play. But it's exciting.

"The mystique — the fans make more of that than the players. If you make mistakes and get behind, every place becomes a tough place to play."

Part of that mystique has to do with Baton Rouge's legendary night games. This one, because it was to be televised by ABC-TV, would be played in the afternoon.

"The LSU fans won't be as drunk at 2:30 as at 7:30," Lassic said. "That's why they play so late, to get the crowd . . .

"Not that everyone at LSU drinks. But you know how fans are."   But the game is not played in the stands or by Mike the Tiger, LSU's Bengal tiger mascot.

"It's on the field," said defensive back George Teague. "We know that."

While the rest of the country was only just now beginning to learn about George Teague, his teammates found out all they needed to know during a scrimmage in spring practice of 1991.

The 6-foot-2, 187-pound Teague went head-to-head with 5-10, 240-pound fullback Martin Houston. And after the dust had settled, only Teague was able to get to his feet.

"People really started to take notice of George when he tackled Martin Houston and knocked him out," said secondary coach Bill Oliver.

More than that, people began to take notice of Teague when he moved to safety in the 1991 season. That year, the Montgomery native really came into his own, with 54 tackles, six interceptions, and 11 passes broken up. Through a quirk of scheduling, where Teague was listed on the roster as a cornerback, he earned All-SEC second-team honors as a cornerback, even though he played the season at safety.

Teague went into the 1992 season listed on everyone's roster as the starting free safety. He moved back to cornerback after the season's first game but wound up the season earning second-team All-SEC and All-America honors at his listed position of free safety.

However, there was much more to Teague than football. Not only was he a Class 6A All-State selection at defensive back in high school, he earned academic All-State honors as well.

And while most football players relish the idea of being known for big hits and big plays, Teague feared being recognized only for his football talents.

"To know me, you have to be around me off the football field," Teague said. "What happens when I'm not playing is the real me.

"I like myself better off the field. I have a different attitude: more caring, more sensitive. On the field, there is a lot of hate. There is a big contrast between my football personality and my real personality."

Off the field, Teague is an accounting major who one day intends to get a degree in engineering. He said the major influences in his life are "my family, the Lord, my fiancé."

And he understands the difficulty people have in separating truth from myth when it comes to football players. Sometimes, he said, the players have the same problem.

"Sometimes people see athletes as nothing more than athletes: dumb jocks," Teague said. "We're seen only as football players, and sometimes that's a negative image that can only hurt you.

"At the same time, some people get caught up in how they are perceived by other people. If you are perceived as a player, as something supernatural, you can get wrapped up in that and carry that image off the field with you. That's not good, either."

It is one of the reasons Teague worked so hard to make a future for himself outside of football. Even though he lettered for four years at Alabama; even though he started two seasons, led the conference in interceptions as a junior, and has a legitimate chance to play pro ball, he has other goals besides success with football.

"Just having other goals than being in the NFL has helped me keep things in perspective," Teague said. "I want to be an engineer. I have plans for a life outside of football. I've always done well in school, and I think that makes a difference."

He is as competitive as any player on the field and hates losing as much as he loves winning.

"But I don't put the game on a pedestal," Teague said. "That's what I think is so strange about fans. It's nice to have fans, and they are important to the game. But it's hard to understand how they can be so excited and wrapped up in the game when they're not part of the outcome. They're not on the field."

As hard as he has tried to maintain a realistic approach to his future, the closer it gets to the end of his college days, the more Teague admits the lure of the NFL keeps getting his attention.

"You can't help but think about it," he said. "You know what you do every Saturday affects your chance to get to play in the NFL. And I'd like to have that option.

"But the most important thing is the rest of my career here. That's what comes first."

Teague's career began in 1989, the last time Alabama won the SEC championship.

He hoped to go out with another SEC ring, and maybe a national championship ring as well.

"That would mean everything to me," he said. "My senior year, the 100th season of football at Alabama — it would be the perfect season."

The perfect season was becoming more and more a possibility now. Alabama would head to Baton Rouge with a magic number of "two" — any combination of Alabama victories and Mississippi State losses that equals two would give the Crimson Tide the championship of the SEC Western Division.

"We've got a chance, and that's all you can ask for," Stallings said. "I've mentioned to the players, the first six or seven games you jockey for position to be in the championship game, and we've done that."

But more than that, Alabama found itself jockeying for position in the national championship race as well.

LSU coach Curley Hallman said the reason for that was simple.

"When this season is said and done, you take the 22 guys playing defense for Alabama and see how many are in the NFL," Hallman said. "John Copeland will go in the first three rounds. Eric Curry will go in the first three rounds. I see talent in the two-deep roster. I see young freshmen coming in and playing well.

"Maybe you don't know all their names right now. But they publicize themselves every time they go on the football field."

Indeed, Copeland and Curry were proving themselves to be the best defensive ends in the nation. After eight games, Copeland had a team-leading 41 tackles, plus six-and-a-half quarterback sacks, three fumbles caused, and two fumbles recovered. Curry had seven-and-a-half sacks, seven tackles for losses, and 17 quarterback pressures.

Cornerback Antonio Langham led the SEC with four interceptions, and safety Chris Donnelly tied for fourth in the league with three.

The team's 25 take-aways led the conference, and Alabama led the league in most defensive categories.

"Their confidence level is extremely high," Hallman said. "And they've got talent."

While there were many doubts about this team through the first half of the season, every week more and more of those doubts were erased as the Tide seemed to get better and better.

"As the season wears on, we're supposed to play better," said assistant head coach Mal Moore. "Hopefully, that's what we're doing. It's what we have to do to win the next three games."

After the second week of the season, Alabama was 2-0 and ranked seventh in the 12-team conference in total offense, ninth in rushing offense, ninth in scoring offense, ninth in first downs per game, 12th in third-down conversions, and 10th in penalties.

Now, at 8-0, Alabama was third in total offense (385 yards per game); second in rushing (221.1); second in scoring (28.25 points); third in first downs (21.25 per game); third in third-down conversions (39 percent); but still 10th in penalty yards.

The difference?

"I think from the first part of the year, we're not making glaring mistakes like we were," Moore said. "That's the trick now — no turnovers, no crucial penalties. I hope we're over that hump.

"It's experience. I think that's the mark of a good team. We've cut down penalties, cut down turnovers, and the offense — we're doing what we've got to do to win."

When the passing game wasn't working, the coaches concentrated on the run.

When teams started lining up to stop the run, the coaches switched the emphasis to the passing game.

"As the season has gone along, Jay (Barker) has improved," Moore said. "That's a plus for this team. The fact that he had the kind of success he had against Ole Miss is going to help as we go along. We still plan to do what we have to do to win, but now we feel we can be effective both ways (running and passing)."

The biggest difference between now and early in the season was that this team was not doing things to beat itself. No more drive-stopping penalties or turnovers, the simple mistakes of alignment and execution.

"Our confidence is better than at any time I've seen it," Stallings said. "We're playing with much more confidence than we ever have before. The defense has played well all year, of course, but the other phases of the game are starting to pick up, too."

The Tide would need every bit of that confidence against LSU.

Maybe it was the week off, maybe it was LSU's seven-game losing streak, maybe it was a case of looking ahead to next week's showdown with Mississippi State.

Whatever the reason, on this Saturday afternoon, the Bengal Tigers gave Alabama everything the Tide could handle. LSU made the decision to take it to Alabama right from the start, winning the coin toss and electing to receive.

Kick coverage had been a weakness for Alabama all year, and it continued to hurt the Tide. Proctor's kick was fielded by LSU's Gary Pegues at the goal line, and the sophomore took it up the left sideline 45 yards before Teague brought him down.

On first down, Homewood, Alabama, native Robert Davis, a freshman who caused quite a stir in his home state when he snubbed both Alabama and Auburn for LSU, took the pitch from freshman quarterback Jamie Howard and went around left end for 16 yards.

The second play was a screen pass to David Butler which picked up 16 more yards, and suddenly, Alabama's vaunted defense was getting backed into a corner.

Looking at a first down at the Tide 23, LSU would get only five yards closer to the end zone. Curry and Lemanski Hall stuffed Davis for a yard gain on first down. Inside linebacker Michael Rogers got outside to stop Davis on a sweep for no gain. Defensive lineman Jeremy Nunley, in for what looked like an obvious passing down, reacted well to the draw play and brought Davis down after a four-yard gain on third down.

But when Pedro Suarez kicked a 35-yard field goal, it marked the first time all season Alabama had been behind in the first half in 1992.

It wouldn't last long. Behind the blocking of tackles Matt Hammond and Roosevelt Patterson, guards Jon Stevenson and George Wilson, and center Tobie Sheils, the Alabama offense marched right back downfield.

Starting at the Tide 26-yard line, nine consecutive running plays — everything from the straight-ahead running of fullback Martin Houston to fake reverse end arounds by David Palmer — carried Alabama to a third down and two yards to go at the LSU 12-yard line.

For some reason, Alabama decided to go to the air on third down, and Barker, rolling right, overthrew a wide-open Lassic, setting up fourth down.   Proctor's 29-yard field goal tied the score at three-all.

LSU's opening offensive drive only served to wake up the Alabama defense. After downing Proctor's kick off in the end zone, the Tigers started out on their 20-yard line.

On first down, Davis fumbled the pitch from Howard, and Lemanski Hall fell on it at the LSU 17. This time there would be no attempts through the air, with Lassic carrying three times and Houston once to cover the distance. Lassic scored on a one-yard dive over the center, and Alabama was up 10-3.

The Tigers tried to catch up in a hurry, with Howard going for it all with a bomb to wide receiver Scott Ray. But sophomore cornerback Tommy Johnson was there to make an over-the-shoulder interception at the two-yard line, falling as he caught it.

Showing just how confident this Alabama offense had become, on first down the Tide ran a play-action pass out of their own end zone, with Barker overthrowing Kevin Lee on a deep sideline route.

As if to prove that wasn't a fluke, quarterback coach Mal Moore called another pass play. Barker changed the play at the line of scrimmage, however, and when he thought Palmer had not heard the change, Barker ended up holding onto the ball too long. He got sacked for a safety, cutting the lead to 10-5.

Although those were two bad plays, they spoke volumes about the change in attitude of Alabama on offense. A year ago, Stallings would never have considered letting Barker throw out of his own end zone once, much less twice. And certainly no one would have given Barker the authority to change the play at the line of scrimmage in such a dangerous situation.

"The play was supposed to go to David (Palmer)," Moore said. "David heard the change, but Jay just held the ball too long.

"Still, Jay made the right decision. He made the right call (at the line). He was right in everything he did, except he held the ball too long."

As far as LSU was concerned, though, all that series meant was that the Tigers would get the ball back in relatively good field position.

Bryne Diehl's free kick following the safety was fielded by Ivory Hilliard at the LSU 37 and returned 13 yards to midfield.

But again LSU went deep, and this time Howard's pass was intercepted by Teague at the Alabama three-yard line.

Poor field position plagued Alabama. The Tide managed to punch the ball out to the five-yard line before punting again, and after the Alabama defense stopped LSU, the Tigers punted to Palmer, who signaled for a fair catch at the Alabama 14.

Then the offense got going again. Lassic picked up six yards on the toss sweep to the left, but was injured and would not return for the rest of the game.

Barker hit Palmer with a quick screen right, and Palmer carried it 12 yards for a first down.

It was run, pass, run, pass for the next six plays, the big plays coming when Barker hit Curtis Brown for 14 yards from midfield to the LSU 36, then Chris Anderson faking the reverse and going 23 yards to the Tiger 13.

From there, it took four running plays before Anderson scored on a two-yard run, and Proctor's kick made it 17-5 for the Tide.

And when LSU responded with a 66-yard drive to the nine-yard line, who else but Antonio London came through for Alabama with a block of Suarez's 26-yard field goal attempt.

That was how the first half would end. Lassic was finished for the day, with 54 yards on nine carries. But his backup, Anderson, would come on to pick up the slack nicely in the second half.

Because LSU had won the toss and elected to take the ball to start the game, Alabama got the kickoff to start the second half. A clipping call against the Tide on the kickoff return pushed Alabama back to its own 15, but it didn't matter. It took just seven plays to go 85 yards, with Sherman Williams getting into the end zone from one yard out and introducing the "Sherman Shake," a sort of herky-jerky dance in the end zone that was his way of putting the exclamation point on his touchdowns.

Sherman Williams, dancing in the end zone?

The sophomore running back from Mobile is the last guy anyone would expect to display that kind of emotion, anywhere.

Williams is normally a quiet, reserved young man who prefers avoiding center stage. However, when you rush for 3,004 yards and score 31 touchdowns as a high school senior, it's hard to avoid the limelight.

As a freshman, Williams showed a knack for finding the end zone, scoring two touchdowns on only 12 carries while seeing action in nine games.

This season, even though he was the team's third-string tailback, the 5-10, 190-pound Williams had scored more points (42, on seven touchdowns) than he had carries (39).

The 'Shake' was just something Williams did after scoring his first touchdown in the Tulane game. It got such a response, he kept it as part of the act.

"We've won all these games in a row," Williams said. "After a while, it gets a little boring. I just thought I'd do something to keep up the team spirit. It's for the crowd and for the excitement. It's just something to talk about and smile about."

The "Shake" is really more of a jerky motion Williams uses to strut through the end zone after scoring. After seeing it for the first time, his teammates began to call Williams "Shakedown," and the fans loved it.

"I got a note from an 89-year-old lady who just loves that dance," said Gene Stallings. "She said she had been practicing to emulate it.

"If I had my rathers, when they scored they would just pitch the ball back to the official. But I would rather see them celebrating for getting into the end zone than coming up short, at the one-yard line."

Williams admits that the "Shake" is not really what he is like.

"It's just the way I express myself," he said. "I realize I'm quiet off the field. I guess I'm just more excited about playing football than walking around doing nothing.

"People think I'm sneaky because I don't say much. My grandmother used to tell me I had sneaky eyes because I never said anything. I'm different when I'm on the field, mainly just because I love the game so much."

Being the third-string tailback at Alabama isn't all bad. The rotation usually has Lassic leading off for most of the first half, followed by Chris Anderson in the third and early fourth quarters, with a fresh Williams coming in to finish off the game when the defense is worn out.

"When I get in there, I just have it on my mind to do what I can to help the team," Williams said. "I'm just like the mailman. He carries the mail, he doesn't write the letters. The rest of the offense writes the letters. I just carry the mail."

Lassic admitted to being a little envious of the sophomore's moves.

"I'm going to get him a white glove," Lassic said. "He's the Michael Jackson of this team."

Some were stunned that Stallings would play Williams as a freshman, figuring there would be more value to redshirting Williams to keep him around an extra year.

But Stallings has always said that if a player shows he deserves to play, he'll play.

"And I knew Sherman was going to be a good player," Stallings said. "The only thing that would keep him from being a good player would be to not give him the ball. If you give him the ball, he runs extremely well, and he has ever since he's been here."

Like Anderson, Williams tries to make every carry count. "I want to be worn and tired out and sore all over the day after a game," Williams said. "I don't want to leave the field until my body feels like it can't play another minute.

"I don't have too many yards, but I have touchdowns. I guess the end zone just wants me to be in there."

LSU got a break two possessions later when, for the first time since the 1991 Fiesta Bowl, Alabama had a punt blocked. Diehl's kick from the 24-yard line was slapped backward by the Tigers' Rodney Young, and LSU took over at the 'Bama three-yard line.

Three plays netted an apparent loss of seven yards for LSU, when Copeland ran Tiger quarterback Jamie Howard out of bounds on third down for a seven-yard loss. But Alabama was flagged for defensive holding, giving LSU the ball on the one-yard line to try third down again.

This time Howard pitched to another freshman tailback, Robert Toomer, who went right and just barely squeezed into the end zone for a touchdown, cutting Alabama's lead to 24-11.

Teague would stop LSU's next offensive possession with his second interception of the game.

The Tide defense would get really nasty after that, ending up with six quarterback sacks, three pass interceptions, 12 tackles behind the line of scrimmage. The Tide surrendered a net rushing total of 22 yards for the game.

"They came out attacking us," said Alabama nose guard James Gregory. "So we figured we had to start attacking them."

The offense joined in as well. Anderson would come on in Lassic's place to rush for 149 yards, and Williams would pick up 69 yards and two touchdowns, the second a 24-yard run in the fourth quarter for the final 31-11 margin of victory, as Alabama gained 301 yards on the ground.

Barker completed 11 of 20 passes for 114 yards, giving the Tide 415 yards of total offense.

It was a particularly nostalgic victory for Barker, who a year ago had made the first start of his career for Alabama, against LSU, in Baton Rouge.

When he walked off the field that night, a 20-17 winner, who knew that not only would Barker continue as the Tide's starting quarterback, but that Alabama would not lose again?

"It seems like only yesterday," Barker said afterward, standing underneath the stadium seats, looking out toward an empty field. "It's great to be back here.

"Last year, it was my job to go in there and not make any mistakes. This time, I was able to make a few plays and I could come off the field knowing I had something to do with the win."

It was Barker's 13th consecutive victory as the Tide starting quarterback, a record unsurpassed in school history.

His position coach, Mal Moore, an ex-Tide quarterback, deserves much of the credit for Barker's success. Knowing he was getting a quarterback with very little experience, Moore designed an offense that would minimize the quarterback position as much as possible. As Barker's abilities expanded, so did the role of the quarterback in this offense.

"A year ago, the offense was limited with him at quarterback," said fullback Martin Houston. "This year, he's running the offense so well, we're able to take a few chances."

Like throwing out of the end zone in the first quarter, something almost unheard of in the past three seasons under Gene Stallings.

And when Barker took the safety, it was a perfect chance for him to fold up into a shell and play caretaker again.

"But he didn't," Houston said. "Jay came right back out there like it was business as usual, like it never happened. He came back like he wanted the chance to do it again."

Barker knew the offense was not as sharp as it could have been.

"We came out a little flat," he said. "I think some of the guys may have been looking ahead."

And then again, LSU threw a few curves that the Alabama offense was not expecting.

Like blitzing. The Tide anticipated blitzes, but not from linebackers, cornerbacks, and safeties.

The fact that Barker saw it and was able to adjust shows just how far he'd come as a quarterback.

"Jay picked everything up," said wide receivers coach Woody McCorvey. "He comes to the sidelines and tells us what he's seeing out there, and because he sees those things, it allows us to make adjustments with him.

"It's not just the passing game, either. In the running game, he makes the right calls at the line and keeps us out of bad plays. That's been a big reason for the success of our running game. Jay has kept us out of bad plays.

"We know he can make the play for us now. And he's not afraid to take a few chances and take the opportunity when it's there."

Just like Barker had taken advantage of the opportunity that was presented to him a year ago, on a Saturday night in Baton Rouge.

"It's exciting," Barker said. "I thank the Lord for just letting me be here, for just having this uniform on. To come back here where it all started and set the record for consecutive wins — it's great.

"But it can't stop here. The will to win on this team is high. Our goals at the start of the year are still realistic. We just have to continue to improve, and everything else will take care of itself."

Even as Barker was talking, things were happening to help those goals fall further into place.

Out in the desert of Arizona, No. 1-ranked Washington was getting knocked off by a score of 16-3.

That meant when the polls came out Monday morning, Miami would be No. 1 and Alabama No. 2, on a collision course for a national championship game in the Sugar Bowl in New Orleans.

"I feel like we're the No. 2-ranked team," said senior Derrick Lassic. "And maybe more."

"Our goals before the season were to win the SEC championship and go to the Sugar Bowl," said John Copeland, who had five tackles — three behind the line of scrimmage — and two quarterback sacks against LSU. "Now we can up our goals to include winning the national championship."

Linebacker Derrick Oden sounded a word of warning even as he talked of how good this team just might be.

"I don't want to sound cocky, but we're a good team," Oden said. "You still haven't seen our best. If we reach the final game, you'll see a great Alabama team.

"But you overlook anybody, and you get beat. We don't look ahead."

12

Setting Up a Showdown

Sure enough, when the polls came out Monday morning, Miami was No. 1 and Alabama was No. 2, and nobody cared about anything beyond that. If those two teams stayed perfect, the bowl coalition had served its purpose to perfection, setting the stage for a national championship game in the Sugar Bowl on New Year's Day.

But the Tide was really into the meat of its schedule now. From the beginning, the predictions were that the Western Division title would come down to either Alabama or Mississippi State, and it did.

Alabama was 9-0 overall, 6-0 in the conference, and traveling just down the road and across the state line to play Mississippi State, ranked 16th in the nation with a 7-2 overall record, 4-2 in the conference.

The Tide had two SEC games left to play, and would have to lose both for State to have any chance of sharing the division title. But if it did happen, if State went undefeated the rest of the way and Alabama lost its last two, then the Bulldogs would be in Birmingham the first weekend in December to play in the SEC championship game by virtue of having beaten Alabama during the regular season.

"This is it, then, on both sides," Stallings said. "They have themselves in a position where they have won two games late and that has put them in position to win the division.

"This is what you play for. It's the kind of game I enjoy. I'm glad we're in this situation."

Wide receiver Kevin Lee came out and admitted this is the game he hoped would happen all along.

"I have been pulling for Mississippi State," Lee said. "I was really hoping it would come down that we would both be undefeated and play this game to find out who is the best in this side of the conference.

"Mississippi State has lost two games, but I know they'll play this one like they are undefeated."

In Starkville, Mississippi State's weekly press release set up the game this way: "Never has Starkville played host to a bigger game than Saturday, when the nationally second-ranked Alabama Crimson Tide enters Scott Field with a 9-0 record and a 19-game winning streak."

In many respects, this was like the first round of a playoff game.

At least, that's how the Tide players were looking at it.

"It feels like a playoff game," Barker said. "This is the game we've looked forward to all year. We realize we can clinch the division title here. It's a big game.

"This team has done a good job concentrating on one game at a time. Really, on one half at a time. Every game we say, 'Let's just win this half.' So we've done a good job of concentrating on the game at hand."

At this point, Stallings's biggest concern was the distraction of all the talk of a national championship game with Miami on January 1.

"I think that kind of talk is a distraction," he said. "But I would rather have that kind of distraction than people not caring about anything riding on the game other than goodwill. You want to be in this situation, yet you don't want to discuss it.

"But people are going to discuss it. It's just how you handle it."

So how would Stallings handle it?

"I like to address it, talk about it, recognize it, then go on to what is important," he said. "These guys are in college, and when they are winning, I'm sure they read as many newspapers as they can find. I'm not going to tell them not to read the newspaper, because that's part of the fun of winning.

"I read them, too, when we win. When we lose, I don't."

Besides, Stallings said, this isn't real pressure. "Pressure is when you're 0-3, not when you are 19-0," he said. "The more you win, the more pressure. But it's a different kind of pressure."

And to be truthful, Stallings didn't mind his players beginning to think about winning the national championship.

"I would hope they are thinking about that," he said. "What's wrong with thinking about it? Good night, we talk about dreaming and dreaming big and having aspirations. Now all of a sudden you want me to tell them not to?

"Let's not be silly. You're 9-0, you've got to give it (the national championship) a little thought. You just can't dwell on it."

The coaches vote in the CNN/*USA Today* poll, and Stallings admitted he had a vote and voted Alabama No. 2.

"I have no idea (if Alabama is really the second-best team in the nation)," he said. "I don't study other teams for that purpose. I saw Nebraska on TV, and they looked awfully good to me. I don't know how they are ranked, but it would take an outstanding football team to beat Nebraska."

But Nebraska did not appear on Alabama's regular-season schedule, and if things continued to work the way everyone on this team hoped, the Tide wouldn't have to worry about the Cornhuskers.

"We're just trying to get through this season undefeated," Lee said. "I'm not looking at this game as clinching anything. It's just another game on the way to an undefeated season.

"I like our position. It gives us something to play for. I like that kind of pressure."

But everyone reacts to pressure in his own way. And typical of placekickers, freshman Michael Proctor had his own way of handling what was going on around him.

He ignored it.

"I don't get mixed up in what people are saying or thinking," he said. "I did that at the first of the season and it got me down a little bit. Now, I just take it one game at a time."

The truth is, Proctor was miserable at the start of the season. He came to Alabama from Pelham High School, hailed as the next Philip Doyle, Alabama's last All-America kicker. And it didn't take Proctor long to decide that anything less than a Doyle-like performance made him a failure.

"I knew at the beginning of the season that people expected a lot out of me," Proctor said. "After the first game (a freshman-record four field goals against Vanderbilt), they expected more.

"People were putting me up against Philip Doyle as a senior and wanted me, as a freshman, to be as good as he was as a senior. And right now, I can't be that good. By my senior year, I hope to be a little better. But right now, that's hard to live up to."

Living up to that pressure was easy after the first week. But the second week, he missed two of three field goals against Southern Miss, followed by another two misses in three attempts at Arkansas.

"That was when the fun stopped," Proctor said. "And this started being a job. I wasn't happy."

And he was trying to be everything everyone wanted him to be. People were coming up to him, acting like old friends. He kept hearing, "Don't you remember me? I met you back . . . ." Proctor would smile and try to act as if he remembered.

"But I really don't know where I met some of those people who say they met me," he said. "I really didn't know who a lot of those people were."

Stallings knew something was bothering his prize recruit. He kept reminding Proctor that this was a game, that Proctor was a freshman, that he was supposed to be having fun.

"Remembering that has made this season more enjoyable," Proctor said.

Not that it's been a bad season. Proctor had made 15 of 23 field goals going into the Mississippi State game, good enough to rank third in the conference and 10th in the nation.

"I think I'm doing fairly well now," he said. "I've not made all my kicks. But I've made the ones we really needed. We needed the field goal on our first drive against LSU, and I made that one.

We needed a field goal against Southern Miss when we were down, 10-7, and I made that one."

But his new philosophy is to not think about the next game until it gets here, not to even consider what might be at stake until its over.

"I'm just having fun," he said. "I don't think about the kicks I've missed. I just think about the games we've won. Victories are fun.

"I don't think about what I could have done anymore. Now, I just look forward to the next game, and go and do my best."

While Proctor talked of not looking back, Mississippi State offensive lineman Mike Montgomery was still haunted by the events of November 2, 1991.

That was the last time Alabama and Mississippi State met. The game was in Tuscaloosa, and with time running out and the Bulldogs trailing, 13-7, State had third-and-goal from inside Alabama's one-yard line, less than a foot from the end zone.

What happened next will never be forgotten by the players on either team who were on the field that day.

The Bulldogs had the Alabama defense on its heels, knocking the Tide backward, heading for what looked like a sure touchdown, and a chance to beat Alabama for the first time since 1980.

The crowd was on its feet, roaring. Players and coaches on both sidelines crowded as close as they could get to that end zone. Reporters and photographers ringed the end zone.

Mississippi State broke its huddle, with the plan for Bulldog quarterback Sleepy Robinson to dive off left tackle, behind Montgomery.

But before Robinson even got to the line of scrimmage, Montgomery fell forward, flat on his face. The line judge threw the flag, and it was illegal procedure on Mississippi State.

That pushed the ball back to the six-yard line, and two plays later Alabama's Stacy Harrison intercepted a fourth-down pass in the end zone to send Mississippi State home beaten, shocked, and dismayed.

The State players were angry. They accused Alabama linebacker John Sullins of calling out the Bulldog snap count to confuse them and make them jump offside. The rumor around Starkville was that Sullins had even admitted to calling the snap count on that play to get Montgomery to jump offside, which would be a penalty if it were true.

"Doesn't matter," said Alabama linebacker Derrick Oden, who was the starter alongside Sullins in that game. "They wouldn't have scored."

"No," said Alabama safety George Teague. "Of course they wouldn't have scored.

"In that last five minutes, there was a little nervousness in our eyes on defense. We knew we had to make a play. But as usual, things worked out for us. They jumped offside and that put the pressure back on them, not us."

Alabama tailback Derrick Lassic, watching from the sideline, wasn't quite as confident as his defensive teammates.

"I remember it like it was yesterday," Lassic said. "I was thinking, 'Let them score so we can get the ball back with enough time to do something.' Then the guy jumped offside and I knew it was over."

"The guy," Montgomery, had to live with that ignominy for a year. He even picked up an unwanted nickname — "offside" — around the Mississippi State campus.

Later that year, at the SEC track meet, when Mississippi State sprinter Kenny Roberts false started in the 100-yard dash, his teammates jokingly blamed it on the Alabama sprinters calling out a false-start cadence.

"I don't take the blame for losing," Montgomery said. "I take the blame for what I did."

It was the one play everyone will remember.

"We know we can beat them," said State center Lee Ford.

But they had to prove it.

"Just because of the way it ended, they'll want revenge," Teague said. "If I was in their position last year, I'd feel like I didn't get a fair chance to get my shot, either. I'd want another chance.

"They've been looking forward to this game to settle it once and for all."

And so the Alabama game became the big game on the Mississippi State schedule, even before the '92 season started.

"I feel it's the biggest game we've played here at Mississippi State," said quarterback Greg Plump. "There is a lot at stake for us. This game says a lot about our bowl chances. For them, it's the Sugar Bowl at stake.

"Everywhere we go, even in class, people tell us this is the big one. It'll be a packed house. Practice this week has been fun. The guys here are excited. My phone's been ringing off the hook with people wanting tickets. I can't help them."

Just as Alabama used the 1991 season as a springboard to its current success, Mississippi State players felt they used last year to get their program turned around, too.

"Beating Florida gave us a lot of confidence," said Plump, who took over for Robinson when Robinson tore up a knee against Florida in a 30-6 victory earlier in the season.

"In the past, Mississippi State didn't win a lot of big games or close games. This year, we've won close games. But more than that, beating Florida let us know we can win big games."

And that is what Bulldog head coach Jackie Sherrill had been looking for.

"This is a team that has brought back respect to their program and is moving in the right direction," he said. "You're looking at a group of guys that have worked very hard. They have won nine out of 10 games they've played at home the last two years. They've been very productive, and they have beaten some pretty good football teams.

"We could sit here and say, 'What if . . . ?' But that's not reality. The reality is that we're playing the No. 2 team in the country, and we're playing them on our field and playing them on ESPN.

"That's a great tribute to these players."

It also made for some very confident players, none more confident than State senior left offensive tackle John James.

"I really don't think Alabama has a chance of coming out of here the No. 2 team in the country," James said. "We've had other ranked teams come in here. Texas came here last year with the No. 1 defense in the country and we kicked the . . . out of them. Florida came in this year ranked in the top five, and we beat them.

"We play well in big games. I expect to come out of here Saturday 8-2 and headed to the Sugar Bowl. Auburn will probably beat Alabama, and we'll play Florida in Birmingham (in the SEC championship game), and Florida doesn't want any part of us again."

The more James talked, sitting in the lobby of the players' dorm in Starkville, the hotter he got. And when someone mentioned that he would be lining up against All-America defensive end Eric Curry, James let it all go.

"This is my third time to play against Curry, and I've done well against him every time," he said. "He'll go in the first round (in the NFL draft) regardless of what happens Saturday. I'm rated low (by pro scouts). I've got nothing to lose.

"I'm rated low, and that's bull . . . . I've been All-SEC three years in a row and I'm rated low? He (Curry) knows me. I put him on the ground five times last year. How can I be rated low? I've got nothing to lose and everything to gain."

The 6-foot-2, 295-pound James said his performance against Curry had as much to do with his earning All-SEC honors as anything he did all season. And he can't wait for the rematch.

"It was a long day last year," James said. "A real four-quarter game. I've seen this year that Curry starts the game and then goes out a lot. But I play every snap. And last year, we played every snap against each other.

"It's good for both of us."

Like his teammates, James believed there was unfinished business between the two teams. In the '91 game, after Montgomery's penalty, State fullback Michael Davis carried the ball to the three-yard line, then Harrison intercepted the fourth-down pass in the end zone.

"That was hard to swallow," James said. "We had Alabama beaten. They know it. You could see it in the expressions on their faces at the one-foot line. They looked sick. Then we had the penalty.

"But last year is last year. This is my last home game, and it's important to beat Alabama. They know we can beat them, and we know it."

James was convinced the play called would have resulted in a Mississippi State touchdown last year.

"How do you keep someone out of the end zone when they are less than six inches away?" James said. "Alabama was beaten. They had the same sick expression on their faces as Florida did this year: shock. They were shocked when we moved the ball on them so quickly.

"It was the same look Tennessee had last year when we were ahead of them in the fourth quarter. The defense was sick because they didn't do their job. I've only seen that sick look three times: Tennessee, Florida, and Alabama.

"Everyone said we'd been looking ahead to Alabama all year. Well, here they are. I'd be very surprised if one of these teams doesn't show up. I know the Mississippi State Bulldogs will."

Eric Curry would show up, too.

It didn't take long for word of what James said to get back to Tuscaloosa. When James's comments appeared in the newspaper, copies were blown up to extra-large size and hung strategically all over the Alabama football building.

But if they were meant to get Curry mad or more ready than usual, they were a waste of time. He and his best friend and roommate, John Copeland, didn't need any outside motivation to succeed — just the fact that they were here, starters on the Alabama defensive line, two players with such ability that NFL defensive coaches could hardly wait to get their hands on them.

It is almost impossible to talk about one without talking about the other. Curry and Copeland were more than best friends. They were kindred spirits, small-town boys who traveled similar hard roads to arrive at the big time together.

It is rare that one team would have two All-America defensive ends in the same season. Rarer still that both players would be rated 1-2 at their position in the country by NFL scouts.

But Curry and Copeland were rare individuals.

"If there are two better defensive ends in the country, I'd like to coach them," said Alabama defensive line coach Mike Dubose, who came to Alabama after coaching in the NFL at Tampa Bay. "These are two of the best I've ever been around. I saw guys in the NFL who were better because of their experience, but I never saw any better from a physical standpoint. And with experience, these two can be as good as any in the game."

It would sound like so much hype, a coach bragging on his players, if the statistics didn't back it all up.

The 6-foot-6, 270-pound Curry would end up the year as a consensus All-America, a finalist for the Lombardi Award, the Chevrolet Defensive Player of the Year and the UPI Lineman of the Year. Despite missing two games with a broken hand, Curry would have 40 tackles, seven tackles for losses, 10.5 quarterback sacks, 27 quarterback pressures, two fumbles caused and one pass breakup.

Copeland, at 6-foot-3, 280 pounds, would end up a consensus All-America, too. He finished with 65 tackles — 11 behind the line of scrimmage — 10.5 quarterback sacks, 22 quarterback pressures, five pass breakups, three fumbles caused, and two fumbles recovered.

Curry played right defensive end, the place for the stronger pass rusher. "He can sit on a corner, put his hand down and the coach is going to say, 'Sic 'em,'" said one NFL assistant coach. "He'll run through traps, play through draws, react to the running game and get the passer."

Copeland was the stronger and more physical of the two. He was the better technician, who could play either tackle or end.

Curry and Copeland didn't become best friends just because of similarities in their ability to dominate on a football field, however.

According to the standardized tests that supposedly measure whether a player has enough intelligence to succeed in the college classroom, both Curry and Copeland were supposed to be failures.

Both failed to make the required minimum on their entrance examinations, Curry getting a 690 on the SAT (700 being the required minimum) and Copeland getting a 16 on the ACT (where 17 is the required minimum).

Curry, from Thomasville, Georgia, elected to go on to Alabama and sit out his freshman year, academically ineligible under NCAA and SEC rules. Copeland, from Lanett, Alabama, chose to enroll at Hinds (Mississippi) Community College so he could play for the next two years, then signed with Alabama as an incoming junior.

Curry quickly proved he could succeed in the classroom as a freshman, and as a sophomore, won the Commitment to Academic Excellence Award from the Athletic Department.

"I didn't think it was fair that I couldn't play football because of a standardized test," Curry said. "But the year away actually helped. It let me concentrate more on my books. When the other guys were going to practice, I could go to my room and do homework. You can reach your goals if you work hard. That's what I learned."

It was on the field that Curry began to have problems. As a sophomore, he broke his foot and missed the entire 1989 season.

"I began to think things were always going to go bad for me," he said. "I had to go to classes on crutches, and I wasn't getting to play any football. I was always falling down on my way to class, and it was frustrating.

"But I never thought of leaving. I couldn't do that. I had too much determination. Plus, people in my hometown look up to me, as far as being a role model and a leader. They put a lot of effort into me going to college. They didn't want to see me come back and do nothing."

In August, prior to the 1992 season, Curry received his college degree, in criminal justice. It took one semester longer than four years, and he became the first person in his family to graduate from college.

"No matter what happens now," Curry said at the time, "I've accomplished something great. I came here as Prop 48, and how many Prop 48s graduate, much less graduate almost on time?

"Some people come to college just to play football. I came not only to play football, but to get my degree. I wanted to be a football player and a student, and I did it."

Did he ever. His calm demeanor hid a quick mind and fierce competitiveness that impressed even his own roommate.

"I think Eric is the best lineman in the country," Copeland said.

And while Curry was often labeled just a pass rusher, Dubose said with a year in the NFL weight room, Curry will get bigger and stronger and be just as good at plugging the gaps and taking on the run.

"He was doing that earlier in the year, before he broke his hand," Dubose said. "Give him a year with an NFL strength coach and he'll be doing it all."

As Curry said, hard work pays off.

"You learn you can't be content," he said. "From early in the season, we had a big reputation on defense. But we had to keep learning.

"We're not supermen. If you stay the same every week, people are going to find flaws in your defense. I tried to improve myself every week. I'd watch John rush the passer and learn techniques from him. He was more of a bullrusher and I was more of a finesse guy.

"I enjoyed playing with him. He's a good guy and helped keep the double-teams away."

While Curry was struggling with his setbacks, Copeland was excelling in the unheralded and unpublicized world of junior college football. He earned Junior College All-America honors at Hinds, with 115 tackles, 10 fumble recoveries, and 13 passes broken up.

"I could have come to Alabama (as a freshman) and sat out a year," Copeland said. "But I wanted to play. I think that helped me out a lot. I got bigger, faster, and stronger."

He had his problems once he got to Alabama, however. That first spring, Copeland was not able to come to grips with the new defensive system put in by Alabama defensive coach Bill Oliver. Add to that a sprained ankle that limited what he could do, and by the end of spring practice, Copeland had his bags packed and was ready to head home.

"I hated it," Copeland said. "I hated Coach Dubose. I was ready to leave.

"But for some reason, I didn't do it. The only reason I think I stayed was Eric. He sort of helped me through it. I just decided to hang in there, and I'm glad. I think about that now, and it would have been the biggest mistake of my life."

By the following fall, Copeland was healthy, and quickly earned the start at left defensive end, opposite Curry.

"That first spring, all I knew about John was that he was mentally tough," Dubose said. "He played every practice, went through every drill with a sprained ankle.

"But it didn't take me more than a few days that fall to realize he was something special. Not only was he a good pass rusher, but he was a strong, physical player at the point of attack. He could play the pass and the run, and that's a person that is difficult to find at any level."

Copeland's strength allowed Dubose to start both players opposite each other, instead of alternating them at right end, traditionally the best position for a pass rusher.

In his coaching career, Dubose has tutored such NFL players as Jon Hand, Curt Jarvis, Anthony Smith, Larry Roberts, Emanuel King, and Cornelius Bennett.

"But as far as doing it all, John is the best I've seen," Dubose said. "His ability to separate himself from the blocker with his hands stands out.

"But what really gets your attention is he has great eyes and a great understanding of the game. He can see little things, like if an offensive lineman's shoulder is slanted a little more than normal, and John knows how to read that and determine where the play is going. That gives him a little jump on people, a real plus.

"It's something I talk to my players about all the time. It's easy to talk about but tough to do on the field because it happens in about a hundredth of a second. I don't know if it's a God-given knack or a learned knack. I've coached players over and over and they still get caught looking, which costs them that extra step which John never seems to have to take."

With Curry and Copeland in the starting lineup together, Alabama went 24-1, including winning 19 games in a row.

What makes the two even more fun is that neither expected this kind of success to happen.

"I think they are both a little embarrassed by the attention," Dubose said. "John is shy anyway, and he is reluctant to do the interviews and be on television. He just wants to do his job as good as he can, and that's good enough for him.

"Neither one of them talks much about what they are going to do, and they never make excuses about what they didn't do. They just do their best on every play, and other than get better, they are the same people they were when they first got here."

That's why the individual wars with opposing linemen like State's James didn't mean much to Curry.

"It seems like there was someone every week — Tennessee, Mississippi State, Florida, Miami," Curry said. "The way I look at it, they had their good moments and I had my good moments.

"They may have won some of the battles, but I feel like I won all of the wars because we won all of the games."

But not all of the games went on on the field.

Just as this game week was winding down, and all the verbal shots had been fired, the Alabama football program was blindsided by one of its own.

Former Alabama player Gene Jelks claimed he had gotten money to sign with Alabama, and he claimed he got paid to play while he was there.

It reeked of the Eric Ramsey affair, in which the former Auburn player taped conversations with former Auburn coaches and then claimed he was getting paid by those coaches. Auburn was under NCAA investigation because of the allegations, which would eventually bring about the resignation of Auburn head coach Pat Dye.

Such allegations directed at their own program brought the Alabama faithful up in arms.

Coach Gene Stallings proudly accepts the coveted National Championship trophy after the Crimson Tide's victory over Miami in the 1993 Sugar Bowl.

Neil Brake—Tuscaloosa News

Alabama Athletic Director Cecil "Hootie" Ingram (above) ushers in a new era of Alabama football as he introduces Gene Stallings as the Crimson Tide's new head coach. Coach Stallings addresses the media at the January 1990 press conference announcing his hiring (below).

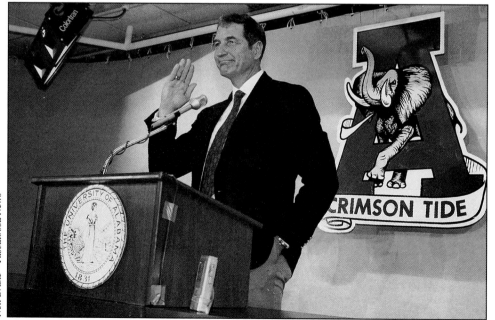

Neil Brake—Tuscaloosa News

Neil Brake—Tuscaloosa News

In the Crimson Tide's 25-8 season-opening victory over Vanderbilt, the Alabama defense sets the tone for the rest of the 1992 season with its dominating performance, as cornerback Antonio Langham (43) intercepts a Vanderbilt pass (left) and All-America defensive end Eric Curry wraps up a Vanderbilt ball carrier (below).

Amy Kilpatrick—Tuscaloosa News

Sherman Williams's (20) touchdown dive helps Alabama run its undefeated record to 5-0 with a 48-7 victory over South Carolina.

Neil Brake—Tuscaloosa News

Coach Stallings discusses the team's offense with receiver Kevin Lee during the Crimson Tide's 17-10 victory over Tennessee.

David Palmer hauls in this second quarter touchdown pass to start the Tide's scoring in its 21-10 triumph over Ole Miss.

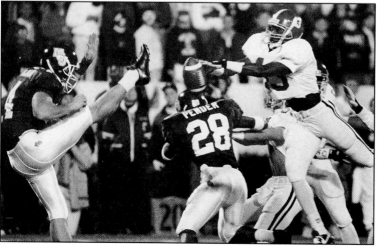

Antonio Langham (43) helps extend Alabama's undefeated string to 10 games with this blocked punt in the Tide's 30-21 win against Mississippi State.

Before a national television audience, the
Crimson Tide whips Auburn to wrap up an
undefeated regular season. Eric Curry (80)
dominates the game with his ferocious play on
defense (above), then celebrates the victory
(right) with fellow All-American John
Copeland (94).

Alabama's swarming defense is in full gear
as linebacker Michael Rogers (52) and nose
tackle Shannon Brown (93) converge on
Auburn fullback James Bostic (33) (left).

Defense continues to dominate in Alabama's 34-13 trouncing of Miami in the 1993 Sugar Bowl. Eric Turner (39), Antonio London (55), and Eric Curry (80) sack Miami quarterback Gino Torretta (left), as the Tide's harassing defense forces Torretta into three interceptions. (Below) George Teague (13), Tommy Johnson (10), and Sam Shade (31) celebrate Teague's spectacular "strip and steal" of Miami's Lamar Thomas to prevent a Hurricane touchdown.

Neil Brake—Tuscaloosa News

Derrick Lassic keys the Alabama offense with 135 yards on 28 carries, the most yards gained by a running back against Miami last season.

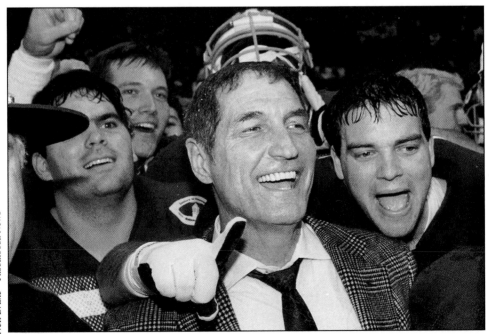

Neil Brake—Tuscaloosa News

As the final seconds tick down in the 1993 Sugar Bowl, Coach Stallings and his players begin to celebrate their 1992 National Championship season, Alabama's 12th national title overall and its first in 13 years.

Michael Proctor (3) and Jeff Wall (16) share the excitement of winning the National Championship.

13

Canceled Checks and Gene Jelks

Alabama fans have long felt that the Atlanta newspaper, the *Journal-Constitution*, was out to get their school. It is a fear whose beginnings can probably be traced to the early 1960s, and the feud that erupted between then-sports editor Furman Bisher and Bear Bryant.

There were several stories that Bisher wrote that Bryant was unhappy with, but the one that brought everything to a head was a story Bisher did for the *Saturday Evening Post* about the brutality of college football, with most of it centered on Bryant, followed by a second story alleging that Bryant and then-Georgia head coach Wally Butts had been involved in fixing the outcomes of college games.

Bryant sued the *Saturday Evening Post*, and, according to his book, *"Bear,"* eventually settled with the magazine for $320,000. Butts received $460,000. And Bisher and the *Atlanta Journal-Constitution* were forever tainted in the minds of many Alabama fans.

Perhaps, too, it is a carryover of a jealousy of Atlanta that many in Birmingham carried with them. Alabamians feel that, up until the 1960s, the cities of Birmingham and Atlanta were equal competitors. Then, in the 1960s, Atlanta took advantage of the racial problems of Birmingham to jump way ahead and become one of the most important cities in the South, if not the nation.

Whatever the reason, Alabama fans have long felt that the Atlanta newspapers were out to get the university and its athletic programs. The season's earlier flap, with Georgia defensive back Ralph Thompson claiming extra benefits from Alabama coaches, broke in the Atlanta paper. And when it turned out to be nothing, the Tide fans chalked it up to the Atlanta newspapers out to get them again.

On November 12, in a copyrighted article, the *Journal-Constitution* claimed that former Alabama team captain Gene Jelks had come forward with tapes alleging NCAA violations by the Tide.

Jelks claimed former Alabama assistant coach Jerry Pullen and others had been paying him throughout his college career, including a $2,100 "signing bonus" after he enrolled at Alabama.

In a statement Jelks signed for the *Journal-Constitution*, and in exclusive interviews, Jelks claimed:

• That Pullen, who had been his grade school coach, and Jelks's own mother, Doris, conspired to get him to sign with Alabama in 1985. Pullen was promoted to a full-time coaching position on then-Tide head coach Ray Perkins's staff at the start of Jelks's career.

• That former Alabama assistant coach Rockey Felker provided Jelks with cash while Jelks was in high school in Gadsden, Alabama, including $583 to buy his mother a Christmas present and $600 for each of the five playoff games won by Jelks's team, Emma Sansom High.

• That Alabama coaches provided Jelks with money he used to make payments on a 1984 Ford Escort, purchased during his senior year in high school. The car was registered to Jelks's mother, but Jelks said it was for his use. Doris Jelks said she made the monthly payments on the vehicle. Gene Jelks said the money was provided by Alabama coaches, and included a cash payment of $2,100 after he enrolled.

• That Jelks received, through the mail, cash in white envelopes, with no return address, while at the university.

• That Gadsden businessmen Alan Cohn and Harold Simmons provided him with money and pay for work he often didn't complete.

Everyone involved issued immediate denials, including Jelks's mother, Doris, who said, "What would I look like, selling one of my kids? I'm not that low."

Jelks claimed that the NCAA had spoken to his attorney, Stan Kreimer of Atlanta, to learn more about the allegations against an athletic department that has never been placed on NCAA probation.

"I was bought and sold to the university," Jelks told the *Journal-Constitution*.

Gene Jelks was one of the most promising running backs in the state his senior year at Emma Sansom High School, when he rushed for 1,491 yards and scored 13 touchdowns to lead his team to a 14-0 record and the Class 5A state title.

Jelks was a consensus first-team All-State running back, who was recruited by every SEC school. When he signed with Alabama, it gave the Tide two of the top high school players in the state, the other being running back Bobby Humphrey of Birmingham's Glenn High School.

Both proved to be outstanding running backs as freshmen. Humphrey was a tougher runner, but Jelks was faster and more likely to break the big run that would bust a game open. Humphrey started the season stronger, and became the first Alabama freshman to record back-to-back 100-yard games when he picked up 106 against Cincinnati and then came right back with 127 yards against Vanderbilt.

But Jelks finished the season stronger, gaining 530 yards in his last four games. Jelks became the first Tide player to gain over 100 yards rushing and receiving in the same game when he ran 18 times for 168 yards and caught three passes for 120 yards against Mississippi State. He earned SEC and *Sports Illustrated* Player of the Week honors for his 192-yard, one-touchdown performance in the 25-23 victory over Auburn.

Jelks led the team in rushing as a freshman with 588 yards on 93 carries, a 6.3 yards-per-carry average, and five touchdowns. In the 24-3 victory over Southern Cal in the Aloha Bowl, Jelks was named the game's Most Valuable Offensive Player for his 79 yards rushing.

But in his sophomore season, Jelks fell out of favor with head coach Ray Perkins, and while Jelks missed the Tennessee game with a sprained knee, Humphrey rushed for 217 yards to claim the starting tailback spot. Humphrey went on to rewrite most of the school rushing records that season, earning All-America honors for his 1,471 yards rushing, the most in school history.

With Humphrey established as one of the top running backs in the country, new head coach Bill Curry had to find a place to play Jelks. That turned out to be in the defensive secondary, where as a junior, Jelks had 65 tackles, four interceptions, one touchdown on an interception return, and another on a punt return, and was named the "Defensive Back of the South" by the Atlanta Touchdown Club.

However, in his senior year, Jelks went down in the first game with a knee injury and would miss that season, taking a medical red-shirt. Humphrey, who missed most of the season with a broken foot, elected to go ahead and turn pro and went on to earn Rookie of the Year honors in the NFL with the Denver Broncos.

Jelks, however, seemed to have lost interest in playing defensive back at Alabama, but the tailback spot was being manned by Siran Stacy, who had sparkled in 1989 when Humphrey went down.

Jelks never quite regained the form he had, even as a junior, and to many was a question mark as an Alabama career that had begun with such promise ended with such disappointment.

After failing to make an NFL team, Jelks returned home to Gadsden and worked a number of jobs, including selling cars in Birmingham for a while and working at a sports memorabilia shop in a mall in Gadsden.

But at 23 years old, it was hard to accept the fact that his athletic life was over. So for the next several years, there were rumors that Jelks was going to strike back at the university with information on what went on while he was playing there.

Rumors of canceled checks had been circulating since 1989. And more than once, Jelks had told reporters who cover Alabama that he was going to "get a few things off my chest" about Alabama.

But each time Jelks was pressed, he backed down.

At Alabama's Sugar Bowl game with Miami in 1989, *Birmingham Post-Herald* columnist Paul Finebaum was sitting in linebacker Keith McCants room when Jelks came in and told Finebaum he was ready to be interviewed, to go public and "rip (former head coach Bill) Curry to shreds."

But, according to Finebaum, once the conversation started, it made little sense, with Jelks accusing Curry of incompetence as a football coach and costing Jelks millions of dollars in the NFL.

There were never any accusations of rules violations, according to Finebaum. Just blame for Jelks's failure to succeed as a football player.

In the succeeding years, Jelks was asked again many times about rumors of checks and rules violations, and Jelks denied it all, even becoming angry with reporters, claiming he would sue anyone who printed such stories.

But in the years since leaving Alabama, Jelks had not been able to hold onto a job for very long, according to some of his former teammates.

"I feel like Gene feels he was done wrong," said Larry Rose, a four-year starter at Alabama who played high school ball with Jelks in Gadsden. "He was booted to defense when he should have been left at running back. They moved him to defense to push Bobby (Humphrey) for the Heisman, and it crushed him.

"I feel sorry for Gene. I'm worried about Gene. He's the one that will end up hurt from all of this."

Former Alabama linebacker Philip Brown said Jelks just felt exploited and was looking for revenge.

"From knowing Gene, he likes to be in the limelight," Brown said. "He's proud of himself. He always wanted to accomplish something. Maybe he . . . a lot of black ball players feel like we were exploited. We played and practiced a lot and got nothing to show for it.

"That's why when you go down there, you have to realize that if worse comes to worse, you can get a degree. Nobody is being used, other than you using yourself."

As far as money was concerned, teammates of Jelks found it hard to believe he was getting anything extra and not telling them.

"If Gene was getting that kind of money, it would have been visible," Rose said. "He would not have been fighting and scratching to get by like everyone else was."

Brown, who like Jelks is black, said there was no money paid to Jelks.

"Having been around him four years, going to bowl games with him, double-dating with him—there was never any money," Brown said. "I roomed with Cornelius Bennett, and if Cornelius wasn't getting money, surely Gene was not. And Cornelius wasn't."

Brown was drafted by the Atlanta Falcons and played a year in the NFL, two in the CFL before coming back to Birmingham to work. He said in all that time of hanging around a lot of ex-Alabama players in the pros, he never saw or heard of players getting money.

"If it had happened, I'd have known because I'd have sought after it, too," Brown said. "I always said a player should get a per diem. The university is making tons of money. Why shouldn't the players get some? But I also see now that it is important to get a degree. I didn't realize that until I got out and got into the working world."

Jelks's bitterness, according to former Alabama defensive back John Cassimus, was the result of the knee injury.

"When everything was going well, Gene was the greatest guy in the world," Cassimus said. "He was everybody's friend.

"But he hurt his knee against Vanderbilt (as a sophomore) and he didn't rehab his leg. He didn't work hard. It was as if he expected it to get better by itself. When he came back, Bobby Humphrey was doing well and Gene was moved to defensive back. He was very jealous of Bobby. He was bitter."

Perkins, who left Alabama to become head coach of the Tampa Bay Bucs of the NFL and then head coach at Arkansas State, denied any wrongdoing in the signing of Jelks out of high school.

"It's unbelievable," Perkins said. "I used to tell our coaches, 'We're not going to cheat, and if one of you does, you'll be looking for another job.'

"This is a tragedy. It's going to hurt Gene Jelks more than he realizes. It's the same with that other guy, at Auburn (Eric Ramsey)."

The denials continued, from everyone accused.

Harold Simmons, the businessman from Gadsden accused of paying Jelks, admitted that he had given Jelks jobs. Simmons is an Alabama fan who never attended the university.

"He (Jelks) is broke, grabbing straws," Simmons told the *Journal-Constitution*. "He had some bad luck. He didn't make it in pro ball. Eric Ramsey hit, and that's the only limelight he sees."

Jelks accused Gadsden businessman Alan Cohn of paying him $100 a week to wash trucks, and Jelks said he would often leave after washing just one truck.

"I don't know what the man is talking about," Cohn said in the *Journal-Constitution* story. "He is mad at everybody connected with the University of Alabama."

As far as the NCAA was concerned, the four-year statute of limitations was almost up on Jelks's allegations. According to NCAA enforcement officer David Berst, the NCAA is prohibited from reviewing matters more than four years old.

But the 1989 allegations fell within that four-year time frame, so the NCAA could look into Jelks's charges.

Alabama athletic director Cecil "Hootie" Ingram said the university has reviewed Jelks's allegations and "will handle them in the proper manner through the SEC and the NCAA."

The matter is complicated because Jelks played for Perkins, who was also athletic director, and then later for Curry, who worked for athletic director Steve Sloan.

The university had even changed presidents during that time, from Joab Thomas to the current president, E. Roger Sayers.

"Personnel changes would not cause the NCAA to avoid looking into the matter if the matter is considered serious," Berst said.

Under a 1985 NCAA rule change, penalties could follow former coaches to their current positions if they are found to be involved in any wrongdoing.

At the time of the accusations, Perkins was head coach at Arkansas State (he has since joined the New England Patriots of the NFL). Former Alabama assistant Jerry Pullen was a graduate assistant at Clemson, and former assistant Rockey Felker was an assistant last fall at Tulsa.

"Assuming the violations somehow involve a former coach, he could be penalized," Berst said. "In order to affect him directly, he would have to have been involved directly in the violation. That's true for an assistant as well as the head coach."

Alabama fans were not the kind to take such allegations lightly, especially not now, when their football team was ranked No. 2 in the nation and the whole program was reunited under Stallings.

Barely 24 hours after the first allegations were out, some Alabama fans were known to have hired a private investigator to look into where Jelks was, and find out who actually was behind it all. The feeling among many was that their hated cross-state rival, Auburn, would ultimately be the culprit.

Jelks's attorney, Stan Kreimer, a University of Virginia graduate with a law degree from Georgia, was the son-in-law of Jack Swertferger, a 1952 Auburn graduate. Swertferger and his wife, Ann, are Auburn season ticket holders and belong to the Soaring Eagles Club, the highest donor level in the Auburn football donor program.

Kreimer, in the *Journal-Constitution* story, said only that the matter was referred to him by a "network of attorneys in Alabama."

He refused to say how he was getting paid or who was picking up the expenses for Jelks, who was now living in Atlanta.

Even Jelks's own family felt something was going on.

"It really disturbs me to hear something like that," said Jelks's father, Dan. "I know we didn't get any money. If we did, we haven't seen it. What bothers me is why did Gene wait so long to talk? Why didn't we hear any of this years ago?

"Something is wrong with this."

But Gene Jelks insisted it was his own idea.

"At this point, I'm 26 and I still have these guys trying to bribe me to keep me quiet," he said. "Giving me $100 here, or helping me out there, or telling me what a great job I'm doing. They feed me a bunch of lies. I'm tired of this. It's time to get on with my life, to take control. Any mistakes now, I have no one to blame. . . .

"This is Gene Jelks's idea. Nobody came to me. This is not the Eric Ramsey story. The (Alabama) alumni, when I called them, they thought that this was a joke. They know Gene Jelks. All they did was buy me off all the time, buy me off to keep quiet."

And that was the most compelling part of Jelks's story: the checks. Somehow, the Atlanta newspapers and Jelks's Atlanta attorney got copies of canceled checks written to Jelks from businessman Harold Simmons.

Simmons doesn't deny writing Jelks checks. He said the checks were for labor provided by Jelks, and anyway, Simmons says, he has no connection with the University of Alabama.

Legitimate or not, six canceled checks written from June 12, 1989, to January 1990 totaling $1,100 would raise eyebrows when those checks were made out to someone as highly recruited and highly regarded a football player as Gene Jelks was.

The last Simmons saw of the checks, they were in possession of either his ex-wife, Carol Simmons, or the lawyer she first contacted about handling her divorce proceedings, Gadsden attorney Steve Brunson.

According to a story by Richard Scott in the *Birmingham Post-Herald*, as late as one week before the story broke, Jelks's Atlanta attorney, Stan Kreimer, was still attempting to get copies of the canceled checks from attorney John Thrower Jr. in the city of Opelika, right next to Auburn.

Thrower said Kreimer contacted him three times between November 2 and 5, by telephone, in person, and by fax, but Thrower claimed he already had destroyed his copies of the checks and refused to help Kreimer.

How Kreimer knew to contact Thrower is another mystery.

All Simmons knows is that at least four people had access to the canceled checks: himself; his ex-wife, Carol Simmons; Brunson, who Simmons's ex-wife first approached about handling her divorce; and Eddie Cunningham, the attorney who ended up handling the divorce for Carol Simmons two years after she first contacted Brunson.

"I had the checks," Simmons said. "They were gotten from me by my ex-wife. She took them to Steve Brunson two years ago. From there, Steve Brunson held them two years. The attorney she hired had to get them from Steve Brunson. That was Eddie Cunningham. The checks were never in anybody's hands but us four people.

"Now, I know I didn't give them to Kreimer. I know she didn't give them to him. I know Eddie Cunningham didn't give them to him. So that only leaves one person."

Brunson did not return repeated requests for interviews on the subject, but a partner in his law firm of Simmons, Brunson and McCain asked for anonymity and told the *Post-Herald*, "Certainly, he nor anybody in this office turned any kind of information over to anybody. We have no business records. We retained no business records. Everyone has accused Brunson of this, but it didn't happen."

Asked if he had any idea how copies of the checks reached Kreimer, the partner said, "That is a concern of ours as well."

But Opelika attorney John Thrower admitted to getting copies of the checks, "through a friend." That's as far as his explanation goes. Thrower and Brunson admit to knowing each other, but Thrower would not say whether he got copies of the checks from Brunson.

But Thrower did tell the *Post-Herald*, "I was approached three times from Monday, November 2, to Thursday, November 5, by Stan Kreimer, and I'll show phone logs, a fax letter I got from him on Thursday, November 5, where he asked for copies and I refused to do so. I had no further communication with Stan Kreimer or anyone since I got that fax letter on November 5. I will swear on a million bibles I didn't give him or anyone copies of those checks."

However, according to the story in the *Post-Herald*, Thrower has been accused by attorneys in the Montgomery area, who are spreading rumors that he gave the copies of the checks to Kreimer.

"I will say this, also: Those other people need to make sure that I'm a private person, too," Thrower said. "I have rights, too, and they better make sure when they say these things that every 't' is crossed and every 'i' is dotted."

Thrower did admit to letting friends see his copies of the checks, but said he destroyed his copies "last March or April" to remove himself from the picture.

"So it went to some other source," Thrower said. "What other source, I can't tell you because I don't know."

That's what everyone wants to know, especially Simmons.

"All you can say is he (Brunson) had the checks and they somehow wound up in all of these hands," Simmons said. "How? How did they get from here to there?"

The following day, Kreimer told the *Atlanta Journal-Constitution* that he and Jelks had met with an NCAA investigator.

Meanwhile, Alabama officials said they had been hearing for two years that Jelks was going to go public with allegations of rules violations by Alabama coaches and boosters.

"The rumors had been out there a long time," said Dr. Tom Jones, faculty athletic chairman. "Each time we heard them, we made inquiries. That's about all we could do since we could never get Gene to return our calls."

Now, Jones said, the university would proceed with a full investigation and file a report with the SEC office and the NCAA.

"My guess is the SEC (officials) will come down to look at our files and see what needs to be done," Jones said. "These allegations are not being taken lightly. We will look to see what the allegations are, but it will be up to the SEC and the NCAA to determine where it goes from there."

A week later, Alabama officials said they had completed the investigation.

"Anytime an athletic director hears anything about his program," said Alabama athletic director Hootie Ingram, "he needs to look into it. Then you put it in the category of whether you need to discuss it with the coach, the school president, the faculty rep, the conference office, or the NCAA, and you do that."

The fact that some Alabama fans and alumni started their own investigations didn't matter to Ingram.

"I don't get into that," he said. "I'm only worried about if I hear any allegations about our program. Then we go through whatever procedure it takes to look into it."

That was all Ingram would say, and the last official word on the subject for quite a while. Eventually, on December 2, Alabama would get an official letter from the NCAA saying the matter was under investigation. But that was all anyone knew.

Meanwhile, Alabama fanatics blamed it on Auburn fans, saying they were just trying to get something on Alabama because of the trouble Auburn was in over Eric Ramsey's allegations.

Auburn fanatics believed the truth had finally come out about the Alabama program.

And the real winners in all this were the sports talk shows, which battled for the latest gossip and rumor to keep the listeners listening and the calls coming in.

CHAPTER

14

A Scare in Starkville

S aturday night in Starkville, Mississippi.

On a cold, clear, night, a crowd of 41,320 — the third largest in Scott Field history — turned out to watch what many felt was the biggest game in Mississippi State history.

And, of course, when Bulldog fans turn out, so do the cowbells.

Ringing cowbells at Mississippi State games is a tradition that dates back to sometime in the 1930s or 1940s. Legend has it that during a home game between the Bulldogs and arch rival Ole Miss, a cow wandered onto the field. State soundly defeated the Rebels that day, and the cow was adopted as a mascot.

Eventually, the cow would be replaced by just the cowbell. And even though the SEC had banned the use of "artificial noisemakers" at all football and basketball games pitting two SEC teams, somehow the cowbells continued to show up at Mississippi State home games.

When Jackie Sherrill arrived on the scene as head coach in 1991, he asked for the fans to bring the cowbells back. His argument was that, at 41,200 seats, Starkville's Scott Field was the second smallest stadium in the conference (Vanderbilt Stadium is the smallest at 41,000 seats). To make up the difference in noise levels between Starkville and, say Tennessee, where Neyland Stadium could seat 91,902, the Bulldog fans needed help — cowbells.

Mississippi State officials posted security at every gate at SEC home games to confiscate cowbells, but it wasn't hard to smuggle the bells in, and it didn't seem as if many were stopped at the door.

At night, the cowbells only seemed louder. Especially this night, when the championship of the SEC Western Division would be decided between the two teams everyone picked to finish 1-2, Alabama and Mississippi State.

The temperature was 45 degrees and dropping quickly as kickoff approached. The wind was out of the southwest at 12 miles per hour, which whipped the flags that surrounded Scott Field as the band played the national anthem.

Mississippi State's captains, Lee Ford, Dan Boyd, Marc Woodard, and John James, were followed to midfield by the other 21 State seniors for the coin toss, which the Bulldogs won and elected to receive.

But all State could get was 10 yards on its first five plays, with one first down, and Todd Jordan came on to punt the ball away from his own 35-yard line.

The Tide's David Palmer caught the kick and returned it three yards to the Alabama 33, where the Tide opened its first offensive series.

Alabama went right to Palmer, who went in motion left to right and took the pitch from Barker, cutting around right end for 18 yards, plus 15 more for an unsportsmanlike penalty on Mississippi State.

That got the Tide into State territory, and on third-and-six Barker hit receiver Curtis Brown for seven yards and a first down. Three plays later, on third-and-10 from the 23, Barker flipped a little shovel pass to Derrick Lassic out of the backfield, and Lassic went 23 yards for the touchdown.

Sherrill countered with a new quarterback on State's second possession, true freshman Rodney Hudson. On first down, Tide linebacker Lemanski Hall dropped running back Kenny Roberts for a loss of three. On second down, Derrick Oden and

Copeland burst through the middle to drop running back Michael Davis for a loss of six on a shovel pass.

On third down, Hudson dropped back to pass and was forced out of the pocket by Curry. His pass, intended for wide receiver Willie Harris, was picked off by Tide cornerback George Teague, except that a penalty on Alabama nullified the turnover and gave State another shot with the ball.

Third down this time resulted in an incomplete pass, which brought on Jordan to kick again. The deep snap also brought Alabama cornerback Antonio Langham right up the middle, and Langham not only blocked the kick, he then scooped the ball up and returned it 24 yards for a touchdown and a quick 14-0 lead by Alabama.

"We worked on the blocked punt all week," said Langham, who had done the same thing against Vanderbilt as a freshman in 1990. "Usually I line up on the outside, but Coach Oliver felt a fast man could get free inside.

"The ball hit me in the chest, and we're always taught to scoop the ball off the ground. We have fumble drills for that type of play. That's why I scored."

Alabama led, 14-0, after the first quarter and seemed well on the way to another victory. The cowbells weren't ringing. Instead, the 10,000 or so Alabama fans who were spread out on either side of the south end zone were on their feet, chanting and cheering.

The second quarter began with Alabama in possession, in the midst of a 51-yard drive. The Tide got to the State 25-yard line, where consecutive plays to Lassic and Palmer netted one yard each. That brought on Proctor, who was perfect on a 41-yard field goal for a 17-0 lead.

The brutality continued on State's next possession, with Copeland forcing a fumble by the Bulldogs' Davis, which Teague recovered at the Alabama 37-yard line.

However, Alabama fumbled it right back in three plays, setting up State on the Tide 40-yard line. The two teams exchanged punts, with Mississippi State getting the better of the deal when Bryne Diehl's punt went 39 yards and State's Tony James returned it 12 yards to the Alabama 36.

Six plays later, the Bulldogs got on the board with a 37-yard field goal, and two possessions later, State passed up a 52-yard field goal attempt with 59 seconds remaining in the half to go for it on fourth-and-two from the Alabama 36. But the Tide's Michael Rogers stepped up and stuffed Michael Davis for a one-yard loss.

Still, with less than a minute to play, State's decision looked good. Alabama was holding a 14-point lead, and had the ball on its own 37-yard line with 54 seconds remaining on the clock. Everyone expected Stallings to order Jay Barker just to run out the clock.

But Stallings didn't. Perhaps sensing that 14 points was not enough, he had Barker throw deep to David Palmer on first down, but the pass was overthrown.

On second down, Sherman Williams got the call on a toss sweep to the right side, and the sophomore tailback burst through the State defense for 11 yards and a first down.

Alabama called a timeout with 39 seconds to play, then Barker dropped back again, looking deep. He was in the grasp of defensive end Jerome Brown when he saw Martin Houston floating free, and Barker lofted the pass to Houston who picked up two yards.

But that play took 21 seconds off the clock, and by the time the Tide got time called, only 18 seconds remained.

On second down from midfield, the play was a heave toward the goal line. Barker dropped back and waited for wide receiver Kevin Lee, one of the fastest members of the team, to streak downfield. Barker's pass was high, almost too high, because Lee had to slow down and wait for it at the five-yard line — which meant the State secondary could hold up and wait for it, too.

That turned it into a jump ball, and Lee won the tip, batting the ball up and then letting it fall into his arms at the four-yard line.

Quickly, Alabama lined up and Barker spiked the ball to stop the clock with less than five seconds left. Proctor ran on, and as time expired, he kicked a 21-yard field goal to put Alabama in front, 20-3.

It looked like another Alabama rout of Mississippi State. The Tide had never lost a game played in Starkville (a perfect 10-0 — the games used to be played in Jackson), and was 62-11-3 overall against its nearest SEC neighbor.

Halftime was a celebration by the Alabama fans, who were

beginning to chant "S-E-C, S-E-C," in anticipation of the division title that would be clinched with a victory over the Bulldogs.

Perhaps the players got caught up in the celebration, too. Over in the Mississippi State dressing room, head coach Jackie Sherrill, who had been bouncing back and forth on offensive sets throughout the first half, decided to go almost exclusively with the wishbone in the second half. State had run the ball well on Alabama in the first half, gaining 74 yards to the Tide's 55.

And State offensive coordinator Watson Brown, former Vandy coach, had figured out what a lot of teams were finally beginning to see about Alabama — that you couldn't run away from Curry or Copeland, so the best bet was to try to run between them.

The area of the field between Curry and Copeland belonged to James Gregory, a 6-foot-4, 285-pound junior nose tackle from St. Louis.

While Curry and Copeland were earning All-America honors, Gregory was having to replace one in last year's starter, Robert Stewart.

Gregory was not as strong or as fast as Stewart, but then few players were. And yet as the season progressed, many felt Gregory might have made the defense better, simply because he wasn't Stewart.

"Robert was stronger, quicker, and flashier," said Dubose, the Tide defensive line coach. "And he made a lot of plays that caught everyone's eye.

"But no one would see how on the next three plays Robert would be out of position. James has more understanding of defensive line play, and of the nose tackle position. For that reason, he's more consistent in making plays."

Stewart, who played linebacker and fullback before being converted to nose tackle, relied strictly on his speed and strength to bust through offensive blocks and chase down the ball carrier.

Gregory grew up a defensive lineman, a SuperPrep All-America selection at St.Louis's Sumner High. Except for a brief experiment at offensive guard in the spring of 1991, Gregory had been the backup nose tackle since signing with Alabama out of high school.

"James understands defensive football better than Robert did," Dubose said. "And he understands reading offenses better than Robert did.

"James will be in a position to help the people around him more than Robert by making calls and communicating more with the defensive ends."

All Gregory lacked going into this season was experience.

"Robert didn't do some things just because he could rely on his strength and quickness," Dubose said. "But James sees things better than Robert did, and being in the center of the field, he's in the best position to communicate with both sides of the defense.

"I think that makes us better on defense than a year ago. Not as flashy, maybe, but more consistent."

The problem came when Gregory went out. Copeland could move to nose tackle and Jeremy Nunley could come in on passing downs, which often happened. But if Copeland needed to stay at end, that left the Tide with the inexperienced Shannon Brown or Elverett Brown, unrelated but both good prospects.

Where Gregory was most needed was in stopping the run.

"James is more consistent against the run," Dubose said. "But his weakness is rushing the passer. He needs to get a three- to four-yard push in there, so the outside guys can close in; and if the quarterback steps up, James is there.

"But he's working on that."

It didn't take long for Mississippi State to silence the Tide fans.

The Bulldogs kicked off to open the second half, and the Tide's first two plays were solid enough — Lassic right for four yards, Lassic left for four more.

But on third down, Barker faked the handoff, stood up, and tried a quick throw to wide receiver Prince Wimbley. However, Mississippi State cornerback Charlie Davidson was waiting for the pass, picked it off at the Alabama 31, and returned it 20 yards to the Tide 11-yard line.

On first down, State got nothing. But on second down, quarterback Greg Plump executed a perfect play-action fake, then fired a bullet to wide receiver Olanda Truitt. Tide corner Tommy Johnson was there to bat the ball down, but Truitt, a

Birmingham native, reached down to make a spectacular one-handed grab, with his left hand, inches above the ground for a touchdown.

"This game means a lot to me," said Truitt, who played at Birmingham's Parker High School, signed with Pittsburgh out of high school, then transferred to Mississippi State after two seasons.

"Ever since I left the state of Alabama, I've wondered if I would ever get to play Alabama. Finally, I get that chance. It's like I'll finally be at ease with myself, knowing I finally got to compete against them."

Truitt would do his best on this night and certainly would have nothing to be ashamed of when it was over. He had three catches for 44 yards and one touchdown, but just as important drew a lot of attention from the Alabama secondary whenever he ran downfield. That would do as much as anything to open the running game in the second half.

His touchdown left State down, 20-9, and Sherrill decided to go for two. Plump took the snap and rolled out, getting pressure from Curry and Copeland, but just before being hit, he got off a pass to tight end Curt Clanton a half step before Clanton would have run out of end zone, and now State trailed by only nine, 20-11.

Chris Gardner's kickoff went out of the end zone, putting Alabama in operation at the 20. Two runs by Lassic netted two yards, then Barker tried to throw a quick screen to Palmer at wide receiver, but the ball got there on one hop.

On fourth down, Diehl got off a 31-yard punt that Tony James returned six yards to the Alabama 47.

State settled into the wishbone attack, but turned it into a passing formation. Plump executed a perfect bootleg pass, hitting Clanton for 22 yards. After a loss of nine on a lateral, Plump faked the option, pulled up, and hit receiver Willie Harris 17 yards downfield to leave third-and-two.

On third down, State took it right up the middle, with Fred McCrary getting four yards and the first down.

Plump executed the option on first-and-10 from the Alabama 13, and picked up 12 yards. On first-and-goal, fullback Michael Davis got nothing, but on second-and-goal Plump dove over the middle for one yard and the touchdown.

The kick was good, and suddenly, it was a ball game again, with Alabama holding a 20-18 lead.

It wouldn't stop there. Starting at his own 20 again, Barker directed Alabama to one first down, hitting Kevin Lee with a nine-yard pass to the Tide 33. Two more running plays netted five yards, then Barker rolled left, waited, saw that Kevin Lee had gotten behind everyone and was wide open at the Mississippi State 30-yard line, and let go with a perfect pass.

Perfect, except for one thing: Lee dropped the ball.

On fourth down, with the sound of cowbells filling the night air and making human sound almost inaudible, Diehl got off a good 41-yard punt. However, James returned it 23 yards to the State 44-yard line, and once again the Bulldogs had good field position.

On first down, Plump tried to pass, and the ball went right to Tide cornerback George Teague, who dropped the ball. Given new life, State began a march to the Alabama one-yard line.

Randy Brown went up the middle for seven yards, then Plump hit Kenny Roberts on a screen that went for 16 more. Michael Davis went up the middle for four, then, after Plump was forced to keep the ball and gain one, Plump popped a quick pass to his tight end, Clanton, for 12 yards and a first down at the Alabama 16.

Brown got the call again, going up the middle for six yards, where he was chased down from behind by Eric Curry. On second, Davis went up the middle for nine yards to the one-yard line, where only Tide safety Sam Shade stopped him from scoring a touchdown.

Now the place was rocking with the noise of cowbells and Bulldog cheers. The Alabama defense had lost linebacker Derrick Oden to an injury on that drive and replaced him with true freshman John Walters. It was as if everything that could go wrong was going wrong for the Tide—dropped passes, dropped interceptions, missed tackles, injuries.

Then it happened. In the press box, Mississippi State officials said it was like déjà vu.

On first-and-goal from the one, Brown burst up the middle for an apparent touchdown. But instead of signaling, the official threw a yellow flag and State was called for illegal participation: 12 men on the field.

Instead of a touchdown, it was a loss of 15 yards. Instead of kicking off with a lead, the Bulldogs were looking at first-and-goal from the 16. You had to wonder how many more chances they would get.

Brown got the ball on a reverse, but Chris Donnelly came up to stop him after a gain of three.

It looked like a costly play for the Tide, however, when nose tackle James Gregory didn't get up. He'd twisted an ankle, and would not return to the game.

On second down from the 13, wingback William Prince went up the middle and was met by Lemanski Hall and Shade, who stopped him after a three-yard gain.

On third down from the 10, Plump dropped back to pass but could find no one to throw to, so he put it out of the end zone.

On fourth down, Sherrill did what he felt he had to do. Gardner kicked a 27-yard field goal and, with a minute and a half left in the third quarter, Alabama trailed, 21-20.

It looked for a while as though State's failure to score a touchdown wouldn't matter. On Alabama's next possession, Barker's pass was behind the intended receiver and intercepted by Charlie Davidson.

And as the quarter ended, State's Randy Brown went up the middle on the Tide defense for four yards, to the 42.

Suddenly, a game that had been comfortably in Alabama's hands was out there for anyone to grab, and it looked as if the Bulldogs were getting the first shot at it.

After three quarters, State had out-rushed Alabama, 120-72, and had 66 yards in return yardage, to only 27 for the Tide. Plump had completed eight of 14 passes for 109 yards and one touchdown, while Barker was nine of 18 for 138 yards with two interceptions, two sacks, and one touchdown.

Clearly, as the teams changed ends of the field and players on both sides held up four fingers, the traditional symbol that said "the fourth quarter is ours," the quiet Alabama fans wondered if this was where the dream would die.

New Orleans Saints scout Hamp Cook was at the game, and he saw something as the teams changed sides that stuck with him for the rest of the season.

"It was the start of the fourth quarter, and Mississippi State is leading," he said. "We see people run down there and put up four fingers, saying they're going to win it in the fourth quarter.

"That's easy to do. The ones you look for are the ones who do something about it in the fourth quarter. (John) Copeland ran down the field clapping his hands. There's nothing bogus about what he's doing. He has an ingredient about him that's sincere. He is a natural leader."

As quickly as things had started going Mississippi State's way, that's how quickly they stopped.

Two plays into the quarter, Greg Plump dropped back to pass and was swarmed by the Alabama defensive line — Copeland, Curry, and Elverett Brown.

A third-down shovel pass by Plump to Davis was dropped, the first mistake the Bulldogs back had made in the half.

A 35-yard punt gave Alabama the ball at its own 20, and Barker directed the Tide across midfield before losing 15 yards while running for his life on third-and-seven.

On fourth down, Diehl came on to punt again, and he got off a 41-yarder to James. James returned it 17 yards, was hit, fumbled, and the ball was picked up by one of his teammates, Johnny Curtis, who went 11 more yards before he was hit and fumbled it again.

This time, the ball went to Alabama reserve defensive back Willis Bevelle, who, after seeing what had happened to the last two guys who tried to run with the ball, simply fell on it, ensuring possession for the Tide.

That gave Alabama the ball at the State 43, and brought the Tide faithful back to life. Two toss sweeps to Williams netted three yards, then Barker sucked the defense in with a play-action fake and threw over the top to Prince Wimbley for 24 yards to the 16-yard line.

Two toss sweeps by Williams netted 12 yards and a first down at the four-yard line, but on a third try by Williams, the Bulldogs' Daniel Boyd shot through the wall of blockers and dropped the tailback for a five-yard loss.

On second down, Barker threw a fade route to Palmer in the end zone, but the pass was overthrown. He came back with a timing route to Lee, but again was off, and on fourth down Proctor hit a 26-yard field goal to give Alabama the lead again, 23-21.

Proctor kicked off to the goal line, where James bobbled the ball, then got it out to the 10 before being brought down by Eric

Turner and John Ausmus. A flag on the play for an illegal block brought the ball back to the State five-yard line.

Plump hit Roberts for 10 yards, then Roberts tried to go up the middle but was nailed for no gain by Lemanski Hall.

Then Plump put up a wounded duck of a pass that Teague settled under at the 19, setting the Tide up with seven minutes to play.

This time it was all Chris Anderson, as the tailback carried four times, the last going over the goal line from three yards out for the touchdown and a 30-21 Alabama lead.

Now the defense was back on its toes, and four plays netted eight yards for Mississippi State, Plump's fourth-down pass getting batted down at the line of scrimmage by Elverett Brown.

Alabama ran the ball seven consecutive times to run time off the clock, and when the Bulldogs got it back, they were down nine points with one minute, 17 seconds to play and looking at 79 yards to the end zone.

The Bulldogs came up 11 yards short. After Plump hit six consecutive passes to move 68 yards, on second-and-10 from the Tide 11, he rolled right, threw right, and once again, the ball wound up in the hands of George Teague.

And that was the ball game.

"When I got to the sideline," Teague said afterward, "Coach Stallings wasn't just excited. He was overjoyed."

The head coach didn't even know the score. He was just glad his team won.

"I hate to ask this question," Stallings said to reporters coming off the field. "But what was the final (score)?"

For the record and for the head coach, it was 30-21. The West was won. Teague rightly earned SEC Defensive Player of the Week honors for his two interceptions and one fumble recovery in the game. The scary part is he had one other interception called back by penalty and a possible fourth interception dropped.

"I thought I played well," Teague said. "But a lot of it was a case of being in the right place at the right time.

"That was a great game for us. It showed that we can get down and still come back."

Never had the Tide defense been penetrated like it had in the third quarter of this game.

"We got rattled a little bit when we didn't need to," said Alabama linebacker coach Ellis Johnson. "Mississippi State is as multiple set-wise and play-wise as anybody we've seen. We went over it all in practice, but it's hard to be ready for it all. And it's a credit to them to be able to run it all."

What shocked the Tide was State's ability to run the ball right up the middle.

"In the wishbone, you've got several things to worry about," said cornerback Antonio Langham. "You've got guys to defend the fullback, the quarterback, and the pitch. And once the ball is snapped, the action is a lot quicker than you see in practice. They were popping it up the middle on us, quick."

It didn't help that the entire third quarter was played on the Alabama half of the field, either.

"That wears on you," said Donnelly, the Tide safety. "The crowd was loud and we were backed up. You start looking for anything to hold onto. It's like a dam was open and they started flooding us."

And even though the Tide was ahead for most of the third quarter, it didn't feel like it.

"You get caught up in momentum," said cornerback Tommy Johnson. "You know you've got to do something to turn it around. But there was no way to take the emotion out of it.

"Field position was critical. We knew they had good speed on offense. We felt they couldn't drive the ball a long way against us, but when they were starting drives at midfield, we didn't handle field position very well."

Finally, the defense ignored field position and started concentrating on reading the Bulldogs' offensive alignments. Once that happened, the flood stopped.

"It just came down to a time when we knew we had to pick it up," said Teague, whose two interceptions gave him six for the year and 14 for his career. "That's when you find out what you're made of."

"A game like this shows we're not invulnerable," Donnelly added. "We're a good defense. But we can improve.

"We haven't been behind like that all year. It makes you check yourself. It's easy to play hard when you're ahead."

State's 301 yards of total offense was the most given up by an Alabama defense since Auburn gained 345 yards in 1991. The

21 points scored on the Tide was the most since Colorado scored 25 in the 1991 Blockbuster Bowl. It was also the first time Alabama had trailed in the fourth quarter of a game all season.

Someone asked Stallings if seeing his team come from behind like that showed him what his players were made of.

"I had a pretty good idea of that already," Stallings said. "You don't win 20 games in a row without having a pretty good idea about your team.

"Now, knowing the results of this game, I think it was good for us. It will help our confidence to know we can come from behind, in a hostile environment, against a good team.

"Of course, I didn't think it was so good for us at the time."

But it did erase any remaining doubts this team may have had about itself.

"You saw the mark of a true champion tonight," said Tide linebacker Derrick Oden, who had eight tackles in the game. "Most people would just lay down and take the whipping. But we fought back, picked ourselves up, and stopped them.

"And now we're moving on."

CHAPTER

15

Trouble on the Plains

There was a time when the Iron Bowl really seemed like a bowl game. The annual contest was always played at Birmingham's Legion Field, that old steel-and-brick structure not far from the old iron ore mines, which once was the basis for Birmingham's economy.

The tickets were split down the middle, half the stadium cheering "Roll Tide" and wearing crimson and white, the other half yelling "War Eagle" and wearing orange and blue.

But like the steel industry that Birmingham was built on, the Iron Bowl has, in a very real sense, fallen victim to a new day and a new economy.

Stadium expansions at both Auburn and Tuscaloosa have meant more money for athletic departments which were claiming they were not making the money they once made. One sure moneymaker on the schedule, however, is the annual Alabama-Auburn game, the Iron Bowl.

When Auburn expanded Jordan-Hare Stadium, athletic department officials wanted the Alabama game to include on its season ticket base on years that Auburn was the home team, and they wanted to move the game to Auburn on alternating years.

Alabama was starting a new donor program called "Tide Pride," and to increase the attractiveness of that program it helped to have more tickets available for the Alabama-Auburn game on the years the Tide was the home team.

So the two schools met and agreed to stop dividing the tickets down the middle and, instead, do the usual home-and-away split on alternating games. When Alabama was the home team, then Auburn would get only 10,000 tickets. When Auburn was the home team, the reverse would be true.

Only Auburn wanted to carry it one step further. Auburn wanted to host the game in a real sense, in Jordan-Hare Stadium, on the plains of Auburn.

Eventually, that was worked out as well. Auburn got its first home game against Alabama in 1989. The agreement was that the game would stay in Birmingham after that until 1993, when it would begin going to Auburn every other year.

Alabama said it would still host the game on its years in Birmingham, but many feel it's only a matter of time before the tradition of playing in Birmingham is stopped completely, and the game alternates between Tuscaloosa and Auburn on a yearly basis.

To the purists, then, the Iron Bowl stopped in the late 1980s, when the stadium stopped being divided equally between fans of the two schools.

Besides, they argued, how could you have an Iron Bowl in Auburn?

Indeed, much was changing the face of college football across the country. Rivalries were dying as teams became more concerned about possible bowl conflicts rather than attractive nonconference regular-season games.

This, then, was really the first year of the alternating series. It just so happened that, as Alabama's home game, the contest would be played in Birmingham by Alabama's choice. Next year, it would go to Auburn. And in fact, both teams would agree to do away with the off week before the game and move the game up a week, in order to have more time to get ready for the SEC championship game that would follow.

The one thing that wouldn't change, however, is the meaning this game carried in the hearts of the fans on both sides.

It is almost impossible to overestimate the hold this game has on the State of Alabama. It is a rivalry that lives 365 days a year, that decorates license plates, T-shirts, hats, throw pillows, and wall hangings. It is a passion that smolders and burns and never dies. It is a storm that brews all year long, building during the regular season, peaking on one day each year, then slowly subsiding through bowl games, final polls, recruiting, and signing day.

Surprisingly, all of that emotion seldom spills over onto the very players who play the game.

"I can't remember — and I played in three of these games and coached in a lot more — I can't remember a game where anything took place on the field between players, any incidents or what we call 'trash' talk," said assistant coach Jim Fuller.

"But I heard (ESPN analyst) Beano Cook say there were six people in the State of Alabama that didn't care about this game, and I think that number may have been a little high."

The most surprising aspect of the rivalry is that it means more to the fans than to the players.

"I learned it's not just our bragging rights, but it's the fans," said George Teague. "I see that now.

"It's for them, so they can brag to the people they work with, the people they live around. And I think the conversation in the stands will be worse than what happens on the field."

Even those players who grew up lifelong fans of one team or the other — for instance, Alabama quarterback Jay Barker — are surprised how it changes when you become a player.

"It was a bigger game to me when I was a fan than it is now," Barker said. "As a player, we're interested in the SEC championship and the national championship. It's a big game, but the fans get more into it than we do as far as getting mad and stuff like that.

"My first game, I thought there would be a lot more going on between the players than there was. Instead, it was just guys playing their hearts out, and then helping each other up. It's more for the fans."

To Fuller, that is the amazing aspect of this game.

"I don't know how the players don't get caught up in it," he said. "But I think there is respect between the players. Besides, it's not uncommon for (Auburn quarterback) Stan White to be here in our dorm, and for (Alabama linemen) Johnny Howard and George Wilson to be down there at Auburn (visiting each other).

There are a lot of guys like that. These guys grew up together. They know each other. They're good friends."

But the fans try to make it big to the players.

"Sure, I hear it all year long," Barker said. "They say you can go 0-10, as long as you beat Auburn. But I know that's not true.

"It just means that much to them to be able to go to work or school and say, 'We beat you.' I thought that way when I was growing up. I wanted to be able to go back to school and say, 'Alabama won, we're better than you.'

"That's why this is more for the fans than the players."

The series had been one that belonged to Alabama until Dye arrived at Auburn. During the decade of the 1970s, when the Tide was winning more games than anyone in the country, Alabama's winning streak against Auburn reached nine. Even before that, Bryant had beaten Auburn more than he'd lost, winning nine of the first 14 times he'd coached against the Tigers.

Auburn had won four in a row in the years before Bryant arrived, but overall, Alabama carried a 32-23-1 advantage into the Auburn game. The Tigers' victories came very early in the series, or very late, after former Alabama assistant Pat Dye took over as head coach at Auburn and broke the 'Bama spell in 1982, beating Bryant, 23-22, in the Bear's last season as head coach.

It was the tradition of the series, by the way, that no coach had won his last Alabama-Auburn game.

Dye and Auburn dominated in the 1980s, beating Bryant's successor, Ray Perkins, two of four and then sweeping Bill Curry's teams three out of three.

During the '80s, it had become a game remembered for one play or one phrase. Every football fan in the State of Alabama knew what "Bo over the Top" meant (Auburn's 23-22 win in 1982), or Rory Turner's quote, "I just waxed the dude," (on his tackle of Auburn back Brent Fullwood to preserve the Tide's 17-15 victory in 1984), or "The Kick," (Van Tiffin's remarkable game-winning 52-yard field goal as time expired in 1985).

But the arrival of Stallings in 1990 brought a change of fortune. The staff he brought with him did not know much about losing to Auburn. They still didn't know after two years back in Tuscaloosa, winning 16-7 and 13-6.

Alabama fans were convinced the series was back under control.

Auburn fans feared they were right.

There was more going on here, though, than just the dying of the Iron Bowl. In the offweek preceding the game, rumors began to circulate about Auburn head coach Pat Dye, the man who had made the Alabama-Auburn rivalry a rivalry again by beating the Tide six of the past 10 games, including a minor streak of four consecutive victories before Gene Stallings arrived on the scene.

Auburn had been under NCAA investigation since Eric Ramsey came out with taped conversations which he alleged were of Auburn assistant coaches and boosters giving him illegal payments. It was an ugly affair that had dragged on for over a year, but which seemed to be coming to a head, now with the NCAA finally involved.

Earlier in November, Auburn University president William Muse announced that Auburn had received an official NCAA letter of inquiry listing nine rules violations described as major.

The allegations were that:

• A representative of the university athletic interests provided cash and merchandise to a student athlete.

• An assistant coach provided cash to a student athlete, some of which came from a booster.

• An athletic staff member provided cash on many occasions to a student athlete.

• An assistant coach provided cash on one occasion to a student athlete.

• The student athlete obtained a loan in violation of NCAA rules.

• The university violated the principle of institutional control.

• Two then-assistant coaches and a staff member erroneously certified compliance with NCAA rules and failed to report violations.

• The head coach and an assistant coach received information about the receipt of extra benefits and did not forward it to the appropriate university officials.

While the 13-month investigation was going on, Auburn changed university presidents, and Dye stepped down as athletic director to concentrate on being the football coach. In his place, Auburn brought in Mike Lude, a former University of Washington athletic director who was believed to be well thought of in NCAA circles.

Upon hearing the alleged violations, Dye's replacement, Lude, said, "There's certainly not anything that was a great surprise in there."

However, the allegation concerning Dye conflicted with the head coach's stance that he had done nothing wrong. Dye reaffirmed his vow that he would not resign, and refused to comment on specific allegations.

Ramsey, a former Auburn defensive back, first made his allegations known on September 27, 1991. He had accused Dye, assistant coach Steve Dennis, former assistant Larry Blakeney, former recruiting coordinator Frank Young, and booster Bill "Corky" Frost of providing him with cash and material benefits in excess of NCAA rules.

Muse said the names of the people included in the NCAA letter were not announced on advice of counsel.

"Up until this time, we have been dealing with rumor," Muse said. "We have not been dealing with specific allegations, certainly not allegations specific enough for us to fully complete an investigation. We now have that information and we'll be able to proceed at that point."

Dye had a clause in his contract that allowed Auburn to fire him if he was found in violation of NCAA rules, but Muse said it was too early to judge whether there would be coaches fired or reassigned.

But asked if he still supported Dye, Muse gave what many felt was a very telling answer.

"I think it would be inappropriate for me to make any evaluation of that relationship," he said.

Dye held his own news conference later that same day and said, "My position is well known and it has been made clear.

There is nothing to gain by saying anything else about this whole matter until it is resolved. Dr. Muse will be Auburn's spokesman, and any questions that come to me will be referred to him."

The Ramsey affair had already had a tangible effect on the Auburn program, however. After a decade in which the Tigers were perhaps the best team in the conference, Auburn was 3-0 when Ramsey went public with his accusations. The Tigers finished the year losing six of their last eight games.

Despite vows of going back to work and putting Auburn back on the right track, the Tigers were on their way to a 5-5-1 season in 1992, 2-5-1 in the SEC.

Dye's health had been the subject of rumor and controversy the past several years, culminating with Dye checking into Emory University Hospital in Atlanta the previous summer to have surgery to reduce the flow of iron to his liver.

There was plenty going on before this game. And despite the distractions Auburn might be facing, there were distractions for Alabama, too.

The Tide players couldn't escape the memory of the last time Alabama was this highly ranked. The Tide was No. 2 in the nation in 1989, having already clinched at least a share of the SEC title, going into the final game of the regular season.

It just happened to be the first game in Auburn, and the Tigers ruined the Tide's dream of playing for a national championship with a 30-20 victory on national TV.

"Most teams that win a championship win it with great defense and an offense that doesn't lose the game for you," said fullback Martin Houston, a member of the 1989 team. "In '89, we had a great offense but couldn't stop Auburn. In the Sugar Bowl, we scored more points (27) on (national champion) Miami than anyone did all year, but it wasn't enough."

There were other differences between the two teams, most stemming from the simple fact that there had been a coaching change — Bill Curry to Gene Stallings.

"The atmosphere around this team is much better," said senior holder Jeff Wall. "All the fans are together and behind us 100 percent. The atmosphere surrounding the program now — it's like night and day, the difference between '89 and now."

Tailback Derrick Lassic, also a member of Alabama's last SEC championship team, agreed with Wall.

"This team is much more relaxed than in '89," he said. "Like going into Tennessee — the coaches (in '89) were real intense, so tight they squeaked. Coach Stallings is relaxed. He prepared just like it was any other game.

"When the coach gets tight, it's like he doubts you. If he's relaxed, we're confident."

Like the '89 team, this Alabama team had wrapped up a title before going into Auburn.

"Maybe it's bad that we won the title before the season was over in '89," Houston said. "We were 10-0 going into Auburn, and we knew we were going to the Sugar Bowl. We could be in that same situation again this year, 10-0 with Auburn left to play."

That was exactly the situation facing the Alabama team this time. And everyone who was a member of that '89 team remembered the season ending with two losses, to Auburn and then Miami.

"Maybe we lost our focus," said center Tobie Sheils.

"At that time, no one on the team had ever won an SEC title, and we did it," Houston said. "But we ended up on a losing note and it didn't feel quite as good. I'd have liked to have won the SEC outright (instead of sharing the title with Auburn). But still, we've got the ring."

If anything, there was the possibility Alabama could look past this game to the SEC championship game a week later, to be played on this same field.

"I hope not," Stallings said. "I'm tickled to death to be in the championship game. And I've heard a lot of talk about it, because we're in it.

"But I'm setting it aside. I don't like to even think about it, about what we're going to do that week, or anything. I don't want it to overshadow this game in any way."

Stallings said nose tackle James Gregory, who sprained a knee in the third quarter against Mississippi State, would be fine. But not in time for this game.

"Other than that, we've stayed healthy," Stallings said. "We've not turned the ball over. We're struggling offensively. But staying healthy and not turning the ball over and playing good defense means you'll be in most games. And we've won the close games. A lot of people haven't."

Starting in Gregory's place would likely be redshirt sophomore Elverett Brown, a 6-foot-4, 270-pounder from Jeff Davis High in Montgomery.

For most of his career, Brown was best known as one of the five Browns on the Alabama team: receivers Curtis and Rick, linebacker Will, and defensive linemen Shannon and Elverett.

Elverett Brown played in four games as a redshirt freshman, but a stress fracture in his foot kept him out of the last six regular season games.

He came back for spring practice and dislocated a shoulder, then dislocated the same shoulder in August, which kept him out of the first two games of this season.

"It was frustrating, because every time I worked my way up to where I thought I could play, I got injured," Brown said. "But what I learned from it all was that it was my fault. It was due to a lack of work in the weight room.

"I'm a lot stronger now. You come out of high school bigger and faster than everyone else, and it took a while to get it through my mind that things were different now. But I spent a lot of time in the weight room while I was rehabbing my injuries, and I see where it's made all the difference."

Brown still was seeing only limited action this season, but he did get his moment of glory in the Mississippi State game, when he batted down a Greg Plump pass to stop a late Bulldog drive.

"I knew I'd play in that game," he said. "But when James went down, it was a real shock. All of a sudden, I knew I'd have to carry the load. The first play, I was so nervous. But after one play, the jitters were gone."

Brown knew he'd be tested by Mississippi State, which continually ran the ball up the middle. Fortunately for him, by the time he was in the game for good, the Bulldogs had fallen so far behind that they had to pass, and didn't really get to zero in on Brown.

"There's going to be pressure on me this week," Brown said. "But me playing against Mississippi State in the fourth quarter helps me understand the pressure. That was a lot of pressure. And I thought I handled it well.

"I expect Auburn to come at me this week. When James replaced Robert Stewart, people wanted to test him. So I expect them to try to run up the middle and test me. Hopefully, between me and our inside linebackers, we can stop that."

Brown said the best advice he had gotten so far came from John Copeland.

"Just play like you're a starter," Copeland said.

"The other players are doing a lot to boost my confidence," Brown said. "I'm just taking it one day at a time, until the time comes. Then, I'll just do the best I can."

Brown would do well to look no further than Alabama outside linebacker Lemanski Hall as an example.

Hall came to Alabama from Lanett, and was a high school teammate of Copeland's. At the time, it was Hall whom everyone wanted, with Copeland the second choice. Hall was thought to be one of the top defensive back prospects in the south at Lanett's Valley High, where he played both quarterback and safety.

As a quarterback, Hall accounted for 1,100 yards of total offense and scored 20 touchdowns. As a defensive back, he picked off 10 passes his senior year.

After being redshirted in 1989, Hall was a backup safety in 1990, and started three games in 1991 before being taken out of the lineup.

The coaches wanted him to move to outside linebacker. Hall wanted to go home.

"I went through a time of frustration," Hall said. "It was real hard. I just wanted to stop playing football. I even called my mom and told her I was coming home."

Instead, he made up his mind that he had come to Alabama to play, and if that meant going to a new position, he'd do it.

"I knew I could hit," Hall said. "It was just getting the coaches to realize I could play a little bit. I had a hard time learning Coach Oliver's (defensive) schemes. It was hard for me.

"But the move to linebacker was a big turning point. If I had stayed at defensive back, I wouldn't be playing here today."

The move was one of necessity for the Alabama defense, which was thin at outside linebackers.

"In our scheme, he was not really suited to play in the secondary," said linebacker coach Ellis Johnson. "He was a good defensive back, but he had some trouble on the deep ball and learning coverages. Plus, we really needed an outside linebacker."

Hall played in 1991 at his safety weight of around 200 pounds.

"I started," Hall said of his redshirt sophomore season. "But basically I was just out there. I didn't feel like I contributed in any way. It was something new to me."

But Hall knew what he had to do. He gave up any hope of being a defensive back and went on a weight gaining program in the off season, reporting in the fall up to 220 pounds.

It made all the difference in the world.

"Now, it means much more to me to be part of this defense," Hall said. "I'm making contributions because I've worked hard to be in the position I'm in now. I know I've got to go out and play the best I can."

Hall let everyone know he'd arrived in the Louisiana Tech game, when he and fellow outside linebacker Antonio London came from either side and caught Tech quarterback Sam Hughes at the same time. The result was a separated shoulder for Hughes, and a new reputation for Hall.

Going into the Auburn game, Hall led the team with 61 tackles, including seven for losses. He had five quarterback sacks and 10 quarterback pressures and he had recovered three fumbles.

Against Mississippi State, Hall had seven solo tackles and assisted on eight others. He had one tackle for a loss of four yards and a quarterback sack for a minus-eight.

"I really prepared myself for the Mississippi State game," Hall said. "I wanted to get something started early and play well the whole game. I ended up with 15 tackles, and I graded out pretty good."

Coming in from the quarterback's blind side, Hall still had his defensive back speed to go with his linebacker size. And he continued to get better as the season progressed.

Hall was just another who fit the Alabama coaches' scheme of moving high school defensive backs up to linebacker. The same had been done with inside linebacker Derrick Oden and was being done with André Royal. And the coaches were playing safety Will Brown as a backup to Hall, who could move over to London's side for his senior year after London was gone.

"If you had told me this story when I was in high school, about how it would work out, I'd have laughed at you," Hall said. "This is not what I expected or planned on."

And if he had quit? If his mother had said come on home and Hall hadn't thought it over?

"Let's just say I'm glad I didn't," Hall said. "It's safe to say things have worked out for the best."

There was no question Auburn was entering this game as the underdog. "People don't think we have a chance," said Auburn offensive lineman Chris Gray. "Heck, our season has not been a very good season at all, up and down, and Alabama, heck, they're undefeated. What would you think?"

Auburn was coming in with a 5-4-1 record, with one of those victories coming over Division I-AA opponent Samford University, coached by Terry Bowden, one of the coaching sons of Florida State head coach Bobby Bowden. Terry's brother, Tommy, was Dye's offensive coordinator at Auburn.

The NCAA had ruled that no team could go to a bowl game without six victories over Division I-A opponents, so in essence, Auburn was coming into this game with a 4-4-1 record and no chance of a bowl.

"So we consider this as our bowl game," said Tiger wide receiver Thomas Bailey. "It would mean a lot to us and a lot of people if we won this game and ended Alabama's undefeated season."

Wide receiver Frank Sanders said that, even though the Tide's defense was ranked No. 1 in the country, he didn't think Alabama was good enough to shut out Auburn.

"You listen to the sportswriters, and it's like they can't be scored on or they're going to shut you down or you're not going to beat them with your offense," he said. "I think that's just a lot of hype. Their defense is good, but not all that great. I haven't seen a great defense all year.

"I don't think their kicking game is as strong as people say it is. David Palmer is pretty good and the other guy (Chris Anderson) is a pretty good returner, but I think our special teams can shut them down just as well as our offense can move against their defense and our defense can stop their offense."

The pressure, Sanders was saying, is all on Alabama.

"In a sense, we really have nothing to lose and everything to gain," he said. "We have a chance to turn our season into a winning season. We have a chance to show that Alabama is beatable. We're not scared to play them. We're just ready to go on the field and play."

A win, said Auburn fullback Reid McMilion, would take away the pain of the last two years.

"And we've had a lot of that," McMilion said. "It's been frustrating. But we know we're good enough to do what it takes to win the game.

"That's exactly what we need to make this season a good one."

It undoubtedly would. But before the game would begin, these Auburn players would have another cause to play for, one more compelling than their own pain or pride.

It would be Pat Dye's last game as head coach.

16

A Tearful Goodbye

When Auburn called a sudden press conference for 10 p.m. Wednesday, the night before the Alabama-Auburn game, everyone knew it could mean only one thing.

University president Dr. William Muse met with reporters in a ballroom of the Sheraton Civic Center Hotel, and in a press conference that was carried live on local television, announced Dye's resignation.

"Coach Dye is a man of strength, conviction, and courage," Muse said. "Throughout his career, he has not been afraid to take stands on issues that he believes to be in the best interest of college football and the best interest of Auburn's program.

"Whether or not one agreed with his positions, one had to admire his strength and the courage of his convictions."

The negotiations had been going on for two days, and resulted in Dye's being awarded his salary for the remaining four years of his contract, plus a settlement estimated to be between $600,000 and $1 million to compensate for the loss of outside income over that period.

"Auburn University has been generous to Coach Dye in the settlement of his contract, but no more so than he deserves,"

Muse said. "Pat has been, and will remain, a part of the Auburn family."

Dye did not attend the press conference. He met with his team shortly after its traditional night-before-the-game meal.

"We were eating dinner," said Auburn placekicker Scott Etheridge. "Usually, after dinner the night before a game, he gives us the OK and we can go. He doesn't usually speak to us. But I had been finished with dinner a long time. In fact, (kicker) Thery George said to me, 'What are we waiting for?'

"Then Coach Dye walked in and I saw his face and knew it. The minute he said 'resign,' tears started coming from everybody. When he was talking, I couldn't even look at him."

The coach who had repeatedly told his team he would never quit, was quitting.

Not that anyone blamed him. But still, there was something disturbing to some of the players that just days after saying he would not resign, Dye resigned.

"When the words came out that he had handed in his resignation, it was a total shock to me and some of the guys," said fullback Reid McMilion. "It just left us blank. There was nothing we could say. Nothing we could do. It just really hit us hard."

Muse said Dye wanted the news out immediately, so that rumors would not spread and follow the team into the next day's game against Alabama.

Dye was expected to wait until after the game to talk about his reasons for resigning. There would be many questions, if for no other reason than Dye had been so adamant about not resigning, even saying he would leave his job as head football coach at Auburn only if he was fired.

However, Muse said Dye had initiated the resignation process a week earlier, and that terms were agreed upon Tuesday. The necessary documents were signed on Wednesday, the day before the Thanksgiving Day Iron Bowl game.

"This is Coach Dye's decision," Muse said. "It was a difficult decision for Coach Dye and Auburn. Coach Dye believes, and I agree, that this decision is in his best interest and in Auburn's best interest."

There is no question the NCAA allegations of major rules violations, one specifically involving Dye, played a role in Dye's decision. After the allegations were made by former Auburn player Eric Ramsey, and tapes were produced which Ramsey claimed backed up the allegations, Dye stepped down as athletic director and was replaced by Lude, a former University of Washington athletic director who had extensive experience in college athletics and a strong reputation among NCAA athletic directors.

In addition, the Auburn basketball team and men's tennis team had gone on NCAA probation under Dye's leadership as athletic director.

Lude said he had talked with Dye twice on Wednesday, the day of his resignation, and described Dye as "a man who is very relieved that he made a decision."

The 53-year-old Dye had produced a 99-38-4 record in his 12 seasons as head coach at Auburn, with four Southeastern Conference championships. He had brought Auburn to a place of prominence on the college football scene, almost winning a national championship in 1983, when his No. 2-ranked Tigers beat Michigan in the Sugar Bowl, only to have Miami leap over Auburn in the final poll with a victory over No. 1 Nebraska in the Orange Bowl.

He had overseen the expansion of Jordan-Hare Stadium to 85,214 seats and led the way in bringing the Alabama-Auburn football series to Auburn's campus for the first time in 1989.

The former University of Georgia offensive guard's success had brought him popularity, power, and an estimated $550,000 a year in salaries and benefits.

After winning three consecutive conference titles from 1987 to 89, Auburn was expected to be strong in 1990, but the Tigers slipped to 8-3-1.

The season was made worse when Dye was hospitalized after vomiting blood. A series of tests in a Birmingham hospital led to rumors of everything from pneumonia to cancer, but Dye was going to Atlanta's Emory University hospital for major surgery to deal with excessive amounts of iron in his blood.

So no one could blame him, in the face of all that, for realizing that discretion is the better part of valor, that there comes a time when you face the inevitable and accept it on the best possible terms.

The decision brought a mixture of sadness and acceptance from Auburn people and a loud cheer in the parking lot of Legion Field from the Alabama fans who were camped out the night before the big game, watching the announcement on TV.

"I told some people who were talking to me, 'If you want to hear a compliment to the kind of coach Coach Dye was and the effect he had on this state, just listen to the other side,'" said Auburn alumnus Paul Spina.

But there were those who believed Dye would fight until the end. Others said the resignation was inevitable, given the investigation and Dye's health.

"He's done a lot . . . that he refused to take credit for," Spina said. "I hope those things will be taken into account. He's an honest man, a good man, and a damn loyal friend. Any smudge or shadow on his career is unfair."

Lyn Seales, president of the Jefferson County Auburn Club, said the fans he was with were stunned and shocked.

"I was stunned personally," Seales said. "I thought Coach Dye could survive this turmoil — I really did — and grow stronger from it."

Former linebacker Quinton Riggins, who was now part of the radio team that broadcast Auburn football games, said the lack of public support from Muse for Dye was a factor.

"I guess that was the kiss of death," Riggins said. "If they said they'll have two or three weeks to hire a new coach, that probably means this had to be planned or thought about a long time ago. The way this came about, there has to be some underlying thing that took place that hasn't come out yet."

Then Riggins turned his anger on Ramsey, a former teammate.

"If Eric wanted this, if he's that kind of person, I feel sorry for him," Riggins said. "This is a direct result of his greed.

"It's sad that a coach has to lose his career for allegedly helping a person put food on his table."

Buddy Moore, a friend of Dye's, said he had an idea this was coming.

"He (Dye) wanted what was best for his family and Auburn University," Moore said. "He was ready to move on to some other things."

Seales said that no matter what, Dye would be remembered in a positive light with Auburn people, and the program would survive.

"Auburn people have always endured and always will," Seales said. "And we'll make it without Coach Dye.

"But I know that Coach Dye is still in the Auburn family and he's going to stay there. He's always been a great asset to the university and he always will be."

In fact, Muse announced that Dye would continue working for the university as a special assistant to the president. Muse said the settlement the school had reached with Dye would be terminated if Dye should choose to accept another coaching job, but Muse said he had no indication that Dye was thinking of such a move.

Of course, anytime a head coach resigns or is fired, it isn't just his own life that is put in turmoil.

In some ways, the assistant coaches pay a higher price. Their contracts are usually on a year-to-year basis, so there is no buyout that could keep them comfortable while they look for other jobs. They are forced into the marketplace against their will, while the head coach can gracefully retire.

Dye would stay at the university as a special assistant to the president. But what about the assistants?

"In this profession, you're used to doors closing," said Auburn offensive coordinator Tommy Bowden, who had been hired only two seasons earlier. "But I believe the Lord will open a new door."

The last two years were just as hard on the assistant coaches. They suffered through the losing. They worried about the investigation. They wondered if their names had somehow, even innocently, popped up on Ramsey's mysterious tapes.

"I don't have a problem with the situation," said Dye's longtime assistant, Joe Whitt. "My concern is for Coach Dye. I hate it for him, to go out with these misconceptions that he's not anything he is. He is one of the greatest football coaches to ever coach the game. He fits up there with all of them and he's a great person.

"Coach Dye is the kindest, most loving man. Even in all of the fire and emotion, he cares about people. That's what he's about.

"For people anywhere to think of him as something other than that, that hurts me more than anything. That hurts me more than not knowing that I'll be at Auburn next week as an assistant."

For all the loyalty, there were their own families to think of, which meant jobs to be looked into.

And of course, there was the possibility that one of them would be named to replace Dye and some of them might get to stay on.

"I'd love to stay," Whitt said. "I love Auburn. But I also understand the reality of the situation."

The players went to bed that night not focused on tomorrow's game, but on their head coach. It made for a fitful night, with long talks between players far past curfew.

"When we first heard the news, it was like a knife going through you," said linebacker Karekin Cunningham. "But there was only one thing on my mind, and that was beating Alabama. That's the only thing we had any control over. We didn't have control over outside factors, but we could go out and win the game."

Over at the Alabama team hotel, Stallings said he didn't know how to react.

"The announcement broke my concentration a little bit," Stallings said. "I don't know what is the best way to handle it. If he (Dye) is happy, then I'm happy. If he's sad, I'm sad."

Fullback Martin Houston said Stallings's mixed feelings came across in a team meeting called to address the situation.

"He just said he was sorry it happened and he felt that Coach Dye had been a plus to the SEC, and he really has," Houston said. "Go back to 1980, when Auburn was struggling. In 10 years he's won four SEC championships. Not too many people can say that.

"I have friends on the Auburn team, and it's not like I'm happy that those guys are suffering because of it. It's a sad situation. It could very easily have been me or any other player in the country. Most of those guys weren't even there when Eric Ramsey was there, and they're paying the price for what he did."

Thanksgiving morning dawned clear and cool, a perfect November day.

The army of Alabama and Auburn fans who'd spent the night in their RVs in the parking lot of Legion Field began their often elaborate pregame celebrations. Many got ready to serve their Thanksgiving turkeys, either precooked and brought along to serve up on outdoor tables or cooked overnight on the grill. There were deep-fried turkeys, with dressing and cranberry sauce, vegetables, pies, and all the trimmings.

Others either celebrated Thanksgiving early or planned to celebrate it late, on Friday or even Sunday.

The important thing to these folks was the game.

Everywhere, football fans mixed and mingled, visiting friends from RV to RV, making new friends along the way, stopping and sampling each other's food spread.

Car horns programmed to play "Yeah Alabama" blared, and were quickly answered with programmed car horns playing "War Eagle." And everywhere, cries of "Roll Tide Roll" and "War Eagle" broke the clear morning air.

Kickoff was set for just past noon, and the stands started filling up even faster than usual. Everyone was talking about Dye's resignation, everyone wondering what kind of effect it would have on the game, on the rivalry, on the balance of football power in the state.

Temperatures were in the 50s by game time, and the wind was blowing 10 to 13 miles per hour out of the northwest. As the players took the field for pregame warm-ups, a horde of photographers gathered at midfield, waiting for the moment when Dye and Stallings would meet, as the head coaches always do.

They didn't have to wait long. Dye, in his usual Auburn blue sport coat and Auburn baseball cap, and Stallings, in his usual game-day conservative, gray houndstooth check jacket, met at midfield.

"I almost didn't want to go out there, before the game, because I kept seeing friends and players and mamas and daddies who have meant so much to me," Dye said. "And I'm kind of sentimental anyway."

Dye and Stallings shook hands, then embraced. Though never close friends, they were never enemies, either. Rather, they respected and admired each other as foes, each sharing a common ground of fighting the same wars. Stallings put his arm around Dye's shoulders and pulled him close. The two talked into each other's ears, keeping their conversation low so that it stayed between them. This, in many ways, was going to be their goodbye.

Stallings hugged Dye again, and Dye's cap slipped off his head. Without the cap, without the shield to hide behind, Dye's emotions were exposed and the tears and pain and sadness were all etched on the Auburn coach's face.

Stallings said later he had a lump in his throat as he told Dye how he felt.

"It was really sad," Stallings said. "I told him we would miss him. I told him college football would miss him. It was probably more of an emotional meeting than I was expecting.

"I told him how I felt. I just hate to see him leave the game like that. I don't know about the NCAA problems, but I feel for Pat, his family, his coaches, and his players."

Composed again, Dye turned and walked back through his team, back into the locker room for one last pregame meeting, to prepare for one last game as head coach.

In many ways, this was the perfect ending to Dye's career. Legion Field was the site of many of his greatest victories, the place where he proved Auburn had arrived when he beat Bryant in the Bear's last Iron Bowl game in 1982.

It was fitting that the opponent was Alabama, the school where Dye was an assistant for so many years. It was even somehow appropriate that the opposing head coach was Stallings. After all, it was Stallings's leaving the staff at Alabama to become head coach at Texas A&M that created the opening for Dye.

The ties Dye had to his cross-state rival were evident during pregame warm-ups. As he strolled around the field, Dye saw Alabama assistants stop whatever they were doing to come over and shake his hand. Bill Oliver, Mal Moore, Jeff Rouzie, Mike Dubose, and Jimmy Fuller had all either coached with or played for Dye during their careers. Time and again, the emotion got the best of Dye, and his eyes watered as old enemies who were also old friends hugged him and wished him well.

"We're old friends, more than anything," Dye said. "We fought them battles when we were on the same side. I got great respect for them and I can guarantee you they got great respect for me. I'll probably go bird hunting with some of them, or fishing or whatever.

"I know the institutions. One's blue and orange and one's red and white. But people are people. That's the way it is."

As Dye made his way back through his own team, the players began calling out to him.

"All right, Coach," said fullback James Bostic. "Cheer up, baby."

Dye smiled. He approached the offense and quarterback Stan White reached out and shook his hand. Running backs Joe Frazier and Reid McMilion gave him hugs.

"You know, you're lucky," McMilion said to Dye. "Some of us only get to play Alabama and be in this atmosphere four or five times. But you've been here 12 times, plus all those others with Alabama."

Dye stopped and looked at his junior fullback.

"You know what I like best about it?" Dye said. "I like playing them in Auburn, but I like playing them here better because it's all red (in the stands). And you've got your little team with your couple of fans, and the odds are all against you."

McMilion said it was a conversation he would carry with him forever.

"He's a fighter," the fullback said. "That's his personality. When his back's against the wall, or he's in a hole, he's going to fight to get out."

When the Auburn team came back out for the start of the game, the players didn't run out. They came out one by one, many holding their helmets up over their heads, as if in salute. It was an emotional tribute to their coach, and set the tone for what would be an emotional day.

There is a saying about emotion and football games. Emotion only carries a player through the first hit, then reality sets in.

And the reality of this game was that it pitted two of the best defenses in the nation. Alabama was ranked No. 1 in defense overall, and led the nation in every defensive category. Auburn was No. 4 overall, not far behind the Tide.

And the first half was one of defense. Alabama came out trying to use as many of its offensive options as possible: Lassic and Palmer on sweeps, Houston up the middle, Barker on rollouts, Barker on passing, even a toss to Palmer who pulled up to pass. The Tide coaches emptied the playbook, probing the Auburn defense and looking for a weakness to take advantage of.

Auburn was going with quarterback Stan White, who was trying to find any and every receiver on the field and even running when he had to.

The closest Alabama got was to the Auburn 15-yard line, on a drive set up by an exchange of great defensive plays.

It began with Alabama's ball on the Auburn 44. Lassic tried a toss sweep, found nothing but orange and blue in front of him, cut back across field, and wound up being brought down by Auburn linebacker Karekin Cunningham for a loss of 16. On second down and 26, Barker tried a play-action pass over the middle, and the ball went right to Auburn linebacker Anthony Harris, who caught it and fell at the Auburn 47.

On first down, White executed a perfect three-step drop and quick throw to the right sideline to wide receiver Orlando Parker, who caught the ball and turned upfield. But after a gain of three, he was hit by Alabama cornerback George Teague, fumbled the ball, and Tide safety Sam Shade recovered at midfield.

On first down, Barker went deep for David Palmer, who caught the ball and stepped out of bounds for a 24-yard gain to the Tiger 26. Houston tried the middle of the line two times for seven yards, and then, with Palmer lined up at quarterback for the first time this season, Alabama was flagged for illegal procedure and penalized back to the 25.

Barker tried a quick pass to Palmer in the right flat, and although the pass was incomplete, Auburn was flagged for pass interference and Alabama had 10 yards and a first down at the 15.

On first down, Sherman Williams got nothing behind left guard George Wilson. On second down, Barker's pass into the end zone intended for Palmer was intercepted by Auburn cornerback Fred Smith.

The first half ended with no points on the board. Barker had completed just four of 12 passes for 43 yards, with two interceptions. Lassic had 11 carries for 34 yards.

Barker's backup, Brian Burgdorf, was warming up in the latter minutes of the second quarter.

"Burgdorf crossed my mind," Stallings said.

"I wouldn't have blamed Coach Stallings for taking me out after the first half," Barker said. "After the interception, I looked back to see if Brian was warming up. The first half was a nightmare, with the penalties and interceptions and incomplete passes."

His counterpart, White, was six of 13 for 39 yards and one interception and two sacks. Tiger fullback James Bostic had seven carries for 24 yards. Auburn had fumbled the ball three times, losing it once.

The best play in the first half for either offense had to be on fourth down. Auburn punter Terry Daniel had five kicks for a 49.2-yard average, while Alabama's Bryne Diehl had five kicks for a 38.8-yard average.

The emotion of the pregame walk was not evident on Dye's face during the first half. Now he was in his arena, and he was fighting. Through the first 30 minutes, his team had managed to stay in the game. Somehow, he was determined to find a way for Auburn to win.

On the other side, the Alabama offensive coaches went over their strategy. The plan going into the game was to be sound, don't make mistakes, be patient, feel out the defense, find the weakness.

"In all close games, somebody makes the big play," said Tide quarterback coach Mal Moore. "It doesn't matter who. It's more important that somebody makes it."

That's what the defensive players talked about in their meeting.

"We knew it would be a defensive game going in," said the Tide's Shade. "Auburn has the No. 4 defense in the country and we're No. 1. It was going to be tough for both offenses.

"At halftime, we started talking about the defense making something happen, finding some way to get some points on the board."

The teams returned to the field for the second half, and wide receiver Rick Brown caught up to cornerback Antonio Langham just before kickoff.

"You've got to intercept one and return it for a touchdown," Brown told Langham.

Langham looked at Brown and said, "I'll do my best."

Alabama kicked off to start the second half, with Proctor's kick coming down to Thomas Bailey at the one. Bailey returned it 24 yards before brought down by the Tide's Willie Gaston.

On first down, Bostic got the call off left tackle and went nine yards before Chris Donnelly and Langham brought him down. McMilion then picked up the first down, gaining three yards up the middle.

Bostic went at right end for seven, and then White, out of the shotgun, rolled right and threw to Bailey for a gain of 17 yards and another first down across midfield.

On first-and-10 from the Alabama 43, Bostic went right at John Copeland and picked up four yards.

On second down and six from the 39, Auburn lined up in a one-back set, with Parker and Bailey split wide left. The play is called "Race over 6 X hook." On the snap of the ball, Bailey would run a hook pattern to the inside of the field, and Parker would cross underneath Bailey with a short "out" pattern to the sideline.

The quarterback, White, would take a three-step drop, keying Langham, who was playing up on the line opposite Parker. If Langham went to the sideline route with Parker, White was supposed to throw to Bailey cutting through the empty space Langham had just left. If Langham went with Bailey, Parker should be open underneath the coverage of George Teague.

But, said Auburn offensive coordinator Tommy Bowden, "the quarterback made the wrong decision. He picked the wrong option."

Langham went with the sideline route, with Parker getting a little out in front of him. White threw it toward Parker anyway, and Langham stepped in front of the Auburn receiver, tipped the ball up in the air once, caught it, and raced 61 yards for a touchdown.

"I saw it coming," Langham said of the play. "I broke on Parker, and when I looked back I saw that Stan had cocked his arm. I knew he was going to throw, so I made my break.

"I wasn't quite there and got one hand out to tip the ball up in the air. I was about to give up on the ball when I caught it. Then I turned the jets on. I saw Stan coming, but I knew it was a foot race and I'd win. It was off to the races."

Parker said he never saw Langham coming.

"I was looking at the ball, waiting to catch it," he said. "He tipped it and then caught it.

"I thought I had a good chance to catch him, but somebody knocked me about 10 yards out of bounds. I believe I could have caught him."

But he didn't. No one did. Another big play for Langham.

It happened right in front of Dye, who stood on the sideline, hands on his knees, and never flinched.

"One of the greatest plays you'll ever see," Dye said afterward. Stallings agreed.

"I know no adjective to describe how big that play was," he said. "I always tell our players they play 55 or 60 plays for the privilege to make one or two." Michael Proctor's kick for the extra point was good, and for all intents and purposes, the game was over.

"That hurt," Bowden said of the interception. "It was very costly. But that's the way the year has gone. A poor decision and we lose the game."

And it changed the game plan for Alabama. Now, said Moore, "we drew the circle a little tighter. We got in position to use the clock."

On Auburn's next possession, White was chased out of bounds once, sacked once for a loss of 10, and forced to hurry throws until finally the Tigers had to punt.

Terry Daniel's punt went 37 yards, and Alabama took over on its own 40-yard line. Now the Tide knew what to do — pound away at the Auburn defense. Seven of the next nine plays were running snaps, with one Barker pass — a 20-yard completion to Curtis Brown, Barker's only pass attempt of the second half — and one sack, the end result being a 47-yard field goal by Proctor to make the score 10-0.

Auburn's next possession was just as futile, and what made it worse was that on fourth down, Daniel shanked a 16-yard punt, giving Alabama the ball at the Auburn 45.

Now it was backup tailbacks Chris Anderson and Sherman Williams's turn. Seven straight running plays, most of them between the tackles, took it down to the fifteen, where Williams scampered in for the touchdown to give the Tide a 17-0 lead.

Now it was futility time for the Auburn offense, and the Alabama defense knew it, zeroing in on the quarterback, White.

On first down, White was sacked by outside linebacker Will Brown for a loss of eight yards. That set Auburn back far enough that the Tigers would have to punt.

Auburn's next possession started with White being sacked by Copeland for a loss of 11. It ended with Patrick Nix at quarterback, throwing two incomplete passes.

In the meantime, White was on his way to the hospital. On first-and-10 from the Alabama 40, Tide defensive line coach Mike Dubose pulled a switch and let Copeland line up on the right side for the first time in Copeland's career.

"If felt really strange," Copeland said. "I didn't even know if I'd be able to get off the ball. Everything looked backwards to me."

Including White, who dropped back to pass and had his back to Copeland's side of the field.

"He was just standing there, with his back to me," Copeland said. "I couldn't believe it. He never saw me coming. I just put my head down and charged. Even at the last instant, I thought he'd step out of the way, but he didn't. I hit him as hard as I've ever hit anybody in my life. I felt like my helmet went through his back and into his chest."

It was brutal. The hit came just as White released the ball. The pass was complete to Bailey for 10 yards. White was down, his right shoulder separated so severely, it would require surgery to fix.

"I didn't slow up," Copeland said. "You have to play physical football. Most times, the most physical team is going to win."

By now, the Alabama fans started chanting, "Hey, hey, goodbye," and even Dye wore a look of resignation.

As the game clock ticked down to zero, Dye stood by himself on the sideline, occasionally glancing up at the clock. When the final horn sounded, he trotted out to meet Stallings again.

The two men shook hands.

"Call me if you need anything," Stallings said.

"All right," Dye said. "I'll do that."

Dye then turned and walked off the field, tipping his hat to the Auburn fans in the end zone as he passed before them for the last time as their head football coach.

"I just love Coach Dye, and it's been hard for this whole team," said Cunningham afterward. "I wanted to give that man a win. There isn't a guy on the team who doesn't love and respect Coach Dye. I just wished we could have given the man a win."

Kicker Scott Etheridge said the players knew all along that this was more than just the Alabama game.

"Coach Dye's resignation motivated us," he said. "You can tell that by the way we played in the first half. I never wanted to win a game more in my life.

"It was the Alabama game, but it was also his game. This was Coach Dye's game. I just wish he could have gone off with a win."

That kind of emotion is what worried the Alabama coaches.

"But Coach Stallings told us that both teams would be emotional today," said Tide linebacker Antonio London. "And you can only rely on emotion for so long. Then, the best team is going to win."

"Everybody was saying they were going to come out and win one for the Gipper," said Martin Houston. "But we were still ready to play, and emotion only lasts for so long. They came out and they were high at the beginning of the game, but when it comes down to it, emotion doesn't win. It comes down to who goes out and hits and executes and does the job."

Or, as Barker said afterward, "We knew the emotion would die out and the better team would win. That's the way it worked out."

The Alabama defense was too much, the Tide offense just enough.

Auburn finished with a total net of 139 yards, an average gain per play of 2.62 yards. White was intercepted twice, sacked five times, forced to run another five times.

"We knew by looking at film that if you hit White or put pressure on him, we could shake him up," Langham said. "He would throw quicker and faster than he wanted to, and into areas he didn't want to. He would have to throw it before he could have time to think."

And throw, Auburn did.

"We thought we had a few things that would work," Bowden said. "But everything we tried, they negated. That defense is as good as what you see on film and what you read and hear.

"We tried all we could. We didn't hold anything back. We threw long, we threw short, we threw to the backs. We ran the draw, we ran screens. We dropped back, we rolled out. We ran inside, we ran outside. We did it all and nothing worked.

"They've got a lot of strengths and all the intangibles. They don't give up yards easily."

Indeed, Dye said, "I've watched Alabama's team evolve this year, and in my opinion, right now they are the best in the country."

It was the first time in Dye's career, a span of 19 seasons as a head coach, that he'd had a team of his completely shut out.

"This is not exactly the way I would have preferred to go out," Dye said. "But I think it's the best of a not too good situation."

Afterward, the horde of media who covered the game and as many Auburn fans and alumni as could get in crowded into the interview room underneath the north end zone of Legion Field.

Surrounded by his family, coaches, and a few selected players, Dye entered the media room to say goodbye. He tried to smile as he faced the reporters who had followed his career for so many years, but there was no holding back the tears.

With his voice cracking, Dye said, "This is one of the reasons why a man's got to do what a man's got to do.

"We've shared enough tears in the last few days to float a battleship, and I probably ain't through yet."

Dye said there were a lot of reasons for his resignation, from his health to the strain on his family to the NCAA investigation.

But, Dye said, he was not forced out.

"I didn't want to hurt my family," he said. "I didn't want to tear down what we built there the last 12 years and I didn't want to leave Auburn on any kind of bad terms. Auburn is my family. It's my family's family."

He said there was nothing staged about the announcement coming out the night before the game. He just wanted the word out once the decision was made.

"And I'm going to tell you something," Dye added. "Auburn did it right."

Dye said he and his family would remain in Auburn, probably in the special assistants role Muse talked about. He said he would spend his free time hunting or fishing and raising his bird dogs. He insisted he would not play any role in selecting the next head coach.

Asked if he would ever return to coaching, Dye at first said no. Then he backed off and indicated he would return if Auburn needed him, or if his family's financial situation dictated a return to the sidelines.

As far as his health was concerned, Dye said it was a factor.

"I knew I had a health problem," he said. "But my health problem wasn't keeping me from working. That's been going back and forth, but it is an uncertain thing. I had a tumor removed from my liver last summer. Some of you may know that, some of you may not.

"I live every day like it's going to be my last day, and I live every day like I'm going to live forever."

But, Dye said, the terms of the settlement with Auburn included the same health insurance he had had for himself and his family since he became head coach.

In the end, it was all those things plus the NCAA investigation that prompted him to quit.

"I think the straw that broke the camel's back was the NCAA letter," Dye said. "I didn't want to get out with that hanging over my head, either. I just hope that when the NCAA and the powers that be look at the allegations, I hope that they'll have some compassion for a team that has suffered through two years of whatever you might want to call it already.

"It's been a very difficult season. The thing I regret most is (the players) never got to experience the thrill and the exhilaration of a big win. That's something I'll always regret because this team worked hard and deserve the right to experience that.

"I don't have to tell them how much they've meant to me in my life as far as that relationship and the loyalty and working together. I'm not smart enough to adequately express what that means to me, but they know."

The tears started from his family — wife Sue, son Pat, Jr., and daughter Wanda. The players behind him were red-eyed; the coaches tried to keep their emotions in check.

"Look, I didn't put ya'll up here on TV for all this," Dye said.

He looked at the players that gathered along side him for this final press conference, and there were several seconds of silence.

"These guys right here, uh, I get too . . ."

Dye swallowed hard, and the tears began to flow.

"I can't look at them," he said.

Fullback Reid McMilion, eyes red, said it for all the Auburn players. "This is part of growing up," he said. "And growing up is not always easy. Things like this do happen and you've got to take it like a man, because he's not going to be there next year for us. We've still got to keep on going and try to pull our team together.

"But we love him and respect him and we're still behind him and he'll always be my coach."

CHAPTER

17

Back to Birmingham

While Auburn was saying goodbye to Pat Dye, Alabama was saying hello to the first Southeastern Conference championship game.

The game would match No. 2-ranked and undefeated Alabama, champion of the Western Division, against No. 12 Florida, the team that came back to share the Eastern Division title with Georgia and earn the right to play in the championship game by virtue of the Gators' 26-24 victory over the Bulldogs in Jacksonville.

Florida was 8-3 going into this game, 6-2 against SEC competition. The Gators, after losing two of their first three games, came back to put together a seven-game winning streak before closing out the regular season with a 45-24 loss to Florida State the Saturday after Alabama's victory over Auburn.

The Crimson Tide was a perfect 11-0 overall, 8-0 in the conference.

Take any previous season in Alabama's 100-year history of football, and an 11-0 record would have the Tide playing for the national championship.

But not this year.

"We've won 11 games and still won nothing," Gene Stallings said. "Oh, we've won the division, whatever that is. But you'd think we'd have at least won the conference."

But the conference had other plans. Expansion meant the SEC was allowed — under an obscure NCAA rule really designed for Division I-AA schools — to divide into divisions and stage its own playoff game. It had never been done before in NCAA Division I-A football, although the national championships for Division I-AA, Division II, and Division III are decided through a playoff format.

So the whole country was watching the SEC's inaugural playoff game. Was it the first step to a national playoff? Would it bring in enough money to start a run on conference realignment? Was it the future of college football?

The Alabama players didn't know, and didn't really care. They were too busy thinking about Florida.

"We want Florida bad," said Alabama cornerback Antonio Langham. "Real bad."

The reason is simple. The last time Alabama lost a football game, it was the second game of the 1991 season, in Gainesville, against Florida. It was more than a beating. It was a 35-0 embarrassment.

"We took a good beating down there," linebacker Antonio London said. "There is a lot of revenge."

"It's a game we've been looking forward to ever since," said Jay Barker. "We were hoping they'd make it. At the first of the year, we weren't sure they would. Now they're here, and it's revenge time for us."

The 29 points Alabama surrendered in the second half to Florida was the most points anyone has scored on the Tide since then.

"I still don't believe they are that many points better than us," Langham said. "It hurt bad, coming home on the plane after that. Not a word was said on the way back. Nothing. It was embarrassing. It was embarrassing to come back to Tuscaloosa after losing that game.

"Florida is coming on strong now. They're not as good as last year. But I still think we've got a lot to prove."

At the time, no one could have predicted that the night of September 14, 1991, would loom so large in the minds of the players on this 1992 Alabama team.

At the time, it was a night everyone wanted to hurry up and forget and be done with.

But now, looking back, Alabama's 35-0 loss to Florida that night at Gainesville's Florida Field might have been the turn-around in a Crimson Tide program that was 8-6 under Gene Stallings, a program that had suffered two embarrassments (Florida, 35-0; Louisville, 34-7) in its previous three games.

"It just got really frustrating," said Alabama center Tobie Sheils. "We were all ready to get out of Gainesville and start the season over, and that's what we did."

The second season started with a 10-0 victory over Georgia, and Alabama hasn't stopped winning since. The Crimson Tide won 21 consecutive games, including this season's 11, going into the SEC championship game against Florida.

"That was a tough game for us," said Antonio London. "We really didn't have an identity on offense. We hadn't decided on a quarterback. And really, we had no identity on defense yet. We were trying to establish ourselves.

"I don't think it took 35-0 to do it. But it did help us down the road."

Most of these Alabama players participated in that game. Yet in many ways, this team has nothing in common with that team on that September night.

For one thing, Alabama was trying to be an option team at that point. After six fumbles against Florida though, the option was soon forgotten.

Jay Barker saw the first playing time of his collegiate career in that game, but it would be six games before he took over as starter, and he has not sat down since.

Defensively, Alabama knew it was good. But the defense also learned it wasn't as good as it thought, as Florida tailback Errict Rhett rushed for 170 yards.

"I'd say the embarrassment of it is what sticks out," said linebacker and team captain Derrick Oden. "We knew we were good. To let a team beat us like that did something to us. We knew what we had to do after that, and did it. But we found out too late for that game.

"Before the game, we knew we had a good defense. But we didn't really play well together. We really came together after that game. I think Florida was trying to make a statement, that our defense was not what it was said we were. And that really hurt me."

Seen from the Alabama side, that 35-0 loss was not really that bad. At the half, Florida led, 6-0, and the Tide, other than not being able to score, seemed in control of the game.

"We had opportunities in the first half," Sheils said. "I know Danny (Woodson, the starting quarterback) and I had two fumbles that really hurt. One they recovered, and one we recovered but killed a drive. There were six fumbles altogether. Our option offense ended right there. We ran it once, fumbled, and didn't run it again.

"In the second half, the game just got out of control. On offense, we were three plays and out. It got to where we were ready for the game to be over with. We didn't quit, but we were ready to get out of Gainesville." The game hurt even more when Florida won the SEC championship and the invitation to the Sugar Bowl.

"Whether or not they were the better team last year, they were definitely not 35 points better," London said.

"No, not 35 points better," Oden said. "We had a lot of turnovers and our defense got tired. But they were not 35 points better. They were good. They had a good year."

This time, Alabama was the one having a good year. Florida could ruin it all Saturday if it beat the Tide and successfully defended its conference championship. That would send Alabama to a secondary bowl, "where we play for nothing but pride," said George Teague.

And although it was a matter of revenge, as the Tide learned last week against Auburn, emotion can only get you so far.

"Revenge can help you prepare the week before the game," Sheils said. "But after the game starts, you don't think about it at all.

"This is a whole new season, a new beginning."

Just like that September night, 21 games ago.

But while the Alabama football team as a whole was enjoying this new beginning, David Palmer was already looking forward to next year.

This was the season Palmer was supposed to be everybody's All-American. This was supposed to be the year he was going to make "The Deuce" a household name, right up there with "The Rocket" and "Magic" and "Air Jordan."

Instead, it had been the worst football season of Palmer's young life.

Off the field, he had the two arrests for driving under the influence of alcohol, and spent a night in jail. He was suspended from playing in the first three games of the season. His every move was watched and studied. He felt as if people were waiting for him to mess up.

On the field, he'd been less than spectacular. After scoring seven touchdowns as a freshman, he'd cross the goal line only twice this season. After averaging 16.1 yards per punt return a year ago, he was down to an 8.9 average this season. His receiving yards were down, his kickoff-return yards were down, his total offensive production was down.

Last year he'd gotten his hands on the ball in some form or fashion 69 times, accounting for 1,113 yards, an average of 101.2 yards per game.

This year, it was 64 plays for 667 yards, an average of 95.3 yards per game.

"It's not been too good of a year," Palmer said. "It's a disappointing year. I thought I'd have a much better year than I've had."

Palmer admitted the off-field distractions were a bigger part of it than he thought they would be.

And on the field, he was being used more as a distraction than an attraction as the Alabama offense improved.

"I'm being used mostly as a decoy," he said. "Anytime I'm in the game, a lot of eyes focus on me. I like that. It's given the other guys the opportunity to do their job well.

"But I don't feel like I've been a factor this year like I was last year. I don't feel like I've been a big reason for this team winning."

His coaches don't agree. Just the threat of Palmer has been a big factor in the progress of this offense, said receivers coach Woody McCorvey.

"I think David's had a good year," McCorvey said. "We've not gotten the ball to him as much as we'd like as a receiver. And some of the things he did last year — lining up at quarterback, running the reverses — everybody expects that now, and they're not going to give it to us.

"But he's helped in other ways. He's been a decoy, and teams have been very much aware of him every time he's on the field. That threat has opened up big plays for Derrick Lassic and Chris Anderson. He's helped us. Just not in as visible a way as last year."

It would have been easy to predict his kick-return yardage would be down this year, because people would naturally kick away from someone as explosive as Palmer.

"After he came back and returned that punt for a touchdown in his first game (against Louisiana Tech), no one's kicked to him," McCorvey said.

"And since missing the first three games, he tried to catch up in a hurry and got a little frustrated."

Palmer said he was more than a little frustrated.

"I haven't been getting the ball like I did last year," he said. "It's been the most frustrating year I've ever had. I just want the ball in my hands more than I'm getting it.

"But every time I go in the game, I hear the defense start yelling that I'm in. They start warning each other about trick plays or reverses. They always point out where I line up. And when they stop me, they're always talking and celebrating, making a big deal out of it.

"It'd be a lot harder to take if we weren't winning. We've got guys like Derrick and Chris and Jay and Sherman stepping up and making big plays for us."

Last year, Alabama needed Palmer in a variety of ways. But with the improvement of the offense, his role has been cut back, even though Palmer is still a backup quarterback and a major part of the offensive game plan.

"As the offense gets better, we have to rely more on David from his position on the depth chart — wide receiver," McCorvey said.

The season wasn't over, of course. The biggest game of the season was yet to come, against Florida in the championship game. If Alabama won, it would set up an even bigger game, against Miami in the Sugar Bowl for the national championship.

"It's important for me to do well from here on out," Palmer said. "Then work hard over the summer. Next year can be a big season for me."

Next year. Maybe by then all the distractions will be behind him and football will be the only thing that matters.

"I just want to finish this season," Palmer said. "I want to do well these last two games and look forward to starting over next year."

The final regular-season loss by Florida to Florida State knocked the Gators from No. 6 in the AP poll to No. 12, and many coaches privately accused Florida coach Steve Spurrier of giving up the FSU game early in order to protect his players and rest them as much as possible for the SEC championship game.

It made sense, in a way. Florida was not going to play for the national championship, no matter what happened against Florida State. What was important to the Gators was winning a second consecutive SEC title, which would be the first two in Florida history. The fact that a Florida win in the championship game would throw the bowl picture out of whack didn't matter to the Gators. They just, rightfully, wanted the title.

There was so much hanging in the balance of this game. This would be the last game played before the bowl matchups could be announced, and it seemed as if everything hinged on this contest.

The winner of the game would go to the Sugar Bowl, the loser to either the Citrus or the Gator, depending on its overall record and reputation.

If the winner was Alabama, it would mean a national championship game with Miami in the Sugar Bowl. But an Alabama loss would put the bowl coalition into a spin cycle, affecting the Cotton, Orange, Sugar and Fiesta bowls.

Top-ranked Miami could refuse the Cotton Bowl, choosing to stay close to home and play the Big Eight champion in the Orange Bowl, on the grounds that the payoff in the Orange Bowl was larger than the Cotton Bowl's.

Or the Fiesta could try to lock up a national championship game between No. 1 Miami and what would almost surely be No. 2 Florida State.

Except that Texas A&M sat there undefeated and ranked in the top three, and if the Aggies should jump over FSU in the polls following an Alabama loss, a national championship matchup of 1 vs. 2 might not happen.

So Alabama's winning became important not just to Alabama, but to the Sugar Bowl, the SEC, and the bowl coalition as a whole.

"I think the most important thing it can do is elevate the significance of the Sugar Bowl, which is good for the recognition of the conference and for our champion to have that opportunity," said SEC commissioner Roy Kramer. "It makes the game more meaningful and, therefore, our championship more meaningful, and if your championship is more meaningful, your whole season is. It's a domino effect."

It focused a tremendous amount of attention on the SEC championship game, as everyone watched to see not only who would win, but how the majority of the bowl picture would come together immediately afterward.

There was no question that Florida would be the bad guys in this game, then. But the Gators were used to that.

Not only was everyone in the conference hoping Alabama would win, but the game was being played in Birmingham, on Alabama's second home field.

"That's great for Alabama," said Tennessee head coach Johnny Majors. "It should be very exciting for Alabama and the Alabama people, to play in one of two home stadiums for the championship.

"That's a very definite advantage for a team that is already good enough."

The Crimson Tide held a 140-48-11 record at games played in Legion Field. Alabama was on a nine-game Legion Field winning streak going into the Florida game, and was 12-1 the past four seasons at the old stadium on Birmingham's Graymont Avenue.

Stallings refused to admit Legion Field was "home," even though everyone else in the SEC knows it is.

"Ask any coach in the country if they want to play on their home field or a neutral site, and you always want to play on your home field," said Georgia head coach Ray Goff. "I think it will be a great advantage for Alabama. When the game was voted to go to Birmingham, you gave either Alabama or Auburn a tremendous advantage. No doubt about it."

South Carolina coach Sparky Woods lost to Alabama early in the season when his team was struggling, then lost to Florida late in a close game, the Gamecocks' only loss in their last six games.

"There will be a lot of great football players on that field," Woods said. "For me to predict a winner would be crazy.

"Certainly Alabama has firepower and the potential to score. I have great respect for Alabama. Their defense is the best I've ever played against. When we played Alabama, I thought their defense was just unmatchable, and offensively, they were very sound.

"Overall, most of the time I give the advantage to the best defensive team. But that's why they play the game. Certainly, Florida has the ability to beat anyone they play."

If you jumped from the start of the season to now, it would look like a ho-hum year. Florida was picked to be the Eastern Division champion, and was the defending SEC champion.

But the season took some strange twists and turns for the Gators. They started out 1-2, losing back-to-back games to Tennessee and Mississippi State after beating Kentucky in the season opener.

At that point, Florida head coach Steve Spurrier said he had to readjust his team's goals.

"After that game (the Mississippi State loss), I told the players to forget the conference championship and try their best to have a winning season," Spurrier said. "If they did that, we'd have a chance to go to a bowl, and that was our goal.

"Then Tennessee lost a couple of games, and we beat Georgia. I'm proud of our team for not faltering, for getting into this position and winning the games we were supposed to win down the stretch to put us in the championship game."

It made for an interesting contrast of styles in the game as well.

Spurrier's teams are known for throwing the ball. Florida led the SEC in passing offense in 1992, the sixth consecutive season a Spurrier-coached team has led its conference in passing.

Stallings's teams are ground oriented. Alabama was third in rushing offense.

"My philosophy has always been you've got to stop the run, be able to run the ball, and then be on the plus side in turnovers," Stallings said. "Florida enjoys throwing the ball, and we enjoy running the ball."

Then there was Florida's defense, which was fourth in the conference against the run and 12th against the pass.

"I just hope we match up better with Alabama," Spurrier said. "We believe we're better against the run than the pass. Hopefully, we can slow Alabama down and not give up a bunch of points."

The Tide had not had consistent success passing the ball, which put in doubt their ability to come from behind.

"We haven't had a lot of success throwing the ball," Stallings said. "And that's what you usually have to do to catch up. My gut feeling is that Jay (Barker, the Tide quarterback) can do it. But I haven't seen him do it enough to say I know he can."

Then there was Alabama's defense, the best in the nation against everything. The Tide went into the SEC championship game ranked first in total defense (allowing 183 yards per game); first in rushing defense (57.27 yards per game); first in passing defense (125.73 yards per game); first in scoring defense (8.0 points per game); first in quarterback sacks (44) and in take-aways (36 — 20 interceptions and 16 fumble recoveries).

In addition, the Tide led the SEC in fewest first downs allowed per game (10.36); third-down conversion defense (22 percent); and turnover ratio (plus-1.45 per game).

However, most coaches will say the forward pass is the great equalizer among teams, and if a team gets going throwing the ball, it's tough to stop.

"Florida really throws the ball well," Stallings said. "They've got a lot of weapons. We've got to pressure the quarterback without blitzing them. (Florida quarterback) Shane Matthews does an excellent job picking up the blitz.

"We've got to keep our blitzing to a minimum and keep pressure on the quarterback with just our defensive line."

Florida was second in the conference in total offense (396.55 yards per game); first in passing offense (286.6 yards per game); fourth in scoring offense (24.27 points per game); first in first downs per game (22.55); first in third-down conversions (42 percent); first in fourth-down conversions (75 percent); but was last in turn-overs (28 — 16 interceptions and 12 fumbles lost) and turn-over ratio (minus .91 per game).

There was also a basic difference in attitude toward playoff games. Spurrier has always been in favor of a national playoff system, while Stallings is against it.

Certainly the playoff concept worked in Florida's favor this particular year. Any other year before 1992, and Alabama would have already wrapped up the SEC title and Sugar Bowl bid. Instead, Florida still had a chance.

"I realize we're the underdogs," Spurrier said. "Alabama is No. 2 in the nation, with the No. 1 defense, statistically. Alabama's offense is pretty good, too.

"But we're excited. If we play the best we can play and Alabama has an off day, we can be OK. We'll go to Birmingham, throw the ball around and see what happens. Alabama is the best in our league, the cream of the SEC. But in a one-game playoff, we've got a chance."

If there was anybody in the country who could prepare a defense for a Steve Spurrier offense, it was Alabama's Bill Oliver.

Oliver and Spurrier have crossed paths several times over the past 25 years. They have battled each other as coach vs. player, assistant coach vs. assistant coach, coordinator vs. coordinator.

And always it seemed that it was Oliver, the secondary coach, going against Spurrier, the offensive coach.

"I've been competing against Steve Spurrier in some form or fashion since 1966, the year he won the Heisman (as a quarterback at Florida)," Oliver said. "I've coached against him from year to year since then. I have as much respect for Steve as an offensive coordinator as anyone. He does a great job regardless of talent.

"I'm tired of looking at him, to be honest. But we have to play."

There are many long-running battles between coaches. But what makes this one stand out is the many different levels at which Oliver and Spurrier have acted out their competition.

It began when Spurrier was a player at Florida and Oliver was the secondary coach at Auburn. It picked up after Spurrier's NFL playing days were over, when Oliver was the secondary coach at Alabama and Spurrier the quarterback coach first at Florida, then at Georgia Tech.

In 1980, Oliver got his chance at being a head coach, at Tennessee-Chattanooga, and Spurrier went to Duke University that same year as offensive coordinator.

Spurrier left Duke to become head coach of the Tampa Bay Bandits of the United States Football League in 1983, and a year later Oliver showed up in the league as defensive coordinator with the Memphis Showboats.

When the USFL closed down before the 1986 season, Oliver landed as secondary coach at Clemson in the Atlantic Coast Conference, and the next year, Spurrier followed him to the ACC as head coach at Duke.

It's been different teams, different leagues, different levels of play, and if Oliver and Spurrier haven't been trying to beat each other on the football field, they've been going against each other in recruiting.

Now they were back in the SEC, Oliver at Alabama and Spurrier at Florida.

"Coach Oliver told us he knew Coach Spurrier, knew his tendencies," said Tide defensive back George Teague. "He really is concentrating on stopping him, on terminating his whole offensive program.

"This seems personal with them. It seems important to Coach Oliver."

For the record, through 1991, the two had competed on the field against each other 12 times. Spurrier won the first meeting, 30-27, against Auburn in 1966 when, with the score tied 27-27, Spurrier convinced then-Florida head coach Ray Graves to let him kick a 40-yard field goal. It was only the second field goal Spurrier had attempted that season, and the first since the first game of the season. The kick was good.

Spurrier also won the most recent meeting, that 35-0 debacle in Gainesville last season.

Amazingly, however, the overall record between the two was a perfect 6-6. They had met on a consistent basis for the past eight years, with Spurrier holding a 5-4 edge (Tampa Bay and

Memphis played twice per year in the USFL, and Spurrier was out of coaching during the 1986 season).

What that means is that Spurrier as offensive coach knows Oliver as defensive coach, and vice versa.

"Steve just has a feel when to do different things," Oliver said. "He knows when to run, to pass, to change the tempo of the game. In watching Steve the past few years, he had developed something he didn't have at one time: a strong taste for the running game.

"What he does is extremely easy. It's just great distribution to a lot of receivers, using the field from sideline to sideline, all the way to the end zone. It's easy, but it's difficult to defend."

The other thing Oliver knows about Spurrier is that what he does one week, he may not do again for a long time.

"I'd be willing to bet the farm we don't see him do the same things he tried to do last week," Oliver said. "They like to counteract week to week. What they did last week, they will do the opposite this week. Steve has a counter to every play he runs, and that keeps you off balance.

"It also makes him a good coach."

Much of Spurrier's offense is based on the quarterback and the receivers making the proper "reads" of the defense at the line of scrimmage. That makes it important for the secondary not to give away what it is trying to do.

And the Alabama secondary was an experienced bunch that had developed a knack for fooling quarterbacks by showing one defense but then executing something else entirely.

"I've tried to cover every base," Oliver said. "He's got better personnel now than he's ever had, except when he was in pro ball with the Bandits."

And Oliver had perhaps the best defensive talent, overall, he'd ever had to work with as well.

It was the kind of challenge that usually brought out the best in both coaches.

And it promised to be quite a show.

CHAPTER

18

"He Must Be Superman"

It is the irony of the SEC championship game format that the Eastern Division champion drew the right to be the host team for the first game. That put Alabama on the visitors side of the field, in white road uniforms, in the visiting locker room, in a stadium that is the Tide's home field three times a year.

"I've never even seen the visitors' locker room," said Alabama linebacker Derrick Oden.

The only thing Florida could find to make it feel like home was the color of the jerseys the Gators would wear. "We're the home team, so we'll be wearing our blue jerseys," Spurrier said. "Other than that, we're treating this as a road game."

For his part, Stallings continued to say he didn't think there was any home-field advantage for his team.

"I don't think it's a clear-cut home-field advantage," Stallings said. "If we were in Tuscaloosa, I'd feel we had that. But we played there Thursday (against Auburn), and I didn't feel like we were at home by any stretch of the imagination.

"It's not a home game. It's the championship game. The Eastern Division champion is the home team. We'll be in the visiting team's locker room.

"I don't know how the tickets are distributed, but Florida may have as many people as Alabama does (in the stands). I just don't know."

The bottom line, however, was that Stallings didn't care. While his team was undefeated and ranked No. 2 in the nation, all that meant was that the Tide had won enough games to get to this one game playoff, a first for Division I-A college football.

"I'm just glad to be here," he said. "I think this is fair. The athletic directors set this up when we all started out. We've got to go with what the rules are. It's been our goal for a long time to get here.

"Realistically, I didn't think we'd be 11-0 this year. I hoped we would. I thought we were a year away. But things worked out for this team."

Things continued to work out for Jay Barker, too.

The sophomore from Trussville continued to mystify most football fans by continuing to not only start for Alabama, but win.

The quarterback of the second-ranked team in the country ranked no better than sixth in his own conference. Florida entered the championship game behind senior Shane Matthews, a Heisman Trophy front-runner at the start of the season, a quarterback who had become the most prolific in SEC history. Matthews finished his career with the conference record for passing yards (9,287); touchdown passes (74); touchdown responsibility (82 — 74 passing, seven rushing, one receiving); pass completions (722); pass attempts (1,202); total offense (264 yards per game); total plays (1,397); passing yards in a season (3,205).

All Barker did was win.

"I grew up in this state, following Alabama as a boy," Barker said. "I realized and appreciated what it means to be the quarterback at the University of Alabama."

Alabama has produced a strong tradition of great quarterbacks, former greats such as Dixie Howell, Bart Starr, Joe Namath, Ken Stabler, and Richard Todd.

"It is a tradition that, hopefully, has influenced generations of kids who grew up hearing about those players and wanted to come to Alabama to be part of that tradition," said Mal Moore, a former Alabama quarterback.

But over the past several years, the top quarterback recruits in the country seemed to have always narrowed their choices to Alabama and somewhere else, then elected to go somewhere else.

Steve Taneyhill chose South Carolina over Alabama. Heath Shuler went to Tennessee instead of Alabama. Stan White picked Auburn over the Tide. Kenny Felder signed with Florida State over the school where his uncle, Walter Lewis, had been a star.

And even when Alabama signed the supposed blue-chipper — remember Gene Newberry, Vince Sutton, Billy Ray, and Jeff Dunn? — where are their names in the record book?

Instead, you find names like Mike Shula, David Smith, and Gary Hollingsworth. Shula had a famous name, but was not a top prospect. Smith was a walk-on. Hollingsworth was an afterthought to a signing class that boasted Ray and Dunn.

"That's hard to explain," said Smith, a walk-on from Gadsden who followed Shula as the Tide's starting quarterback. "We talk about that ourselves. Why would a top quarterback prospect not want to come to Alabama? They know they're going to win."

Maybe, say the ones who did go to Alabama, winning isn't everything with many of the top quarterback prospects coming out of high school.

"I think one of the biggest reasons is that Alabama has never concentrated on the individual," said Hollingsworth, who quarterbacked the Tide to the SEC championship in 1989. "Alabama has never really concentrated on running Heisman campaigns.

"It's more of a team concept. You fit in and help the team. You may not have the stats, you may not throw the ball as much as some places. And for a high school kid coming out, he sees passing yards equal individual awards. But if someone wants to go somewhere and win, he goes to Alabama."

Smith, Hollingsworth, and Barker all think the edge comes from having grown up in the state.

"You have to understand what Alabama football has done," Smith said. "By being from instate, you understand the tradition and know what kind of player succeeds at Alabama. You know you'll go and win a lot of games and probably never come up for the Heisman, but the team will win, and that's the most important thing."

Which is what Barker has said all along.

"Since I was five years old, I told my parents I was going to play at Alabama," said Barker, who was signed only after Gene Stallings took over and was desperate to get some quarterbacks.

"I told the kids in my neighborhood and they snickered. But I stayed focused on my goal, and now, it's so rewarding to be here because I wasn't highly recruited.

"In fact, maybe Jay Barker shouldn't be here at all. But I am."

Perhaps the secret is that the guys who end up playing at Alabama are guys who just want to win, who are dedicated to playing for Alabama, and nothing more than that.

"I was just a small part of all the success we had my junior year (1989)," said Hollingsworth, who was elected by the fans to be the quarterback of the team of the decade. "We had Siran Stacy, Kevin Turner, Lamonde Russell, Craig Sanderson, Roger Shultz — a lot of guys doing their job. I just fit in, and everything kind of clicked.

"It's just like Jay now. He's won 15 in a row, and he's not necessarily putting up the numbers a quarterback like Shane Matthews is, but the object is to win, and he's able to help his team do that."

Alabama's starting quarterbacks have traditionally been small-time recruits with big-time hearts.

"The big-name guys out of high school want to continue all the attention and hype," Barker said. "They are more interested in what they do than what the team does.

"The other guys follow their hearts. They want to win. They go to Alabama."

A full house of 83,091 packed ancient Legion Field on this December afternoon for the first-ever SEC championship game. The press box was filled to capacity, and the SEC Media Relations Department had to set up an auxiliary press box to handle requests that came from all over the country.

A national television audience would tune in the game on ABC-TV to see whether this was, indeed, the future of college football.

It was 46 degrees at kickoff, with a brisk wind that came out of the north and gusted up to 15 miles per hour. By the fourth quarter, with darkness falling, temperatures would drop into the mid-30s.

Alabama won the coin toss, and deferred to the second half. That would mean Florida would take the ball, and the game would start with strength vs. strength: Alabama defense against Florida offense.

Harrison Houston returned Michael Proctor's kick to the Gator 23, and the game was on.

Right away, you knew this game would be something special. Florida lined up in the 'I' formation, and Alabama came out in a four-man front, with London and Copeland as the ends and Curry and Jeremy Nunley as tackles. On first down, tailback Errict Rhett took a quick handoff up the middle — a lesson no doubt learned from watching Mississippi State work on the Tide defense — for six yards. He came back on second down and picked up one to the right side.

Then Florida tipped its hand as to what its strategy would be for most of the game. On third-and-three out of a two-back set — facing a three-man front of Curry, Elverett Brown, and Copeland — Matthews dropped back to pass. Curry was taken wide on the pass rush, and the Florida quarterback flipped a shovel pass to Rhett, who ran right through the hole where Curry would normally be for 13 yards and a first down.

Rhett lost two yards on his next carry, then Matthews hit a quick out to the left side in front of cornerback Antonio Langham for six yards, and Florida got the first down on the next play when Alabama was called for jumping offside.

Matthews rolled left on the next play, and was chased by London, but managed to get off a 13-yard gainer to tight end Charlie Dean and it was first down at the Alabama 32-yard line.

Matthews hit Willie Jackson over the middle for 17, followed with a quick throw left to Dean again for 13, and suddenly, the Alabama defense was backed up into its own end zone.

Two plays later, Matthews ran the shovel pass again, and Rhett scored, giving Florida a 7-0 lead less than five minutes into the game. The drive was typical Florida: seven pass plays and five running plays.

The ease with which the Florida offense moved the ball on

that first drive had Tide fans worried. Could the Alabama offense possibly respond?

Yes. There would be no feeling around, trying all the angles, probing for a weakness in this game. Alabama went right to work with the bread and butter, and Lassic took his first carry right up the middle for seven yards, then took his second carry behind left tackle Matt Hammond for eight yards and a first down.

Florida had come out in a five-man front, but now shifted back into a four-man front, bringing up linebackers to shoot the gaps. It was obvious the defensive plan was to stop the run.

"It was an insult, the way they played us," said Alabama wide receiver Curtis Brown. "It was like they didn't have any respect for our receivers."

"Their safeties were sitting down, challenging us," Barker said.

But scheming to stop the run and actually stopping the run can be two different things. Lassic carried again, the third play in a row, and picked up three yards. Then it was Martin Houston's turn, running a draw for six yards and then a straight-ahead smash for three and a first down.

On first down from the Florida 45, Barker took a quick step back from center and fired a pass to Palmer, who went 17 yards to the Florida 28. From there, Lassic got the call four times, hitting the left side for eight, the right side for eight, the left side for seven, and finally cutting back on a toss sweep and going straight up the middle for three yards and the touchdown to tie the game, 7-7.

It was classic Alabama offense: nine running plays, one pass.

Alabama stayed in a four-man front on defense now, and began to bring in different combinations of defensive backs, going up to six or seven at one time. Florida drove the ball across midfield, to the Tide 42-yard line, but then London batted down a Matthews pass at the line. Copeland stopped a draw play behind the line of scrimmage for a four yard loss. Matthews had to hurry a throw that fell incomplete, and now it was fourth-and-14 from the 46.

Only Steve Spurrier would try a fake kick at this point in this big of a game. Punter Shayne Edge took the snap, but before he could do anything, Dabo Swinney was on top of him for a 12-yard loss.

Alabama could not take advantage of the field position, and the two sides settled down into the defensive struggle everyone expected. The Tide was running the ball almost exclusively, and Florida was trying a more balanced attack, an almost equal number of runs and passes.

The first quarter ended with the score tied, and the second quarter began with more of the same until Florida punted to Palmer, who returned the ball 20 yards. Alabama picked up 15 more on a face-mask call against the Gators.

That put Alabama on the Florida 42-yard line, and Barker immediately hit Palmer with a quick pass to the left side for nine yards. Lassic and Houston failed to gain on successive plays, and finally, it was Alabama's turn to go for it on fourth down.

Chris Anderson got the call going to the right side, and was stopped. However, Florida was flagged for an illegal substitution, a five-yard penalty which resulted in an automatic first down for Alabama.

On first-and-10 from the 28, Lassic went up the middle but was thrown back for a loss of two yards.

Then Barker saw what he was looking for, faked the handoff, and lofted the ball toward wide receiver Curtis Brown, who was racing down the left sideline. Brown ran under the pass and carried it into the end zone for the touchdown, and Alabama was on top, 14-7.

"He made a tremendous throw," Brown said of Barker. "I ran a post route and he led me to the outside. That was a good place to throw it.

"The score was tied at seven, and we felt if we kept it a touchdown ahead, we'd win."

That's how the first half would end. Alabama had 79 yards rushing, with Lassic picking up 60 of those on 12 carries, including one touchdown, to just nine yards rushing for Florida.

But the Gators had 132 yards passing, with Matthews having hit 12 of 17 with one touchdown. Barker was not throwing as often, but it was evident he had risen to the occasion for Alabama, having completed five of five for 88 yards and one touchdown in the first half.

At halftime, Florida coach Steve Spurrier felt he had the game right where he wanted it. Alabama was sitting back in a

zone on defense, letting Matthews have the short stuff, and
Spurrier, as offensive coordinator, was about to start letting
Matthews take all the short stuff he could get.

"We knew what they were going to try to do," Langham
said. "With our strong pass rush, they'd try to take that short,
three-step drop, and pick us apart underneath. Or maybe get us
to bite and then go over the top on us. We had to be patient and
not gamble."

But Oliver was beginning to wonder if he wasn't being too
patient on defense, that maybe it was time to gamble.

However, with the entire season riding on this one game,
this wasn't the time to take chances. So Oliver decided to stay
with what was working and worry about adjustments when the
time came.

For a while, it looked as if he may never have to.

Alabama played almost exclusively a four-man front, using a variety of defensive back-linebacker combinations to keep
Matthews from being able to throw very far downfield. With
linebackers like Lemanski Hall, Will Brown, Michael Rogers, and
Derrick Oden — converted defensive backs — the Tide was able
to go into a lot of different coverages from a lot of different looks.

From the Florida standpoint, the game was in Matthews's
hands now. He came out on the first drive of the second half and
threw for five, scrambled for four, threw for five, was sacked for
a loss of 13, and then tried the shovel pass to Rhett again for a gain
of six yards.

On the other side, Alabama's offense was getting stuffed on
its first two possessions — three plays and a punt. Barker's
second pass of the half, a quick hitch to Palmer, was too high; it
was his first incomplete pass of the game.

The Gators moved the ball in short chunks, taking the short
passes the Alabama secondary was giving them. But always the
Tide made the play to stop Florida before the Gators got too far.

On Matthews's second possession, he took Florida as far as
the Alabama 27-yard line, where on third-and-10 he was sacked
for a seven-yard loss by a blitzing George Teague. On fourth
down, Judd Davis's 51-yard field goal attempt — surprisingly,
the only field goal attempt of the game — was short.

That gave Alabama the ball on its own 34, and on first
down, Barker, seeing Florida in a blitz, pump-faked the quick

pass to slow down the rush, then hit Palmer for a 39-yard gain to the Florida 27. It was "The Deuce's" fourth catch of the game, for a total of 94 yards.

Lassic went right for nine yards on first down, then Houston went up the middle for two and the first down at the 15. The next play was for Lassic, who ran the sweep to the right side of the field, the short side, and the senior cut up when he saw a gap, burst through the defense, and scored on a 15-yard carry.

The extra point was not automatic, however. Proctor's first kick was nullified and Alabama backed up 15 yards for a personal foul. His second kick was a 40-yard attempt, and it was nullified by Alabama being offside.

Finally, he was looking at a 45-yard extra point. But it didn't matter to Proctor. He booted his third consecutive kick through the uprights, and Alabama led, 21-7.

Then came an unusual defensive series for Alabama. The Tide defensive coaches put Curry and Copeland inside at tackles, with Dameian Jeffries and Nunley at the end positions. London and Hall were out, with Will Brown and André Royal in at outside linebackers.

Matthews saw that and went to work. He dropped his tight end, Greg Keller, over the middle and hit him for a 19-yard gain on first down, carrying Florida to midfield. Rhett went up the middle between Curry and Copeland for 12 on the next play, and the Gators were looking at first down at the Alabama 37.

Matthews ran a play-action fake and hit fullback Kelvin Randolph over the middle for five yards, then came right back over the middle to hit Rhett for four more yards.

Curry burst through the line to stop Rhett for no gain on third down, but on fourth-and-one, Matthews took a three-step drop and hit Willie Jackson with a quick pass in the right flats for three yards and a first down.

Now, Alabama put London back in the game and went to the base three-man defensive front, with Curry, Elverett Brown, and Copeland. Matthews countered with the shovel pass again, Rhett taking the ball right to the hole vacated by Curry's rush for 14 yards and a first down at the Alabama 11.

Same defensive lineup, same offensive play, and Rhett picked up seven yards to the four.

And on the next play, Alabama tried to get aggressive and blitz from the right side. Matthews burned the Tide, pulling up and hitting Jackson with a quick sideline pass into the end zone for four yards and the touchdown to cut the lead to 21-14.

As the third quarter drew to a close, it was as if Alabama went into a panic. With Florida blitzing on just about every play, Barker came out throwing. He overthrew Prince Wimbley, was forced to scramble and picked up two on second down, then hit Sherman Williams on a screen pass that picked up 11 and a first down.

From midfield, Barker tried to go deep for Palmer but overthrew him. He then tried a quick out to Palmer on the left side that picked up six yards. But his third-down pass to Wimbley was incomplete, and Alabama had to punt.

It was a most un-Alabama-like series, a drive of six pass plays called. And it ended in near disaster when Bryne Diehl shanked his punt 16 yards, giving Florida a first down at the Gator 31-yard line.

The third quarter was not the fourth quarter, and both sides were playing with a sense of controlled panic. Time was running out, but not fast enough to suit the Tide.

The defense stuffed Florida again, but the Alabama offense was falling apart. Senior guard George Wilson was called for jumping offside. Barker was underthrowing receivers. And again, on fourth down, Diehl shanked a punt, this one going 20 yards to the Florida 49.

With Hall out and Will Brown in, Alabama went with five defensive backs and a four-man front. Matthews hit Jackson for nine on first down, and got the first down with a short pass over the middle to Rhett for six.

The shovel pass picked up four, and then Spurrier tried some trickery, with Matthews handing off to Rhett, who pitched back to Matthews, who threw it back to Rhett over the middle. The whole thing netted only five yards, however, so on second down, Florida went conventional, and Rhett took the toss sweep to the right side for four yards and the first down.

On first-and-10 from the Alabama 23, the Tide jumped offside, giving Florida five yards. Matthews threw a fade route to the end zone for Jackson, who was out of bounds when he caught the pass. On second down, Matthews was flushed from the pocket by London, but found Jackson for a 16-yard gain down the right side.

Two plays later, Rhett scored from one yard out, and suddenly, it was a new game, a tie game, with eight minutes, nine seconds left to play.

Up in the press box, the Sugar Bowl representative excused himself to go to the bathroom. A scout from another bowl said, "I bet he already has."

Sugar Bowl executive director Mickey Holmes was in Atlanta for the bowl coalition's announcement of the bowl pairings the following day. He couldn't watch the finish.

"We had so much riding on it," he said. "Alabama wins, and we have the national championship game. Alabama loses, and we probably have a Florida-Syracuse matchup."

On the Alabama sideline, defensive line coach Mike Dubose gathered his players around him and relayed a message from Oliver, who was in the press box.

"This is your team," Dubose told the defense. "You've got to win the game. Somebody's got to make a play."

Out on the field, Barker was getting sacked twice and throwing it away on third down, and Diehl shanked another punt, putting Florida in position at the Alabama 40-yard line.

The Tide defense did make the plays, however. Matthews's first-down pass was overthrown. On second down, Rhett tried a draw up the middle, but Oden was there and stopped him after a three-yard gain. On third down, Matthews was pressured by Curry and forced to hurry his throw, which fell incomplete.

The Florida punt went into the end zone for a touchback, and Alabama took over at the Tide 20. After gaining two yards behind guard George Wilson, Lassic took the ball and stretched the defense out, cutting up when he saw a gap and racing 25 yards to give Alabama some breathing room.

That was all the Tide offense could do, with Anderson losing three yards and Barker overthrowing receivers on the next two plays. And this time, Diehl got off a respectable 35-yard punt that the Gators' Monty Duncan caught and downed at the Florida 21.

In the press box, SEC officials began preparing for Division I football's first overtime game. The SEC had determined that if the game was tied, each team would get the ball at the 10-yard line and get four plays to try to score. Both teams would get one possession, and if it was still a tie game after that, the same procedure would be used until the first team scored and won.

On the field, Langham, the hero of the Auburn game, was thinking it was time to get aggressive.

"To tell the truth," he said. "I was frustrated. All the defensive backs were tired and mad. We were ready to prove something. Matthews kept throwing it short, throwing it short, and after a while we thought we were going to jump on one.

"It was getting close to the end of the game and they had the ball. We'd been dropping back all night in our zone, but I figured I had safety help, so I decided to gamble. I relied on Sam Shade to get over the top."

On first down, three minutes and 16 seconds away from overtime, Matthews, the leading passer in SEC history, took the snap, looked right, then left, and came back with the throw, a quick out to the right side intended for Monty Duncan.

"I thought I could pop it for five yards," Matthews said. "It was my mistake. I made a bad decision. I should have thrown it somewhere else."

Langham was up on the line, squatting down so that maybe Matthews wouldn't see him.

"Shane never saw me," Langham said. "But I saw him. I read his eyes and made the play Coach Dubose said we had to make.

"They'd been running that little hitch route all day. This time, I played it differently, and when he (Matthews) released the ball, I broke on it. I knew I had it. I remember a smile hitting my face when he let it go. You play football to make a great play. To make it for a touchdown is a cornerback's dream."

Langham just stepped around Duncan, took the ball in and sprinted 27 yards to the end zone.

"He must be Superman," said linebacker Derrick Oden of Langham. "I swear, if he pulled up his shirt, I think it would have a big 'S' on it."

Langham was mobbed in the end zone. The Tide fans mobbed each other in the stands. The Sugar Bowl officials mobbed each other in the press box.

"After I crossed the goal line," Langham said, "I turned around and saw nothing but all these white jerseys coming toward me. They lifted me up off the ground and pinned me up against the fence. I thought they were going to throw me over."

When he finally started making his way to the sideline, he found Eric Curry waiting on him, holding the football. "They ain't getting this ball back," Curry told him. "It's yours."

And then Curry hid the ball until the game was over and he could give it to Langham to keep.

Of course, it wasn't quite over just yet. There was still three minutes left on the clock, and all Florida needed was one touchdown.

The Gators took over at their 22-yard line, and on first down, Matthews hit Jackson for 17 yards. The next play was an incomplete pass.

And on third down, Matthews's pass was batted up in the air by Derrick Oden and Michael Rogers intercepted it at the Florida 48.

Now the game was over.

"I feel so bad for the guys because it ended up that way," Matthews said. "We played our best game of the year. We played right there with the No. 2 team in the nation. There was no way we were going to lose this game. No way.

"I made a bad play and it cost us the game. One bad play."

Spurrier was asked about Matthews's play afterward.

"He . . . played well," Spurrier said, hesitantly. "He's played some better ones.

"It's one thing to get beat. And it's one thing to give it to them. We're disappointed to lose, but we're more disappointed in the way it happened."

Florida was so close. The Gators pushed the Tide as no one else had all year, had them on the edge of the cliff, hanging on by a fingertip.

But when that fingertip belongs to Antonio Langham, it's all a team needs.

"It's going to take us a while to get over this one," Matthews said, his head down, arms crossed in front of him. "I can tell you that."

For his play — eight tackles, one interception — Langham was named the game's Most Valuable Player.

"This is a players' dream," he said. "I wanted to make that play."

Bill Oliver couldn't believe the way it ended.

"If I were a betting man, I would have bet 10 to 1 that Shane Matthews has never thrown an interception on that route. The degree of difficulty on that play (for a defensive back) is a 10.

"Matthews just doesn't make that mistake. It's like having a guy that coaches under center. He just doesn't do that."

But he did.

"It was a great football game," Matthews said. "It came down to one play. They made the play and won the game."

Derrick Lassic was named the ABC Chevrolet Player of the Game after rushing for 121 yards on 21 carries for two touchdowns. Barker finished by hitting 10 of 18 passes for 154 yards and one touchdown. Palmer had five receptions for 101 yards.

Matthews finished the game hitting 30 of 49 passes for 287 yards and two interceptions. The 49 attempts was a career high for him. He went out having set 18 SEC records and 47 Florida records.

Meanwhile, the Tide clinched its 20th SEC championship. Alabama won the first ever SEC title in 1933 and now was the first team to win the SEC championship game.

Alabama's nine wins against SEC competition was an SEC record. Only three teams in league history have won as many as eight games in one season, and Alabama did it two of the three times.

The victory was the 12th of the season for Alabama, tying a school record. The Tide would go on to have a chance to become just the third team in NCAA football history to post a perfect 13-0 record.

The Tide's 22-game winning streak is the second longest in the nation, behind Miami.

"I feel very proud, I know that," said Stallings, accepting the SEC championship trophy from SEC commissioner Roy Kramer. "We're glad to be representing our school and conference in the Sugar Bowl. We had goals at the beginning of the year, and winning our conference and going to the Sugar Bowl was one of them.

"I thought it would be almost impossible for us to go 12-0, but it took every one of those wins to put us in a position to play for the national championship. That was one of our goals, too."

It was a close game, closer than any Alabama had had all season.

"But we knew we'd find a way to win the game," said David Palmer. "We are Alabama, and Alabama stands for championships. We weren't going to lose."

Or, as Stallings said, "If you're going to be champions, you've got to win games like this."

Now it was up to the AP voters to make sure there was a national championship game, pitting No. 1 Miami against No. 2 Alabama.

"I don't have any control over what happens in the polls," Stallings said. "But if I remember right, didn't Florida State lose a game earlier this year? And let's see — aren't we 12-0 and No. 2 in the nation?

"I expect we'll get the opportunity to play Miami. I hope we do. I think it would be a great game, with Miami's 28-game winning streak and our 22-game streak."

That is, of course, exactly what happened. When the final polls came out, Miami was No. 1, Alabama No. 2, and the rest of the top 25 didn't matter.

The fight for the national championship was on.

CHAPTER

19

Attitudes

W hen the bowl pairings came out the Sunday after the SEC championship game, it was a great day for the SEC. Six conference teams were invited to participate in bowl games, the fourth time since 1986 that six member institutions played in postseason events.

Florida (8-4) would play North Carolina State in the Gator Bowl. Ole Miss (8-3) was paired with Air Force in the Liberty Bowl. Tennessee (8-3) and Boston College were in the Hall of Fame Bowl. Georgia (9-2) and Ohio State would meet in the Citrus Bowl. Mississippi State (7-4) and North Carolina were in the Peach Bowl.

But the only game that mattered was the Sugar Bowl, where No. 1 Miami (11-0) would meet No. 2 Alabama (12-0) on New Year's night, at 7:30 CST in front of 75,000 fans and a nationwide TV audience, courtesy of ABC.

It was the match made in college football heaven. The team of the '70s, Alabama, would play the team of the '80s, Miami, to see who would become the team of the '90s.

No college football team had ever won more games in a decade than Alabama of the 1970s. The Crimson Tide went 103-15-1 over that 10-year period, winning eight conference championships and three national championships.

The decade of the 1980s belonged to Miami. The Hurricanes boasted a 99-19 record with three national championships.

Miami added its fourth national championship in 1991 with a perfect 12-0 record, and was riding a 28-game winning streak going into the Sugar Bowl, the longest winning streak in the nation.

Alabama was on a run of its own, having won 22 in a row going into the 13th game of the season.

This Sugar Bowl would mark the first time two undefeated teams had met in a bowl game since the 1987 Fiesta Bowl, when Penn State defeated Miami for the national championship.

When Alabama ticket manager Tommy Ford arrived at his office Monday morning after the championship game, he heard the phones ringing before he got inside.

Figuring the answering machine would handle the call, Ford walked over to discover that the answering machine had already reached the end of its recording loop and could take no more messages.

"As fast as we can hang up a phone," Ford said, "it rings again."

The phones weren't just ringing in the ticket office. They were ringing in just about every office on the Alabama campus that was even remotely related to the athletic department.

"I've had phone calls all day," said Steve Wilson, manager of Coleman Coliseum, the building where the ticket offices are located. "They can't get through to the ticket office, so they call me. They're calling anybody they can think of."

Calls were coming in to the workers at Bryant Hall, the athletic dorm; to the athletic academic support staff; to Bryant Museum; even to head coach Gene Stallings's office.

And all the callers were after the same thing: Sugar Bowl tickets.

In fact, the demand started as soon as the championship game was over. When athletic department officials arrived back on campus following Saturday's game, university students were already lining up outside Coleman Coliseum to wait for student tickets that would not go on sale until Sunday afternoon.

"It was cold and raining," Ford said. "But the longer the evening went on, the longer the line got. The students had tents set up, some had those big beach umbrellas, others just had sheets of plastic to keep the rain off.

"They were cooking out, sitting around hibachis with their lounge chairs, grilling steaks and baking potatoes. By the time I got back here Sunday morning at 7:30 a.m., they were lined up all the way to the back of the Coliseum."

Wilson said it looked like a refugee camp you see on television from some foreign country.

"There were people sleeping on the ground, bunched together, covered by a quilt, with a big sheet of plastic over that to keep the rain off," he said. "It took us four hours to clean it all up. We had three bonfires to clean up, plus cups, food, plastic — and all of it soaking wet."

Once the tickets went on sale, they didn't last long.

"We sold 2,200 tickets from one to six o'clock that afternoon," Ford said. "One per student."

Ford said he could have sold more, but he didn't have anymore student tickets to sell. They were gone, just like most of the 17,500 tickets Alabama received from the Sugar Bowl.

"Our policy is well defined as to who gets tickets," Ford said. "But we could probably sell 100,000 tickets to this game if we had the time and the tickets."

Across the hallway in the offices of Tide Pride, the athletic department season ticket program, Wayne Atcheson would do little else but answer phone calls.

"People are calling saying, 'I know you can get me some tickets,'" Atcheson said. "But I can't. We've got a priority program for our tickets, and that's one advantage of being a member of Tide Pride."

Over in Stallings's office, his secretary, Linda Knowles, said it was very much like the 1970s, when Alabama seemed to be playing for a national championship every year.

"It's not a whole lot different," said Knowles, who was Bryant's secretary during those days.

"If you win, people get excited and want to be there. People are calling, wanting tickets, wanting to know where the team is staying, wanting to talk to Coach Stallings.

"We've gotten tons of mail already. And people call who just want to talk to Coach Stallings just for a minute, who say they are the biggest Alabama fan in the world and they just want to talk for a minute. And they are big fans."

Some of the calls to the ticket office were outrageous.

"I had one gentleman call and not only request but expect 40 tickets to the game," Ford said. "I checked and his priority enabled him to order two. His chances of 40 were zero.

"We're trying to help people. We've got the number of the University of Miami ticket office and started giving that out, thinking maybe Miami had tickets. But about 20 minutes later, Miami called here and said, 'Thanks for sending us business, but stop. We're looking for more tickets, too.'"

Some people just wouldn't take no for an answer.

Others just wanted to say thanks.

"I had one man call and say, 'I'm on top of the world, and I don't care if we win another game,'" Knowles said. "Then he said, 'Of course I want us to win, but no matter what, it's been a great year.'

"That's how they all feel."

Derrick Oden was surprised to be so excited about playing in the Sugar Bowl.

"All my life, I wanted to play at UCLA and in the Rose Bowl," said Oden, who was born in Pasadena, and lived there until he started high school.

"My high school always played its last game of the season in the Rose Bowl. We called it the 'Turkey Tussle.' But I never got to play in a high school game there because we left."

After his seventh-grade year, Oden's family moved from the Pacific Coast to the banks of the Warrior River and Tuscaloosa, where Oden became a three-year starter and two-time all-state selection at Hillcrest High School.

Despite those honors and his 140 tackles as a senior, many scouts felt Oden was too short, at 5-feet-11, to play linebacker at the major college level. Fortunately for him and for the Tide, Bill Curry's Alabama staff didn't feel that way and signed Oden to a scholarship in 1988.

He became a starter in his sophomore year. As a senior, Oden was elected one of the team captains and was the third leading tackler on the team with 65 stops, two quarterback sacks, and one forced fumble.

And although he missed out on both UCLA and the Rose Bowl, Oden had learned to love the idea of playing in New Orleans on January 1.

"This is what we've been working for all year," he said. "We've got a chance to win the national championship. It's a chance to show off."

There isn't much showing off to do for an inside linebacker in Alabama's defensive scheme, not with players like Curry and Copeland, London and Hall, Langham and Teague on the outside.

"I think I've been pretty steady," Oden said. "It's been a solid year. I don't give myself many minuses. But when I look at our defense, I never single out any one person. Especially not myself. I look at the defense as a whole, and whether I did what I was supposed to do in the overall scheme."

And in the overall scheme of things, Oden felt as if he was right where he belonged.

"I've been chosen team captain and we've won the SEC championship," he said. "If we win this next game, it will be like a dream come true."

Playing this Alabama defense was like a dream for some people. Except it was a dream that quickly became a nightmare.

In the final NCAA statistics, Alabama led the nation in total defense, rushing defense, and turnovers created. The Tide ranked second in pass defense and second in scoring defense and had earned a place among the great defenses of all time.

Alabama fans know something about great defense. The Tide's national championship teams of the past had always been built on great defense. Two of the greatest were the 1961 team, led by future NFL Hall of Famer Lee Roy Jordan, and the 1979 and 1980 team, which won back-to-back national championships.

"Defense is an attitude," said Billy Neighbors, All-America defensive tackle for Alabama in 1961. "It kills you if someone scores on you. That's the way we were."

That '61 defense still holds the school record for fewest plays allowed per game (52.4), fewest rushing and passing touchdowns allowed (three) and most shutouts in a season (six). Alabama led the nation in scoring defense that year, allowing just 2.2 points per game.

"For a while, Alabama defenses played with this idea of 'bend but don't break'," said Mike Clements, a starting defensive back on the 1979 team. "But with our defense, there was no such thing as bending. We were supposed to stop the offense right there, three plays and out. And someone always made the big play when we needed it. That was something we did quite a bit."

That '79 defense holds school records for most interceptions in a season (25), and fewest touchdowns allowed rushing (two). The Tide led the nation in scoring defense that year, too, giving up an average of 5.3 points per game.

But members of both those teams say this 1992 defense, which came to be called "The Bullies of Bryant Drive," may be the best of all time.

"I think this defense is as good as we've ever had," said Jordan, one of the greatest linebackers to play the game. "Overall, they've got tremendous balance, with excellent corners, excellent linebackers, and two great defensive ends.

"And they've got the right mentality. You can tell all 11 guys believe someone is going to make the play, no matter what the situation. They look around the huddle and they see 11 guys who can do it."

Alabama quarterback coach Mal Moore played on the 1961 team and was an assistant coach during the 1970s.

"All those defenses played with a great amount of confidence," Moore said. "But this defense has a little more versatile ability. They rush the passer extremely well, where the '79 defense didn't face the kind of passing game we face now. This defense may be more capable playing against different schemes of offense.

"But the great teams have an attitude, no question. All great defensive teams have that. Each player plays with a high level of confidence. Each player knows his teammates can carry his load. The common thread between that '61 team, the '79 team, and this team is confidence."

This defense posted three shutouts, recorded 47 quarterback sacks, led the conference in interceptions with 22, and had two players — Teague and Langham — who shared the conference lead in interceptions with six apiece.

It was a defense that scored knockouts of such quarterbacks as Tennessee's Heath Shuler, LSU's Jamie Howard, and Auburn's Stan White.

"Our players are confident," said Bill Oliver, who calls the shots for this defense on game day. "We talk about that all the time. Something always seems to happen good for this team, by somebody."

Neighbors said there is no question this team is better than the one in '61.

"This team has a lot more talent than we had," he said. "Langham is one of the best defensive backs that ever played at Alabama. Eric Curry and John Copeland are probably the best defensive linemen that have ever been there. They have great outside linebackers, solid inside linebackers. Teague holds everyone in the secondary together.

"Everybody is bigger and stronger. Lee Roy was the backbone of our defense, no question. But these guys are just better."

Clements feels one of the advantages this team has is that players grow up playing defense now, instead of being converted to defense once they are in college.

"This team has more quality people at every position, and they've grown up more specialized," he said. "But they also have more to contend with now than we ever did."

Still, if it comes down to attitude, Alabama has it.

"We go on the field knowing we can win," Copeland said. "It doesn't matter what the situation is. We're confident."

Moore summed it up best.

"This," he said, "is a very, very capable defensive football team."

The University of Miami had proven to be pretty capable, too — at both defense and offense.

The 'Canes ranked eighth in the nation in total defense, fifth against the pass, eighth against the rush, and third in scoring defense (11.5 points per game). And as a team, Miami had created 29 turnovers, and ranked third in the nation in turnover ratio.

But of course, most of the attention at Miami went to the offense and Heisman Trophy-winning quarterback Gino Torretta. The 'Canes averaged 436.5 yards, 32.4 points per game, and Torretta had completed 56.7 percent of his passes for 3,060 yards and 19 touchdowns.

He had four receivers who each had over 40 catches, led by Horace Copeland's 47 receptions for 769 yards and two touchdowns and Lamar Thomas's 47 catches for 701 yards and 10 touchdowns.

"In a way, I'm glad we're playing Miami," said George Teague. "I'm glad he (Torretta) won the Heisman. He's been named the best player in college football. That's a challenge for us.

"It gives us a chance to prove whether or not we can play against someone of that caliber. We've played against good people. But to play against a Heisman winner is exciting."

Teague was a freshman defensive back when Alabama played Miami in the 1989 Sugar Bowl. The 'Canes won that one, to win their third national championship, but it wasn't easy. Alabama wasn't intimidated by the Miami image then any more than the Tide players were intimidated now.

"When I hear Miami, all I think of is cocky, flashy, great talent," Teague said. "I've never gotten caught up in that."

Miami has had a hard time getting away from that image, helped along when the Hurricane players walked off the team plane at the 1987 Fiesta Bowl wearing Army fatigues and carrying toy guns.

The 'Canes got into a brawl with Notre Dame players coming out of the tunnel for the opening kickoff of a regular-season game.

The "Miami Rule," which outlawed taunting, was adopted by the NCAA. It was drawn up after the 'Canes were flagged for over 200 yards in unsportsmanlike conduct penalties in the 1991 Cotton Bowl against Texas. And while Miami head coach Dennis Erickson has worked to change that image, the Miami players still love to talk.

"And it's hard not to get caught up in that," Teague said. "It's hard to stay quiet, to mind your own business."

If that is Miami's image, what is Alabama's image?

"Totally different," Teague said. "I see a good team with a lot more class."

Indeed, Alabama has always liked to think it is the image of how a football team should handle itself: play hard, play clean, stay quiet. Knock your man down, help him up. Score a touchdown, hand the ball to the official.

Of course, it doesn't always work that way. A new generation of players has come in who grew up on dancing in the end zone and strutting over fallen opponents. But still, Alabama probably does it less than most teams.

There would be confrontations leading up to this game, once both teams got to New Orleans. But true to form, Alabama players saved their talk for the game.

Miami offensive tackles Mario Cristobal and Carlos Etheridge did not seem too concerned about Alabama's defensive end duo of Copeland and Curry.

"We've watched Curry and Copeland on film and they deserve their All-America honors," Cristobal said. "They are two great players.

"But we wouldn't have come to the University of Miami unless we wanted to play for the best. We're looking forward to playing them."

The two Miami linemen were no strangers to big games, however.

"These kids are veterans," said 'Canes line coach Gregg Smith. "Cristobal is in his third year as a starter. They've been to a lot of bowl games. They're just excited to go play."

Because Miami's first-team offense usually worked against its first-team defense in practice, Cristobal and Etheridge had to face the best defensive ends Miami had — Kevin Patrick and Darren Krein — every day.

"Those guys have gone against the best for the last three years," Krein said of Cristobal and Etheridge. "I don't think this will be any different for them. I think they'll have success. They know what it's like to go against fast and strong guys like Curry and Copeland."

Chris Donnelly, the transfer from Vanderbilt, was discovering what it was like to play in big games—bigger than any he'd been in before.

"I don't know that I've ever had a chance to play for a title, a championship," Donnelly said. "We played in the state championship game my sophomore year in high school and lost. I guess that was the last time."

In the space of a month, Donnelly had played in and won the SEC championship game and was preparing to play for the national championship.

"As a football player, you grow up looking forward to a game of this magnitude," he said. "That's what we practice for and prepare for, games like this. It's what we play the game all our lives for."

But too many players never get the chance, just as Donnelly wouldn't have if he had not transferred from Vanderbilt, where in two years the Commodores won two games and lost 20.

"They say winning is contagious," Donnelly said. "Well, losing is, too. It gets to a point where it is expected, where if something goes wrong, everyone said, 'Oh no, not again.' And the game is over."

Donnelly started every game at free safety in 1992, and he played despite a left knee that was already scheduled for arthroscopic surgery on January 7.

"We never even talked about surgery during the season," Donnelly said. "I think the doctors knew there was no way I was going to miss the rest of this season. And they said all along it was something that I could play on, something that could be taken care of after the season ended."

This season meant too much to Donnelly. Everything had fallen into place for him, and his team. He went from playing for pride to playing for the prize, and it is a distinction Donnelly wanted to savor and remember forever.

"I know Miami is good," he said. "They wouldn't be here if they weren't.

"But we've got a good team, too, or we wouldn't be where we are, either."

The week before the team headed south to New Orleans, starting tackle Roosevelt Patterson's grandfather passed away.

Then early on Christmas morning, the day before the team was to depart for the Sugar Bowl, inside linebacker Michael Rogers was seriously injured and another person killed in a one-car accident near his home in Butler County.

Rogers was listed in serious condition with cuts, bruises, and a concussion.

"It's my understanding that it knocked him out, and he's been in and out of consciousness," said Tide secondary coach Bill Oliver. "He won't be able to play. But the big thing is, he's alive. He's lucky to be alive."

The friend killed in the accident was sitting next to Rogers in the back seat of the 1985 Buick Electra.

According to police reports, the car was traveling toward Rogers's hometown of Luverne about 3 a.m. when it went off the road, hit a culvert, and flipped.

"Rogers was thrown from the car and somehow pinned under the car," Oliver said. "The car caught on fire, and the two cars of kids coming up behind them were there to get everyone out."

Police said Rogers and the others were on their way home from a nightclub in Greenville.

The 6-foot-1, 220-pound Rogers started 11 games during the regular season, and was second on the team in tackles with 68. He had 10 tackles behind the line of scrimmage, one sack, two interceptions, and he also broke up one pass.

Oliver said Mario Morris would likely step in to start in Rogers's place.

"That's where we'll look first," Oliver said. "But that really is something we'll have to decide when we get back to practice."

The Alabama team had put two weeks of work into getting ready for the Miami game, then took the Christmas holiday off. The team was to meet in New Orleans the day after Christmas and resume workouts there.

Rogers's absence meant the defensive schemes that had been put in to take advantage of his speed and athletic ability were useless. Morris, while a smart linebacker, was not the athlete Rogers was, and couldn't be expected to do the same things.

When Stallings arrived in New Orleans, he was repeatedly asked if the players were going to do anything to honor Rogers, such as wear a decal with his number on their helmets.

Stallings graciously said no. But he had to be thinking: Why would they honor a player so stupid as to be out at three o'clock in the morning, racing in a car, one week before the biggest game of his life?

"Losing Michael is a big blow to this team," said linebacker coach Jeff Rouzie. "But we feel good about the guys we have, Mario and (freshman) John Walters. They've worked hard. You always know something like this could happen, and these guys have got to be ready to play.

"We'd love to have Michael there. But the game is business as usual. The next guy has to step up and do the job."

Morris will have no problems making the defensive calls that Rogers is responsible for.

"I think one of my strengths is that I can direct traffic," Morris said. "I can recognize situations and check the defense. That's perhaps my best asset."

The weakness would come in pass coverage.

"Mike could do a lot of things in coverage," Rouzie said. "But in today's defense, with all the substitution we do, there are ways to work around certain things. We've got extra defensive backs we can use, or (outside linebacker) Will Brown can play the run as well as cover. There are options."

One thing the Miami offense was known for was finding a weakness and putting its best guy out there on the weakness, one on one.

"They isolate you," Rouzie said. "And they've got a great quarterback and great receivers to do that with."

The pressure would be on Morris because Miami puts its best receivers to work on the inside of the field, trying to get the matchup with linebackers.

"I'm sure Miami will try to pick on the linebackers," Morris said. "I imagine they'll test me first. But I believe I'll be ready. I'll play the defense the coaches call and do my best. I'll be OK."

Alabama fans started pouring in around Christmas. While the bulk of the Tide faithful would not arrive until the day before

New Year's Eve, enough were in New Orleans early so that when the players arrived, they were greeted by a large contingent of fans.

"Miami, they don't bring the fans like Alabama does," said a guy named Jimmy, who was putting out T-shirts to sell in a shop along Bourbon Street. "I ordered three times as many Alabama T-shirts as Miami shirts."

For that reason, most of the shop owners and business people in the French Quarter were Alabama fans.

"Whoever brings us money, that's who I want to win," Jimmy said. But many Tide fans came with their own T-shirts, either in red or white, and with a variety of sayings.

Such as the one that had the Alabama logo on the front, just above the words, "We're not snobs." On the back was the rest of the message, "We just think we're better than you."

Everywhere, there were signs, "Need tickets." There were few offers.

And as game day drew near and more and more Alabama fans arrived, New Orleans became a sea of red, where the greeting wasn't "Happy New Year" but "Roll Tide."

Miami fans, decked out in their team colors of green and orange, hung together as much as they could.

But Jennette Penn, who came to the game from Miami, said the 'Canes fans didn't pay attention to all the Alabama support.

"Miami fans," Penn said, "are never overwhelmed."

Fans weren't the only ones pouring into the city for the game.

"We've issued press credentials for 600 people for this game," said Sugar Bowl spokesman Chris Menninger.

"For any other game, our press box would be adequate. But for this game, we're using our regular press box, and our auxiliary press box, plus two rooms inside the stadium where we'll pump the game in on video screens."

Everyone was there, it seemed. "This is much more intense because of the national championship," said Associated Press sportswriter Mary Foster.

"The AP has six or seven writers here this year. Normally, we'd have two."

The *Birmingham Post-Herald* had 11 people down to cover the game. The *Birmingham News* had six. The two main Birmingham television stations sent staffs of seven, including satellite trucks for live broadcasts. And Birmingham sports talk-show host Matt Coulter was doing his call-in show live all week from the bar in the Alabama team hotel.

Both teams were allowed out to see New Orleans and Bourbon Street in the evenings, particularly earlier in the week, before most of the fans had arrived and curfews were pushed back to 1 a.m.

Invariably, the two teams ran into each other on the street in the Quarter, and confrontation took place.

"I'm going to knock somebody's head," yelled Miami linebacker Rohan Marley. "We're going out Friday to kick. . . ."

"They're just trying to intimidate us," Derrick Lassic told his teammates. "And they can't."

According to Lassic, the confrontation that took place near Pat O'Brien's, started out as "yakkety-yak and all that stuff," then got personal.

"They were saying 'Mississippi State who? Who is Florida? You ain't beat anybody. I don't even know why you showed up. You can't beat us,'" Lassic said.

Miami receiver Lamar Thomas got up in Lassic's face and screamed, "You know me. Everyone knows me. But who are you?"

Lassic said it was hard not to respond.

"I didn't know who he was until I saw his number," Lassic said. "His jacket number was 36. He was acting like he was a god or king."

Marley saw the 290-pound Patterson and screamed, "You must be an offensive lineman, you fat, sloppy ———."

Marley, the diminutive son of the late reggae star Bob Marley, had plenty to say about Alabama.

"We came here No. 1. We came here to take the ring back to Miami and we will, whether they like it or not.

"We're going to beat them. We're going to kick their ass."

Someone asked Marley if he wasn't concerned about the Alabama players hearing what he had to say and coming after him.

"They'll see this on TV tonight and they'll love it," he said. "They better love it."

According to Lassic, Marley was the loudest of the group during the confrontation.

"I don't mind the jawing," Lassic said. "But when somebody thinks they're better than you are, like a god or a king, that irritates me. I was brought up to be more humble.

"That little kid (Marley) is a real loud and different individual. The way he was talking, you'd think he was L.T. (Lawrence Taylor) or something. Well, he'll have a lot to prove to back up the statements he made.

"Maybe once the game starts, I'll have something to say to him. Maybe as I run by him for a touchdown, I'll sing him one of his father's songs: 'We Be Jammin.'"

Miami defensive end Darren Krein thought the Alabama offense just wasn't going to be much of a test for the Hurricane defense.

"We think they are pretty one-dimensional," he said. "The passes they caught in the Auburn and Florida games were a lot of luck."

The Miami players wore their reputation on their sleeves and weren't afraid to give anyone the finger — especially the one wearing past national championship rings. Thomas walked into a pregame press conference and put his two national championship rings on either side of the microphone in front of him.

"The third one," Thomas said, "will be icing on the cake."

Meanwhile, Lassic got in one good shot of his own.

"What are the Miami colors? Orange and green?" he said. "Those are cute colors. Girls' colors."

Gene Stallings had little use for such verbal confrontations.

"The game will be settled in the arena," he said, when told of the verbal jousting. "Not in Pat O'Brien's. What some rookie wide receiver says doesn't mean much to me."

Alabama wide receiver David Palmer gave another example of his ability as an athlete during practice one day in the Superdome.

Palmer was running a deep sideline pattern, and the ball was thrown just a little bit out of bounds. Palmer reached out and caught the ball and his momentum carried him full speed across the sideline, and right into a young boy who was standing too close to the field, watching.

There was no way Palmer could avoid hitting the boy. So as he did, he dropped the football, clutched the boy to his body so tight the boy barely moved, and executed a perfect forward roll, protecting the boy all the while with his body.

The boy got up shaken and looked as if he wanted to cry, but couldn't, really, because he wasn't hurt.

Alabama head coach Gene Stallings made sure the boy got a T-shirt and cap, and a lot of the players came by to check on the boy and make him feel better.

But as Stallings walked away, he was shaking his head over Palmer's presence of mind to handle the situation.

"That was unbelievable," Stallings said. "He hit that boy going full speed, but wrapped him up so tight, the boy never felt a thing."

Perhaps the best story of the season was that of Alabama offensive guard and team captain George Wilson.

Wilson probably had no business even being on this football team, much less starting. He was lucky to be walking, much less running.

In June of 1989, after being redshirted his freshman season, Wilson accidentally shot off half his left foot while coming home from hunting in the woods around his family's home near Abernant.

Surgeons took a section of muscle from around his chest and a skin graft from his calf and did their best to give Wilson as much of a foot as possible. But the big toe was gone, along with the ball of his foot.

Three years later, here he was, starting for the No. 2 team in the country, a two-time Academic All-SEC selection and second-team Coaches' All-SEC pick.

"I'm in awe of him," said his father, former Alabama halfback Butch Wilson. "I know two days after the accident, he told his mother he would play football again, and we said, 'Sure.' Then we looked at each other and both of us were just hoping he'd be able to walk again.

"I told him he didn't have anything to prove and not to do it for me. He said he had to prove it to himself and if he didn't at least try, he'd go through the rest of his life wondering if he could have done it."

Butch Wilson was always aware of the pressure that George might feel, growing up as the son of a football player. Butch Wilson was All-State, All-South, and an honorable-mention All-America selection as a halfback at Hueytown High School.

He signed with Alabama in 1959 and was a starter by his sophomore year. When he left after the 1962 season, the teams he had played on had gone 29-2-2 with one national championship. Butch Wilson was drafted by the Baltimore Colts and played five years there, finishing his NFL career after two seasons with the New York Giants.

"My father never talks much about his playing career," George Wilson said. "When he does talk, I listen. He's played a lot longer than I have. He's seen just about everything.

"He's always low-key. He has things (from his playing days), but he doesn't flaunt it."

The reason was George.

"I low-keyed it because I didn't want George to try to compete against me," Butch Wilson said. "If he wanted football, I was for him 100 percent. If he didn't, I was still for him 100 percent. Wherever he went to school, I was behind him. Whatever he wanted to do, that was fine with me and his mother."

George did elect to play football, however, and was an All-State selection at Jess Lanier High in Bessemer. He was rated the top offensive center prospect and one of the top 10 college prospects in the state.

Everything pointed to his matching his father's athletic accomplishments, until that summer day.

"What happened was very humbling to me," George Wilson said. "It's easy for an athlete to get that 'take on the world' attitude. Then something happens to pull the reins back on you and make you realize you are vulnerable, that you are just a person like everyone else.

"It made me look at the reality of life. It gives you a different perspective."

It changed priorities for everyone in the Wilson home.

"Football didn't seem so important," Butch Wilson said.

"People would ask me if George would play again. I'd say I don't care, I just hope he walks.

"I asked him one day why he was putting himself through so much just to play again, and he told me, 'Dad, other guys are hurting just as bad as me. There are guys with bad knees, hurting just as much as I am, paying their price to play.'

"He was right. Everyone has their problems. I went through it. I have bad knees. But I never lost a foot. I had bruises, but I never lost part of my body. It's unbelievable, how much determination he has."

George Wilson's attitude was a reflection of this whole Alabama team, which is why he was elected one of the permanent team captains.

"You have to have a certain amount of confidence," he said. "If people say you can't do something, like you can't beat Miami, then you say, 'I'll at least try and go down fighting.' "

Butch Wilson wished he could be right there beside his son. As game time drew nearer, he found himself going to the jewelry box, pulling out his national championship ring, and rubbing it for luck, hoping that soon there would be another championship ring in the family, belonging to George.

"I don't wear this (ring) much," Butch Wilson said. "But I'm hoping it's a good luck piece this week.

"I'm tickled to death, but I'm scared to think about it. I hate to say anything. I guess I'm superstitious. I don't want to jinx anything."

Butch Wilson could feel the old fire burning again. He saw his son out there, battling on half a foot, unable to push off right or left at times, getting the job done on sheer guts and determination.

"I wish I could help him," Butch Wilson said. "I told him I'd be good for one play, then they'd probably knock my head off. But I'd stick it in there for one play if they'd let me.

"A national championship is special. I can't even comprehend it. If it happens, it'd be so great.

"I don't know what it will take, but I know this team will do whatever it takes. That's what champions do."

That's what George Wilson did. Of all the things Butch Wilson gave his son, the heart of a champion was the greatest gift of all.

20

National Champions

Game day.

All the talk, all the hype, all the practices, all the schemes — it was all over now, except to see who could back it up and who couldn't.

Both teams would have last-minute meetings, of course, to go over one last time what they had to do to win.

The Alabama coaches didn't break it down this simply for their players, but essentially, they went into the game with five keys to winning it:

1. Seven-play drives. If every offensive possession takes at least seven plays, then chances are, if Alabama has to punt, the Tide will be able to pin Miami back in bad field position.

2. Create turnovers. The Tide had lost six games under Stallings. In all six, the Tide lost the ball more than they caused the other team to lose the ball.

3. Run the ball between the tackles. Miami's defense is built on speed. The one way to neutralize speed is to run straight at it.

4. Consistent punting. In a game expected to be this close, field position is everything. Tide punter Bryne Diehl can't afford those 16-yard shanks he sometimes gave up in big games.

5. Stop the long pass. In other words, make Miami put the ball in the air often, but for short distances. The more the 'Canes throw, the more chances Alabama has to intercept.

The big number the Alabama defense was concerned with was 3.5 — as in 3.5 seconds — the time it takes a good quarterback to set up and release the ball.

"If I can get 3.5 seconds, I'll take it every time," said Torretta. "I don't think it's taken me 3.5 seconds to get rid of the football at any time this season."

As the week went on, the Alabama defensive coaches became more convinced that Miami was not even considering getting involved in a smash-mouth, run-up-the-middle kind of game with the Tide.

"They are going to throw the ball," Bill Oliver said. "They play from endline to endline, sideline to sideline, exploit the whole field.

"When you play a running team, they will use a limited amount of the field. But when a team spreads it out like Miami, it becomes tougher to defend."

Passing games are different. Florida's passing game was built on many formations, out of which the offense could run the same play. What made the Gators' offense so tough for Alabama in the championship game was that Spurrier was using formations and personnel in ways he'd never done before, and the Alabama defense, relying so heavily on recognition, got fooled.

Miami, on the other hand, was a one-back offense. The 'Canes liked to line up basically the same way every time, but had the capability to run 40 different plays from every set.

"It is really simple if you sit down and coach it," Oliver said.

And Oliver and his staff had gone over it carefully, coming up with a scheme they felt would create as much havoc as they could with the Miami offense. The plan was to make Torretta have to read and reread the Alabama defense, to keep the quarterback and receivers from reading the same things and making the same adjustments.

Because if the Miami offense clicked, the way it ran routes that interconnected all over the field, it was almost impossible for at least one receiver not to get open.

That's what Miami was counting on, anyway.

"Our quarterback takes shorter drops and gets rid of the ball quicker in order to neutralize the hard pass rush of Alabama," said Hurricanes quarterback coach Rich Olson. "Gino has the ability to read coverages, and the receivers have options and adjustments at the snap of the ball."

The night before the game, the Alabama team went to see Tom Cruise, Jack Nicholson, and Demi Moore in the movie "A Few Good Men."

Miami went out of town for the night, staying in a hotel in Baton Rouge, to get away from the distractions of New Year's Eve.

Hurricane coach Dennis Erickson said he doesn't sleep the night before a big game.

"I'm too nervous," he said. "I'm nervous as hell. When I quit being nervous, I shouldn't be in coaching."

Stallings sleeps like a baby the night before the game.

"I tell my wife it's because I have a clear conscience," he said. "She says it's because I have no conscience. I'm not sure."

In the Miami locker room, tailback Darryl Spencer unpacked his lucky underwear, the same underwear he wore for every Miami game.

"It's worked for two years, because we haven't lost yet," Spencer said.

"It's a superstition of mine. I probably could play without it, but it would definitely be in the back of my mind."

Down the row of lockers, linebacker Rohan Marley had on headsets, listening to the reggae music of his father, Bob Marley.

Linebacker Michael Barrow was taking a bubble bath and listening to music by the group Public Enemy.

Defensive end Kevin Patrick would be putting a rubber band on his right hand, as he had done for every game since high school.

"It's my little thing," Patrick said. "It's kept me from being injured, knock on wood."

The Alabama players had their rituals, too.

John Copeland got ready by listening to rap. Jay Barker would pray and then visualize what he had to do.

George Teague prayed "to keep myself from getting hurt and to play the best I can," he said. Placekicker Michael Proctor had a teddy bear dressed up in Alabama paraphernalia sitting in his locker.

"The first time I saw it, I laughed," Teague said. "Then I thought, if that's what it takes for him to kick a long field goal and win us the game, it's all right with me."

Linebacker Lemanski Hall would take the field and immediately begin looking for his parents and younger sister in the stands.

"That's the only thing that brings me good luck," Hall said. "I always find them in the stands, and they'll wave or stand up or something. I've been doing that since junior high, and I'm still carrying it on."

Cornerback Antonio Langham usually dreamed about a game the night before, and swore his dreams have a way of coming true.

His dream for this game?

"I'll tell you afterward," he said. "I don't want to jinx it."

Stallings said he thought the game would be high scoring. Erickson disagreed.

"You watch their defense and our defense, and you think it will be low scoring," Erickson said. "Coach Stallings seems to think there will be a lot of points scored. If there are a lot of turnovers, it could be high scoring.

"Our ability to protect the passer is key. We've got to run the football to slow down their rush. We've got to stop their running game, because if they can run, they can work the play-action passes.

"But most of all, we've got to be able to throw the ball. That's what we do for a living."

Miami went into the game an eight-point favorite. Stallings laughed.

"I wouldn't trade my team for Miami's," he said. "I don't think we're underdogs. I think we've got a good chance."

The Miami team was after more than a win, more than just beating Alabama.

The Hurricanes were after history.

"They talk about the great teams in college football, the

Oklahomas and all that," said Lamar Thomas. "I want them to talk about the Miami Hurricanes."

The 'Canes put a lot of stock in their tradition of winning, a tradition that started with the 1983 national championship team. Since then, Miami had gone 107-13, and the seniors on the squad were looking at a 45-3 record for their careers, if they beat Alabama.

A national championship would give Miami consecutive national titles, three in four years, four in six years, and five in the past 10 years. The most recent team to win back-to-back titles was Alabama, 1978–79. Only Notre Dame had won three titles in four years. No team had ever won four titles in six years.

"We know what we're playing for," Erickson said. "We're playing for a national championship. We're playing to make history in college football. We're very aware of where we're at. We know that we can go down in history, and that's very important to us."

What the 'Canes wanted was the word "dynasty" to be associated with their program.

"We need to win this one right here to put an exclamation point on this dynasty," said linebacker Michael Barrow. "I think we've done everything to be considered a dynasty, but to be mentioned with the Notre Dames and the Alabamas and the dynasties of the past, we have to win this game."

In the final minutes before taking the field for the start of the game, it was so quiet in the Alabama locker room, you could hear every buckle snap. No one was talking. Players were staring at the floor, staring at the ceiling, staring into space.

"All we could picture in our minds was beating Miami," Lassic said. "We were focused on Miami and what we had to do to win. Maybe we were obsessed."

Stallings gathered his team around him for one last talk before taking the field.

"I didn't have much to say," Stallings said. "I told them it wasn't enough to just want to win. I told the team it was going to take more than that. We were going to have to leave everything on the field."

When the Alabama team raced onto the field, the Miami players, already out there, turned their backs.

When the Crimson Tide went through warm-ups, Miami players watched and laughed.

"In all my years," said Bill Oliver. "I've never heard such stuff. They laughed at us when we were warming up. Imagine that."

When the team captains went out for the pregame coin toss, the Miami captains refused to shake hands with Alabama's George Wilson, Prince Wimbley, Derrick Oden, and George Teague.

And the fire burned inside every Alabama player.

"We wanted to shut them up," said Barker, usually the quiet quarterback. "We wanted to beat them up so badly they couldn't talk."

Alabama, the home team, won the toss and elected to defer to the second half. Miami chose to receive. Once again, the game would start with strength vs. strength, the Hurricane offense against the Crimson Tide defense.

Miami didn't even try to get a running game going. First down was a screen pass for three yards. On second down, Alabama lined up in a three-three defense — three down linemen and three linebackers. Torretta lined up in the shotgun, and when the Tide dropped just about everyone into coverage, the Miami quarterback was forced out of the pocket and nailed by Alabama cornerback Tommy Johnson for a three-yard loss. On third down, Torretta was pressured again and forced to hurry his throw, which fell incomplete.

On fourth down, Miami punted. Paul Snyder got off a 44-yard kick that David Palmer fielded at the Alabama 38, and then The Deuce nearly cut loose, going 38 yards back upfield to the Miami 24.

There were no surprises from the Alabama offense. Lassic went up the middle for four yards. Lassic went around right end for 14.

And Miami used its first time-out, not even three minutes into the game.

On first down at the six-yard line, Barker rolled right and had Lassic wide open in the end zone. All he had to do was loft the ball over safety Casey Greer's head, but he didn't, and Greer batted it down for an incomplete pass.

Lassic gained three yards on a second-down sweep, and on third down, Barker rolled out on a bootleg to the right. No one was in front of him, so he tried to make it to the end zone himself. But linebacker Robert Bass caught him from behind after a gain of only one yard.

So Michael Procter came on and kicked a 19-yard field goal for a 3-0 Alabama lead.

The Hurricanes took over after the kickoff at their 21-yard line, and on third down, wide receiver Kevin Williams got loose down the middle and hauled in a pass for a 34-yard gain. Miami picked up 10 more yards on a pass to tailback Jonathan Harris, down to the Alabama 24. From there, it was nothing on three plays, and Miami kicker Dane Prewitt, a Birmingham native, kicked a 49-yard field goal to tie the score.

For all the talk about defense, there wasn't much for the first three possessions. Alabama took the ball and, behind four consecutive carries by Lassic, moved from the Tide 26 to the Miami 49. But from there, the Tide tried to go to the air. Barker missed Chris Anderson with a shovel pass. Barker was sacked. And on third down, Barker threw deep for Kevin Lee, overthrew him, and Greer intercepted for the Hurricanes and returned it 26 yards to the Tide 39-yard line.

Was this the mistake Alabama couldn't afford to make?

Not with the Tide defense coming on the field. On first down, Torretta hit fullback Donnell Bennett for three yards to the 36. On second down, Torretta hit Lamar Thomas over the middle, and Thomas had a clear field down the middle, except for one thing: cornerback Tommy Johnson.

Johnson came up from behind Thomas and punched the ball out of his hands at the Alabama 23. Willie Gaston recovered it, and disaster was averted by the Tide defense.

Johnson, a sophomore from Niceville, Florida, was playing the game of his life. He had a quarterback sack in Miami's first offensive series, two tackles in the second, and now caused a fumble in the third.

But that was nothing compared to growing up the son of a Baptist minister.

Johnson had to walk a very straight and narrow path, with curfews that had to be obeyed.

"When you start getting older, you start getting a lot of peer pressure," Johnson said. "And you got frustrated by the way he did things, him being a minister.

"He was real strict. I was in the 12th grade, and my curfew was 11 o'clock. Staying out late was the main thing I tried to do."

Alcohol was out of the question.

But coffee wasn't. Coffee was what the elder and younger Johnson drank when it was time for a fatherly lecture.

"He'd say, 'You better tighten up or we're going to drink some coffee together,'" Johnson said. "I hated drinking that coffee, because I knew I was going to get that long lecture, too."

Yet when it came to football, the elder Johnson was behind Tommy all the way. His father had played college football and semipro ball in the Philippines. He volunteered to coach Tommy's peewee league team, and gave his son nothing but support and good advice.

"My father taught me a lot of things," Johnson said. "He said it was all natural, you know, you were born with the talent and it's God given.

"He gave me a lot of support in high school. My freshman year he used to take me out to jog, and I'd jog with him just so I could listen to him talk and he could give me some encouragement after we finished."

It was a life of discipline that now, Johnson said, he can see paid off.

"My freshman year, I saw the reason for it all," he said. "And I love him for that."

Bill Oliver loves what he sees in Johnson at cornerback.

"He is a good athlete," Oliver said. "He could play wide receiver. He could play a variety of places on offense.

"But we recruited him to play defense. That's where I wanted him all along."

After the fumble recovery, Alabama was able to meet one goal: a seven-play drive. The Tide kept the ball for eight plays, before Barker was intercepted again, this time by Ryan McNeil at the Miami 23.

"If you'd told me before the game I was going to throw two interceptions in the first half, I would have said we're going to lose the game," Barker said.

But his teammates on defense were just getting warmed up. On first down, Torretta, for the first but not last time, came to the line of scrimmage and saw Alabama with all 11 defensive players on the line of scrimmage. It was as if the Tide was daring Miami to go long, daring those receivers to see if they really were faster than the Alabama secondary.

Torretta tried to go long on first down, but overthrew Horace Copeland.

The next time the Miami quarterback came to the line, he was looking at 11 defenders strung out on the line of scrimmage again — three down linemen, two linebackers, and six defensive backs.

He called time out.

"Alabama was putting a lot of pressure on him (Torretta)," said Miami receiver Kevin Williams. "They were moving to a lot of different formations. I don't think he was picking it up too well."

After the time out, Miami came out and tried a reverse in an attempt to catch Alabama overrunning its pursuit. Instead, defensive back Alvin Hope nailed Kevin Williams for an eight-yard loss.

Torretta's third-down pass was too high for Williams, and Miami was forced to punt.

That started the Tide on a 10-play, 46-yard scoring drive, and one of the most confusing penalties of the night. Lassic picked up 35 yards in three carries, the last one for 10 yards to the Miami one.

Brought down so close to the end zone, Lassic put the ball down on the ground, then gave it a spin. The referee took that as a bad sign and flagged Lassic for unsportsmanlike conduct, a penalty that confused everyone.

"It confused me," Stallings said. "Believe me, we (Stallings and the officials) talked about it."

To no avail, of course. Backed up 15 yards, the Tide got to the Miami six before Proctor was called on to salvage the drive with a 23-yard field goal and a 6-3 lead.

Miami took over on its own 28, and seeing that same 11-man front, Torretta tried a quick throw to the right side that was so hurried it was hard to tell who it was for. All Torretta knew was that Eric Curry was coming, and he didn't want any part of Curry.

"I told him I'd be back," Curry said. "I told him to get used to it, because I'd be in his face all night."

On second down, Torretta looked over the 11-man front and stopped when he saw John Copeland staring straight at him, as if there was nothing in his way.

"Torretta looked over at me, and he froze for a second," Copeland said. "I could see the fear in his eyes."

The Miami quarterback dropped back to pass, then tucked the ball under his arm and began to run. He got 15 yards before Sam Shade and Eric Turner brought him down.

Now, it was first down at the Miami 43, and suddenly, Torretta was looking at a five-man front, with two linebackers and four defensive linemen. The straight-ahead handoff to Bennett gained six.

On second-and-four, Miami went to the shotgun, but Torretta couldn't tell what he was looking at. He called time out again, the third and final time out of the half, with nine minutes and 20 seconds still to play.

"We threw a lot of looks at them," Teague said of the Alabama defense. "We never came back with the exact same thing twice in a row. Coach Oliver did a great job of mixing up the coverage and confusing them."

Torretta came out of the shotgun, but was so anxious to drop back, he fumbled the snap and was forced to fall on it for a five-yard loss. On third-and-nine, looking at a four-man front with two linebackers and five defensive backs, Torretta tried to go deep, but the only person back there to catch the ball was Alabama safety Sam Shade.

Shade, a former high school running back, brought the ball back to the Miami 33, and in four carries Lassic had it down to the two-yard line. From there, Sherman Williams came on and scored the first touchdown of the game, and while the Sherman Shake was going on throughout the stands, the scoreboard said: Alabama 13, Miami 3.

Now, Miami felt pressured into throwing the ball. But Torretta never knew what kind of defense he would be throwing into. On its next possession, a three-down-and-out series for the

'Canes, Torretta came out looking at a 4-2 defense on first down, a 4-1 with six DBs on second down, and a 3-1 with seven defensive backs on third down.

The net result for Miami was three yards and a punt.

Miami got the ball back one more time before the half ended. Operating almost exclusively out of the shotgun now, and facing that 3-1-7 defensive alignment by the Tide, Torretta threw nine times, completing six, for 59 yards. But with one second left on the clock, Torretta had no choice but to spike the ball and let Prewitt come on to kick a 42-yard field goal as the half ended.

Alabama was disappointed to have not scored more than one touchdown in the first half, but couldn't be too unhappy with a 13-6 lead.

Especially considering the way the defense was playing. At half-time, Miami had only six yards rushing, while Torretta had completed 12 of 25 passes for 127 yards, with one interception, one sack, and innumerable pressures.

The Tide defensive staff was more convinced than ever that Miami wouldn't run the ball, and the Alabama secondary realized the Hurricane receivers weren't superhuman after all. So, Oliver decided to go with that 11-man front, defensive backs staring into the faces of the receivers.

"We took some chances," Oliver said. "But you've got to do that against the kind of talent Miami puts on the field. I saw our kids making as many big plays as I've ever seen.

"I just felt we could make Torretta think we were in man coverage when we were really in zone, and vice versa."

Alabama's base defense for this game revolved around a five-man secondary and a four-man defensive front, although one of those four down linemen was often a linebacker, either Antonio London or Lemanski Hall. But Oliver mixed in six, sometimes seven defensive backs, constantly changing, with the change not based so much on field position or down and distance as on instinct.

To increase the chances of that pressure, Tide defensive line coach Mike Dubose often had Curry and Copeland line up side-by-side, to eliminate the double-team of both of them.

"You play percentages," Oliver said. "You look at the charts, and they pass 13 or 14 times and run two times. Even first-and-10, they pass. So you have to stop the pass.

"You mix it up. You go at times with maximum pressure, a maximum blitz. But you don't do it too often. You can't go to that well too many times."

The challenge of the 11-man front was whether Torretta's receivers could get past the Tide defensive backs and if Torretta could get the ball off before the oncoming rush got to him. More often than not, it didn't work out that way for the 'Canes.

On the other side of the ball, Alabama had rushed for 152 yards in the first half, with Lassic getting 106 on 17 carries. With Barker having completed only two of eight passes for 12 yards and two interceptions, there were no secrets as to what either side was going to do in the second half.

Alabama received the kickoff to start the second half, and basically got nowhere in three plays.

Diehl got off a 44-yard punt, only his second punt of the game, and Miami started its comeback attempt on its own 39-yard line.

On first down, Torretta tried a quick pass in the left flat for Williams, and Tommy Johnson was ready for it. Johnson stepped in front of Williams like a man who knew the route beforehand, and returned the ball 23 yards to the Miami 20.

On first down, Lassic went left for no gain. On second, Lassic went right, faked the reverse to Palmer, who was crossing back to the left, and picked up seven yards to the 13. On third down, Barker dropped back to pass, was pressured, and ran nine yards for a first down to the four-yard line, and a Miami face-mask penalty took it to the two.

On the third try, Lassic ran directly behind right tackle Roosevelt Patterson, that "fat, sloppy (obscenity)," according to Rohan Marley, for one yard and the touchdown.

"You should have seen Roosevelt before the game," Lassic said. "He was going crazy."

Following Proctor's kick, Miami took over on its own 29-yard line. On first down, Torretta tried a quick pass over the middle for Jonathan Harris, but George Teague broke in front and picked it off, racing 31 yards for the first touchdown of his college career.

"They were hitting the underneath routes, so I played a little guessing game with Torretta," Teague said. "I've never been in the end zone with the football before. I hate it had to come to my last year in my last game."

Proctor's kick was good, and suddenly, five minutes into the second half, Alabama was up, 27-6, and Torretta, the Heisman Trophy winner, was in a daze.

Desperate to make something happen, Williams took Proctor's kick at the one-yard line. He got as far as the 11 before he was brought down by Michael Ausmus.

On first down, Bennett went up the middle for no gain. And then on second down, came the play of the game, the one Alabama fans will talk about forever.

Torretta dropped back, hit Lamar Thomas with a strike after Thomas had blown by a fallen Willie Gaston. Thomas was on his way to the end zone when Teague, fresh off his touchdown run, caught up to him and stripped him of the football, stripped Thomas naked right there at the five-yard-line, embarrassed him for the whole world to see.

"He made the catch in my area," Teague said. "The way I saw it, if he scored, it was going to be my fault."

Thomas, one of the fastest men on the field, had a six-yard head start on Teague, considered one of the slowest of the Tide defensive backs.

But Teague did it. Not only did he catch Thomas, but as he was catching up, for some reason, he decided to not settle for the tackle but go for the ball instead.

"I just thought about it and did it," Teague said of the steal. "And the ball came right back in my belly."

Thomas never knew what happened. The play was so unbelievable that it had to be seen over and over to really be appreciated.

"That may have been the greatest individual effort in Alabama football history," Oliver said.

"To have the play come against Thomas made it that much sweeter," said Tommy Johnson. "He talked the most all week. It couldn't have happened to a better guy.

"And caught from behind? He wasn't just caught from behind, he was caught from behind badly."

The play never counted, however. Alabama was offside back at the line of scrimmage, so Miami got the ball back, got the down back.

But whatever momentum that play might have given the Hurricanes was lost forever. This game was as good as over.

Miami would add a late touchdown on Kevin Williams's 78-yard punt return, a touchdown Alabama would answer right back with a bone-jarring, crushing 59-yard, 12-play drive that ended up with Lassic going in to the end zone from four yards out. It was 12 running plays, without a hint of a pass, a one-dimensional offense at its best.

"Now I see why Alabama doesn't need to pass," said Miami linebacker Michael Barrow.

"They thought we'd be intimidated," said Alabama center Tobie Sheils. "Instead, we wound up intimidating them with the running game."

"My linemen were coming back to the huddle saying they didn't think Miami's players wanted to get hit anymore," Barker said. "They'd had enough."

The Tide started celebrating. The coaches tried to keep them calm, to tell them there was still a lot of time on the clock.

"But it wasn't any use," said Lassic, whose 135 yards rushing and two touchdowns earned him the Sugar Bowl MVP. "We were going around giving high fives and hugging each other. We were elated. We'd won, we knew it. It was over. We were national champions."

Alabama had rushed for 267 yards while throwing for only 18 yards. And although Torretta had thrown 56 times, completing 24 for 278 yards, for the first time in his career as a starting quarterback he had failed to guide Miami's offense to a touchdown. It was the first time Miami had failed to score an offensive touchdown since 1984.

"I think he was confused," Shade said of Torretta. "He was falling backwards, missing exchanges, throwing a few bad passes. We got to him.

"He thought we were in zone when we were in man, and in man when we were in zone. I know in the first half we confused him."

Indeed, when it was all over, Torretta said he didn't remember much about the second half, "The whole game was a blur. It was all or nothing, and we got nothing."

And as for tradition and history . . .

"Miami feels they have this Miami mystique, that when they step on the field, the game is over," Shade said. "Well, we have some tradition, too. And ours is a lot deeper than theirs."

Or, as Mal Moore said when asked about Miami's talk of tradition, "I think Alabama's tradition is way, way beyond that of Miami's. Miami is not as old a program.

"It takes years to acquire the kind of tradition Alabama has. You can't purchase it in three or four years. You have to earn it over a period of time."

It was 11:24 p.m. when the game was officially over. It was also the end of the first day of a new year, and the first day of a new century of football for Alabama.

The second hundred years began the way most of the first hundred were spent: with the Crimson Tide as national champions.

The first thing Gene Stallings did after he left the field was hug every member of his family.

"Great job, Pop," said his son, John Mark, who has Downs Syndrome. "You did OK, Pop."

Stallings looked at John and placed a national championship cap on his head.

"We're national champions, partner," he said. "The national championship, son. That's big."

Then he went out to face the waiting media, who wanted to know how he did it.

"If you go back and check, you'll see I never said we were the underdog," Stallings said. "First of all, I didn't believe we were the underdog. I felt we had a good football team and a good chance to win the game.

"Miami's a good football team. I thought they were well prepared. But deep down, I didn't think they were better than we were. I felt we were a pretty good defensive team. I felt we could do some things to keep them off balance. Even though you don't win with schemes, I thought we had a good scheme.

"I don't consider this an upset."

EPILOGUE

"We did everything we set out to do."

That was the one quote Gene Stallings repeated over and over, from Friday night after the game to Saturday when Alabama was officially named college football's 1992 national champion.

He wanted to make sure everyone knew it wasn't an accident, that the Tide didn't just stumble into its 12th national title. He wanted to make sure everyone knew that this Alabama team had earned it.

Thirteen victories. Nine SEC wins. The first SEC Western Division championship, a victory in the first SEC championship game. A solid thumping of defending national champion Miami.

When someone showed Stallings a copy of the final poll Saturday morning, he only looked as far as No. 1.

"That's all that counts," he said. "I told the players this week that we hadn't played our best game yet. I think now we have."

It was a good year for the SEC after all. Of the six teams that received bowl invitations, only one lost.

And the big one was claimed by Alabama; it was the one the SEC was afraid no SEC team could win because of the toughness of the conference schedule, coupled with the championship game at the end of that.

The Tide extended their own NCAA records for most bowl appearances (45), bowl victories (25), seasons with 10 or more wins (23), seasons with no more than one loss (37), and undefeated regular seasons (14). It was a team that was honored for its achievement, individually as well as collectively.

Michael Proctor set a freshman scoring record with 94 points. Antonio Langham set a record for touchdowns scored by a defensive back in a season (3). David Palmer set the record for most punts returned for a touchdown in a career with his fourth.

Eric Curry and John Copeland were consensus first-team All-America selections, and would be the fifth and sixth players taken in the NFL draft.

Curry earned the Chevrolet Defensive Player of the Year; the Pigskin Club of Washington, D.C., Lineman of the Year; the UPI Lineman of the Year; and was a finalist for the Lombardi Award.

Copeland was the finalist for the *Football News'* Defensive Player of the Year.

George Teague earned second-team All-America honors and was also taken in the first round of the NFL draft, the 29th pick, by Green Bay.

Langham earned third-team All-America honors.

Copeland, Curry, Lemanski Hall, Langham, Lassic, Antonio London, Derrick Oden, Tobie Sheils and Teague all earned first-team All-SEC honors.

And Stallings won the Paul Bryant Award as the Coach of the Year by the Football Writers Association of America.

"Only in America can you be fired twice, then win a national championship and be coach of the year," Stallings said. "I was embarrassed about my record. But I was never embarrassed about the way my teams performed. Still, it's gratifying to win the national championship."

Stallings has always worn the Super Bowl ring he earned as an assistant with the Dallas Cowboys. He was asked where he would wear his national championship ring.

"I'm going to wear it right there," he said, pointing to the finger where the Super Bowl ring resided. "And I'm going to put this Super Bowl ring to bed."

It was a victory that was celebrated long into the new year. There was a parade and pep rally in Tuscaloosa that drew an estimated 10,000 fans. The awards ceremony was moved into the basketball arena and televised live on pay-per-view. *Sports Illustrated* put out a special issue just on Alabama's season, the first time the magazine had ever done that for any team.

"It seems like the celebration never stopped," said Antonio Langham, on the first day of spring football. And indeed, spring football practice was interrupted by a trip to the White House, where the national champions were honored by President Bill Clinton.

Meanwhile, the loss ate at Miami coach Dennis Erickson. "I'm not over it," Erickson told the *Fort Lauderdale Sun Sentinel* on the eve of his own spring game. "I don't know that you ever get over something like that.

"Our goal is to compete for the national championship and win the Big East. But I'm not so sure our ultimate goal isn't to get an opportunity to play Alabama again, to go back to the Sugar Bowl and play them.

"I'd like to have one more chance to play them before I die. Heck, I'd play them in Tuscaloosa if they wanted."

There's an old saying that fits here. Winners tell jokes, while losers cry, "Deal again!"

But of course, there would be no "deal again." Not with the same two teams, anyway. Alabama would lose Curry and Copeland, Teague and Oden, Wilson and Busky, and Lassic and Houston.

Still, the question was inevitable. Could Alabama repeat? Could the Crimson Tide do what no team had been able to do since 1978–79, when one of Bear Bryant's finest teams won back-to-back national championships?

It's entirely possible.

Almost the entire offense returns. Only George Wilson will be gone from the line, and Alabama has stockpiled offensive linemen the last two years. Both backup tight ends are bigger and faster than Steve Busky, the 1992 starter. The loss of Prince Wimbley at wide receiver could be compensated by the fact that

Alabama is loaded at that position with David Palmer, Kevin Lee, Curt Brown, and Rick Brown.

Barker returns at quarterback, along with his backup, Brian Burgdorf, the MVP of the following spring's A-Day game. While Lassic and Martin Houston are gone, Tarrant Lynch has experience at fullback, and Chris Anderson and Sherman Williams return at tailback.

On defense, only Teague is from the secondary, while Chris Donnelly, Antonio Langham and Sam Shade return, along with Tommy Johnson, Willie Gaston, and Eric Turner.

At linebacker, Lemanski Hall is back, along with Michael Rogers. Mario Morris and John Walters can play Derrick Oden's position, and Andre Royal and Will Brown return at outside linebacker to compensate for the loss of Antonio London.

James Gregory is back at nose tackle. Curry and Copeland are gone, but Jeremy Nunley returns, as does Dameian Jeffries, Elverett Brown, and an outstanding prospect in Kendrick Burton.

Both kickers are back. And Alabama has had three outstanding recruiting years under Stallings. The schedule is the same, with one exception: more home games. So could Alabama be back?

"I haven't even thought of next year," Stallings said.

But he was reminded of something he said back in the summer of 1992, before the season started, when everyone picked Alabama to win its division and Stallings smiled and told all the prognosticators that they were premature, that the season was still, in his own words, "a year away."

Stallings smiled when reminded of that statement. "I shouldn't have said that, should I?" he said.

One thing will be different, though.

This time, everyone will be able to see that Alabama is coming.